Studying
YOUR OWN

• SECOND EDITION

School

To Lisa, Lucas, and Maya

• SECOND EDITION

Studying
Y O U R   O W N
School

An Educator's Guide to
Practitioner Action Research

GARY L. ANDERSON
KATHRYN HERR · ANN SIGRID NIHLEN
Foreword by SUSAN E. NOFFKE

CORWIN PRESS
A SAGE Publications Company
Thousand Oaks, CA 91320

For information:

Corwin Press
A Sage Publications Company
2455 Teller Road
Thousand Oaks, California 91320
www.corwinpress.com

Sage Publications India Pvt. Ltd.
B 1/I 1 Mohan Cooperative Industrial Area
Mathura Road, New Delhi 110 044
India

Sage Publications Ltd.
1 Oliver's Yard
55 City Road
London EC1Y 1SP
United Kingdom

Sage Publications Asia-Pacific Pvt. Ltd.
33 Pekin Street #02-01
Far East Square
Singapore 048763

Printed in the United States of America

Library of Congress Cataloging-in-Publication Data

Anderson, Gary L., 1948–
Studying your own school : an educator's guide to practitioner action research / Gary L. Anderson, Kathryn Herr, Ann Sigrid Nihlen. — 2nd ed.
    p. cm.
Includes bibliographical references and index.
ISBN-13: 978-1-4129-4032-0 (cloth)
ISBN-13: 978-1-4129-4033-7 (pbk.)
    1. Action research in education. 2. Education—Research. I. Herr, Kathryn. II. Nihlen, Ann Sigrid. III. Title.
LB1028.24.A53 2007
37.7′2—dc22   2006030723

This book is printed on acid-free paper.

10   11   10   9   8   7   6   5   4   3

Acquisitions Editor:	Rachel Livsey
Editorial Assistant:	Phyllis Cappello
Project Editor:	Astrid Virding
Copy Editor:	Barbara Coster
Typesetter:	C&M Digitals (P) Ltd.
Proofreader:	Scott Oney
Cover Designer:	Rose Storey
Graphic Designer:	Lisa Miller

Contents

Foreword

It has been over 10 years since I was asked to write a foreword to the first edition of *Studying Your Own School.* Since that time, I have used the book many times in my courses in action research, which most often include school practitioners as well as graduate students headed toward positions in teacher education in universities here in the United States and abroad. There has been almost total agreement that the first edition was a really useful text. So I am very pleased to have been asked to write a foreword to this new edition. It is an opportunity to consider not only the work itself but the contextual changes in the field over the past decade. Much has changed, but much has also remained the same.

Over the past two decades there has been a quiet, yet substantive change in the role of practitioners in educational research. Grassroots efforts in action research and other forms of practitioner research have highlighted the importance of educators' own understanding of their practice, both in the United States and internationally. Research by practitioners in education has been widely recognized and accepted from the local level to conference presentations at the annual meetings of major research organizations. Within the research and teacher education institutions, and most recently from within the state, have come endorsements, exhortations, and reward structures claiming the benefits of researching one's own practice. This increasing attention from many levels has recognized action research (individual and collective) as a means for teacher development, knowledge generation, and educational reform, often including attention to the need for greater social justice in and through education. This remarkable growth in projects involving educational practitioners in various aspects of research has run parallel with increased understanding of the multiple meanings of terms such as "action research" and "practitioner research." Indeed, the shift in the use of the term "action research" from the earlier reference to "practitioner research" stands as evidence of a change in the context of research in education.

In this context, as in the context of the earlier edition, this new edition of *Studying Your Own School* makes new and important contributions. It draws on the scholarship on the comparative history of action research without assuming a parochial stance. The work highlights important and complex historical, epistemological, and methodological questions in an accessible style. Yet it also draws on the decade of work in presenting new material that responds to the needs of practitioners doing the work in schools and classrooms.

It is ironic that all too often the literature on practitioner research reproduces the same separation between theory and practice that it seeks to subvert. Those writing about it do so within the language and publication systems of universities. As such, there is a separation between abstract works about practitioner research and "practical" guides. In the latter, there is a tendency to reduce its complexities to the level of a "how to do it" manual, with brief references to the complex core of personal, ethical, and political dimensions that are central to practitioner research. In this book, however, there is a balance between thorough access to the vast international academic literature, a strong narrative text that allows readers to "feel" how research proceeds, and a good introduction to issues of data collection and analysis. Questions of paradigmatic status, validity, and the politics of knowledge production are addressed alongside examples of the lived experience of doing research. Methods of engaging in research are usefully summarized but within a framework, reminding us that the techniques for practitioner research are not merely a parroting of those of traditional social science but rather are emerging in response to educational lives and concerns. There are, in this new edition, materials related to the messiness of getting started on action research projects as well as attention to ethical issues specific to this research strategy and new insights into how issues such as "validity" should be considered.

Studying Your Own School can assist teachers and other educators, collaboratively as well as individually, in using research to improve both the quality and the justice of education in all of our own schools. In the foreword to the first edition, I commented on the era as one in which the danger for practitioner research was clearly the same as that in other then contemporary reforms, such as shared decision making and school-based management. Yet the problems in education are not confined to school buildings. The larger political and economic context of schooling (which has worsened since the first edition) is one in which poverty and racism are central dynamics. For many works on practitioner research, the process of engaging in action research has been reduced to a few short steps, individually taken, to improve the technical efficiency of one's practice. In actual practice, practitioner research is much more. It can offer a collaborative means to richer understandings of education and to the identification of what I refer to in my own work as the "spaces for ethically defensible, politically strategic action" (Noffke, 1995). In decision making, in management, and in research there must be a focus on understanding technical, social, and political aspects of issues as they emerge in action.

The second edition of *Studying Your Own School* does what the first one did: it builds on the experiences of practitioners, potentially enhancing both understanding and action. Yet it also gives clues on how to respond to the current context in which "data-driven" reforms are sought as an antidote to institutional and structural and now global issues. It offers insights into how practitioners can ask, through action research, the really hard questions we all need. I look forward to using this new edition in my classes with both teachers and teacher educators.

Susan E. Noffke

Acknowledgments

All of us owe a debt to our students, many of whom are practitioner action researchers, for pushing our thinking and sharing their experiences with us.

Thanks to Rachel Livsey of Corwin Press for her persistence regarding a new edition of this book; we appreciate her belief in our work.

I owe a considerable debt to the teachers, principals, and school leadership teams of Emerson Elementary School. They have always welcomed me, allowed me free access to whatever they were doing and planning, and allowed me to wander their halls. When they asked me to teach a course for them on-site, we began a journey that includes, but does not end, with this book. As teacher researchers, they shared their perspectives and hopes for developing practitioner research. For this, I thank them.

I also want to thank the many students who have taken my qualitative research courses over the years; I have learned a great deal from their questions as well as from their research. I would also like to thank Shelley Roberts for her input.

Ann Sigrid Nihlen

We are grateful to Owen Creightney and "the boys' group" for sharing this journey with us.

Kathryn Herr and Gary L. Anderson

The contributions of the following reviewers are gratefully acknowledged:

Diane Yendol-Hoppey
Associate Professor
School of Teaching and Learning
University of Florida
Gainesville, FL

Rob Walker
Director, Centre for Applied Research in Education
University of East Anglia
Norwich, United Kingdom

Terry Morganti-Fisher
Education Consultant
Morganti-Fisher Associates
Austin, TX

Randi Dickson
Assistant Professor of English Education
Queens College/CUNY
Flushing, NY

Janna K. Smith
Director of Professional Development and Assessment
School District of Clayton
Clayton, MO

Preface to the Second Edition

We began the preface to the first edition with the following quote from a teacher researcher and an optimistic prognosis for action research in education:

> For me, it [teacher research] was part of learning how to be a learner again and thinking about what made that exciting for me. Then, when you get back into that mode, you think, How can I create that for my students? . . . I enjoy what I'm doing again, I'm not just making it through the day anymore.
>
> Stephanie Mansdoerfer, teacher
> La Cueva High School, Albuquerque, NM

The above testimony by a high school teacher captures the kind of excitement we have encountered regarding action research, both within the academic research community and within the public school system. Practitioners are excited because such research can lead to professional renewal and improvement of practice. Academics are excited because action research represents, among other things, a more grounded approach to the creation of new knowledge about educational practices.

We have attempted to create a book that is the result of a dialogue between the experience-based insights from the world of practice and the methodological and theoretical insights of the academic community. Although representing different professional cultures, those who work in colleges of education and those who work in schools are beginning to recognize that they each have a different kind of knowledge—each with its own criteria of validity—to share. School practitioners are beginning to demystify the hierarchical nature of the so-called expert knowledge of academics, and academics are beginning to realize that the old model of knowledge creation (in universities), dissemination (through academic journals), and utilization (by practitioners) is not working.

A growing number of teachers, counselors, and administrators are collaborating with universities in a variety of capacities. Colleges of education are increasingly demanding that their faculty have extensive and recent practitioner experience and that faculty spend greater amounts of time in schools. Although ivory tower college of education professors who have not set foot in a school in 20 years can still be found, they are nearing retirement.

As we reread the original preface of *Studying Your Own School* 12 years later, we were struck by how optimistic we were in 1994, in terms of both the extent to which action research would be a pathway to professional renewal for school practitioners and the extent to which university academics would embrace it. While in some ways the last 12 years has confirmed this optimism, in other ways there is room for considerable skepticism.

There is much evidence that school practitioners are embracing action research. Since 1994, there have been many advances in the number of publication venues, in theoretical developments, and in professional development opportunities. Several new action research journals have come into existence, and both academic and practitioner journals are publishing more action research. Although in 1994 books on action research were exclusively written by university academics, today there are many book-length action research studies written by school practitioners, published primarily by Teachers College Press and Heinemann Publishers. In 1994 we scoured dissertations, conference papers, and fugitive documents for examples of action research, but today we can point to a strong body of published action research scholarship. Theoretical developments in situated and distributed cognition and Freirian pedagogy have helped to justify the formation of practitioner "learning communities," such as critical friends groups and teacher inquiry or study groups. Whole-school leadership teams have appropriated action research's use of data and cycles of inquiry as a way to strengthen organizational learning. Finally, while old-style inservice "talking heads" still exist, teachers have tended to take greater control over their professional development hours and are increasingly likely to engage in group inquiry. Even individual teachers can often list classroom action research as part of their professional development plan in many school districts.

The context of teaching has changed, though, since we wrote the first edition of the book. We now live under No Child Left Behind legislation, which has intensified previous tendencies toward increased standardization, high-stakes testing, scripted instructional materials, and increased surveillance over teachers. In this context, the promotion of action research with its empowering potential for school practitioners can be a cause for concern to a top-down reform movement. When action research is incorporated into reform movements, its empowering potential is often stripped away. One of the most intractable problems in education is the difficulty of making successful practices more systemic, or what some refer to as "ramping up" innovations. Consultants who promise 5 or 7 or 10 steps to effective action research become a logical result of large-scale reform. In the context of pressures to meet Annual Yearly Progress under No Child Left Behind, action research becomes in some schools a popular name for merely poring over test score results. While action researchers would certainly not overlook test scores as a source of data, they would tend to see them as one among many indicators of student success. Innovative possibilities like action research become imposed on a school community and in the process run the risk of losing the sense of an organic change process instigated by invested stakeholders. As action research becomes mandated on a larger scale, it can become contrived, as teachers learn to implement the form without the substance.

The positive response of university academics is also a mixed blessing. While courses in action or teacher research have multiplied, particularly in teacher education departments, they are too often assigned to faculty with little experience with action research, because few university faculty have done action research or had any exposure to it in graduate school. In fact, this book was written in part for those very well-meaning faculty and their students who need a crash course in action research. In some cases, because action research challenges their sense of expertise, faculty refuse to consider it genuine research. Institutional review boards, often staffed by faculty unfamiliar with this research approach, are often woefully unprepared to think through the ethical issues associated with it. "Suggestions" for improvement are offered or questions are posed that are baffling and/or unhelpful. These issues result in some universities and school districts all but banning action research as a legitimate form of research. Anderson (2002) and Anderson and Herr (1999) have written extensively on the ways that action research challenges the positivist assumptions built into the university's view of legitimate knowledge. So while we are encouraged by action research's growing popularity, our concern is that it be an empowering practice for school practitioners, not absorbed into or derailed by current accountability systems.

Besides the usual updating and revising associated with second editions, we have made some significant changes to the book. First, we have added Chapter 5, titled "The Research Question, Ethical Considerations, and Research Design." Practitioner action research is a complex undertaking, and we wanted to honor the complexity in discussing at length some of the initial issues to be taken into consideration. These include the early evolution of a research question and some sense of the ethical dilemmas that one encounters along the way. This early stage of research is often the longest and most difficult for many practitioners. In addition, we have added some new examples of action research studies reflecting the development of the field and how the context of schools has changed, based on the reality of current educational reforms.

TOWARD A NEW PARADIGM
OF SOCIAL INQUIRY

The conventional weapons of research are cumbersome; heavy field pieces dragged slowly into position hardly suitable for the swift-moving, rapidly changing targets of an action programme. (Smith, 1975, p. 94)

For too long researchers in colleges of education have felt like second-class citizens with regard to their university colleagues in the arts and sciences. They have sensed that their research in action-oriented settings and their split commitment between the scientific and practitioner communities made their research not so much inferior as fundamentally different. School practitioners, who could be characterized as third-class citizens in this academic pecking order, felt the same tensions with regard to educational researchers in universities. Most graduate courses in research are designed to teach practitioners how to consume research done by academic researchers. Seldom is it even suggested that practitioners could do research themselves unless they were to enroll in a university doctoral program.

Books have been written by academic researchers in the last 30 years about the differences between positivistic and naturalistic (qualitative) paradigms. By now, most educational researchers have made their peace—at least rhetorically—with the legitimacy of both. Now academics are watching the emergence of a third way of knowing education—research done by educational practitioners. Although it bears some resemblance to the naturalistic paradigm, it differs in several important ways:

1. Knowledge is not produced only for a scientific community but rather for a broader community, consisting primarily—though not exclusively—of school practitioners.

2. Unlike naturalistic research, which involves the observation, description, and interpretation of educational settings, action research aims primarily at the transformation of these settings.

3. Unlike naturalistic research, action research is done within an action-oriented setting in which reflection on action is the driving force of the research. This tension inherent in combining action and research is captured in the term traditionally used to describe this type of inquiry: *action research.*

We believe it is time for educators—both academics and practitioners—to stop apologizing for our research and clinging to paradigms that do not necessarily fit our reality. Lindblom and Cohen (1979) long ago called into question the usefulness of most social science research, which approaches social change through top-down, outside-in models of "social engineering" like the current

No Child Left Behind reforms. Modernist paradigms in the arts and sciences are falling like dominos. When the smoke clears, social scientists may understand that while they have been defending their modernist canon, educators, researchers, and practitioners have collaboratively been exploring a new paradigm of research with the potential to bring about social change from the bottom up and the inside out. We hope this book moves us closer to that goal.

DESCRIPTION OF CONTENTS

In Chapter 1, we provide the reader with a loose definition of practitioner action research. The purpose of providing a definition is not to fix parameters but to give the reader who may be encountering action research for the first time some general categories with which to approach subsequent chapters. We also lay out a series of assumptions about teacher research. These are themes that serve as a subtext for the rest of the book.

Educational practitioners have been doing some form of systematic inquiry for as long as there have been schools. However, the notion of inquiring practitioners has been written about and studied only relatively recently. In the first section of Chapter 2, we provide a review of the various ways that action research has manifested itself in different times and social contexts. It is a paradigm of research that has surfaced at different times and in different places over the past 100 years. We feel it is important that the beginning action researcher be aware that he or she is engaging in work that has a long, important, and controversial history.

In the second and third sections of Chapter 2, we provide the reader with a sense of the epistemological and political issues associated with action research. We agree with Cochran-Smith and Lytle (1993, 1999) that teacher research represents a potential new knowledge base in education and that we must begin to discuss how this new knowledge, which emerges from action and from inside schools, is created and shared. We also discuss the ways that action research is political. By political we mean not only the ways that action research can be viewed as a threat within institutional and district politics but also the "politics of knowledge," in which school practitioners struggle to legitimate the currently devalued knowledge base that exists in schools.

In Chapter 3, we present a diversity of current approaches to action research by summarizing a variety of action research studies. Throughout the book we cite numerous other studies that the reader can access. We believe that the best thing aspiring action researchers can do is to read other practitioners' studies. For the first time since action research appeared many decades ago, there is a critical mass of published books, articles, and conference papers that report action research in education.

In Chapter 4, we bring previous themes together through a process-oriented narrative of a three-year action research study undertaken by coauthor Herr. This chapter focuses on the research process with an eye to opening a window onto the decision making of an action researcher as Herr encounters the ever-changing, action-oriented, and political nature of the setting in which she was both practitioner and researcher. Herr describes the ways that goals of empowerment and the defensive mechanisms of institutions create an environment in which the action researcher must tread with care. This chapter also graphically illustrates what we reiterate several times throughout the book—that action research is seldom neat and tidy.

Chapter 5 fills a gap in the first edition of the book. The biggest struggle for most action researchers is getting clear on the focus of the study and developing initial research questions. In this chapter, we focus on areas for consideration prior to beginning the research, including research question creation, ethical considerations, and processes of gaining approval from research offices for the inquiry.

In teaching courses on action research, we have found that practitioners have made important modifications to traditional qualitative research methods. In Chapter 6 we provide the reader with a user-friendly guide to qualitative methods while at the same time indicating how practitioners are modifying these methods to meet the constraints and opportunities they encounter in their schools.

About the Authors

Gary L. Anderson is a former teacher and principal who is currently a Professor in the Steinhardt School of Education at New York University. Among his books are *The Action Research Dissertation: A Guide for Students and Faculty* (2005, with Kathryn Herr), *Performance Theories and Education: Power, Pedagogy, and the Politics of Identity* (2005, with Bryant Alexander and Bernardo Gallegos), *The Micropolitics of Educational Leadership: From Control to Empowerment* (with Joseph Blase), and *Educational Qualitative Research in Latin America: The Struggle for a New Paradigm* (with Martha Montero-Sieburth).

Kathryn Herr is a former teacher, school counselor, and grade dean. She is currently a Professor in the College of Education and Human Services at Montclair State University. She continues to study the same issues she addressed as an action researcher in her middle school work site: the disenfranchisement of whole groups of students in the current structures of schooling and institutional changes. She recently published (2005, with Gary L. Anderson) *The Action Research Dissertation: A Guide for Students and Faculty*. She is the long-standing editor of *Youth and Society*, a multidisciplinary journal that focuses on issues of youth growth and development in their social contexts.

Ann Sigrid Nihlen is an Associate Professor in the Language, Literacy, and Cultural Studies Program at the College of Education at the University of New Mexico. She has taught at the State University of New York at Buffalo and was the Coordinator of Women Studies at the University of New Mexico. Currently she teaches courses on qualitative and teacher research, anthropology and education, issues of sex and gender, and social class and education. She has published in the areas of gender, teacher research, and women's studies. Her current investigations include work with the Emerson Elementary School Oral History Project, where she is a coresearcher with several teachers. The group is writing a book titled *Teacher Talk: Our Story of School Restructuring.* She is also preparing a manuscript of an ethnography of white, working-class, first-grade girls that will incorporate her more recent collaborative work with teachers in a community college.

C H A P T E R   O N E

What Is Action Research?

Most researchers attempt to study social reality either by decontextualizing variables or by being a fly-on-the-wall observer of a natural setting. These are the hallmarks of objectivity in quantitative and qualitative research methodologies. Action researchers, on the other hand, study social reality by acting within it and studying the effects of their actions. All three of these approaches to research have their particular strengths and limitations, but what sets action research apart is that it generates knowledge out of ongoing problem solving in social settings. Action researchers can be outsiders to the setting who collaborate with insiders, or they can be insiders working alone or in collaboration with others. In schools, action researchers tend to be teachers or other school professionals doing what is often called practitioner, teacher, or action research.

While *action research* remains the most common term across most disciplines, variations of this type of research go by terms such as *action science, participatory action research (PAR), community-based action research, cooperative inquiry, self-study, emancipatory praxis, autoethnography,* and, as is more commonly the case in education, *teacher, practitioner,* or *action researcher.* As we make clear in Chapter 2, each of these terms connotes a different emphasis. In many cases, each represents different research traditions that grew out of very different social contexts.

In the first edition of the book, we used the term *practitioner research* because we wanted to place practitioners at the center of the enterprise and because we thought it was emerging as the term of choice in education. However, the term *action research* seems to have held up among educators, and placing school practitioners at the center of the enterprise can sometimes obscure the centrality of action as well as displace other participants, such as students, parents, and community members. Therefore, we have used *practitioner action research* in the book title, although in the text of this edition we tend to shorten it to *action research* for the sake of brevity.

Although the plethora of terms used to describe this research also reflects wide disagreement on many key issues, we provide below a working definition of practitioner action research, as well as a few of our working assumptions, that are used throughout the book. Action research is a living, growing movement that is in the process of evolving; it is this evolution that we describe in subsequent chapters.

DEFINING ACTION RESEARCH

In attempting to provide a working definition of practitioner action research, we want to make it clear that every point in the following definition is hotly debated in the burgeoning literature on action research. Thus, we attempt to provide a snapshot of how the definition is taking shape.

In the field of education, the term *action research* connotes "insider" research done by practitioners using their own site (classroom, institution, school district, community) as the focus of their study. It is a reflective process but is different from isolated, spontaneous reflection in that it is deliberately and systematically undertaken and generally requires that some form of evidence be presented to support assertions. What constitutes "evidence" or, in more traditional terms, "data," is still being debated. This is particularly the case in self-study forms of action research that rely to a greater extent on experience and narrative.

As mentioned above, action research is oriented to some action or cycles of actions that practitioners wish to take to address a particular situation. For this reason, the term *action research* has traditionally been used for this type of research.

Action research is sometimes described as an ongoing series of cycles that involve moments of planning actions, acting, observing the effects, and reflecting on one's observations. These cycles form a spiral that results in refinements of research questions, resolution of problems, and transformations in the perspectives of researchers and participants.

Some, including the authors, argue that action research is best done in collaboration with others who have a stake in the problem under investigation, such as other educational practitioners in the setting, students, parents, or other members of the community. Sometimes collaboration involves outsiders (e.g., university faculty, consultants, evaluators) who have relevant skills or resources.

Like all forms of inquiry, action research is value-laden. Although most practitioners hope that action research will improve their practice, what constitutes "improvement" is not self-evident. It is particularly problematic in a field such as education, where there is no consensus on basic educational aims. Action research takes place in educational settings that reflect a society characterized by conflicting values and an unequal distribution of resources and power. Currently, most educators are working with imposed accountability systems based on standardized test scores that may or may not reflect school achievement or improvement from a practitioner's point of view.

More concise definitions exist in the growing body of literature on practitioner action research. For example, McKernan (1991) describes practitioner action research as "a form of self-reflective problem solving which enables practitioners to better understand and solve pressing problems in social settings" (p. 6).

McCutcheon and Jung (1990) provide the following definition: "Systematic inquiry that is collective, collaborative, self-reflective, critical, and undertaken by the participants of the inquiry. The goals of such research are the understanding of practice and the articulation of a rationale or philosophy of practice in order to improve practice" (p. 148).

Kemmis and McTaggart (1982) provide a definition with social justice at its center:

[A] form of *collective,* self-reflective enquiry undertaken by participants in social situations in order to improve the rationality and justice of their own social or educational practices, as well as their understanding of the practices and the situations in which these practices are carried out. Groups of participants can be teachers, students, principals, parents, and other community members—any group with a shared concern. The approach is only action research when it is *collaborative*, though it is important to realize that the action research of the group is achieved through the *critically examined action* of the individual group members. (p. 6)

While we prefer to remain as eclectic as possible with regard to a definition, we would also like to lay out a few assumptions that form the foundation for this book.

WORKING ASSUMPTIONS

Following are a few assumptions that we share about action research. We feel that these assumptions are also widely shared within the action research community. Throughout this book, we use *action research* to denote insiders doing research in their own settings, though we realize the term is also used more broadly. For a more complete discussion of insider and outsider action research, see Herr and Anderson (2005) and Noffke (1997).

Action Research Differs From
Traditional Academic Research
Without Necessarily Being Less Rigorous

Although action research can borrow appropriate methods from university-based research, it is different from academic research in that it represents insider or local knowledge about a setting. There is no way an outsider, even an ethnographer who spends years as an observer, can acquire the tacit knowledge of a setting that those who must act within it daily possess. This creates obvious advantages for the insider action researcher, but it also makes it harder for the practitioner doing research to step back and take a dispassionate look at the setting. This subjectivity is one of the reasons some recommend that practitioners do research in collaboration with outsiders or with a *critical friend*. This critical friend may be another insider who plays a devil's advocate role. The implications of the differences between insider and outsider research are continuing to be discussed. We review these epistemological (how we acquire and share knowledge) issues in more detail in Chapter 2. It is important to add that action research is not less rigorous than traditional academic research but rather defines rigor differently.

Action Research Is Political

In fact, any research that makes knowledge claims is necessarily political, but action research is political in a double sense. It is political in the obvious sense that asking critical questions about one's practice, classroom, and school can offend those with a stake in maintaining the status quo. But it is also political in the sense that practitioners creating knowledge about their own practice challenge those who view practitioners as passive recipients of knowledge created in universities. As school practitioners find their voice, they are in a position to challenge reformers who view them as scapegoats for low student achievement.

As mentioned in our definition, we believe that no research is neutral; therefore, researchers should not be naive about how their research will be received within their setting. Although action researchers need techniques for gathering and analyzing data, they also need an understanding of the ways in which action research often threatens the vested interests and ideological commitments of some groups and individuals. Chapter 2 addresses in more detail the "politics" of doing action research.

In Chapter 2, our goal is to discuss epistemological and political issues in a straightforward and clear manner. Many books that deal with these issues, although excellent accounts that are valuable resources for academics, tend to turn practitioners off because their discourse is pitched at academics rather than practitioners (e.g., Carr & Kemmis, 1986; Kincheloe, 1991; Winter, 1987). We want language to serve as an aid rather than an obstacle to understanding for practitioners.

On the other hand, we are disturbed by a growing anti-intellectualism on the part of some who assume that educational practitioners only want a nuts-and-bolts, "what-I-can-do-on-Monday" recipe for answering "safe" and narrow questions limited to the four walls of a classroom or school. We find this trend toward "deskilling" insulting to educational practitioners, who, in our experience, desire a better understanding of their practice and its social effects. We also understand, thanks to Argyris and Schön (1974), that there is no such thing as practice that is nontheoretical. Many of the recipes and tips for teachers that appear in practitioner journals are dripping with theoretical and ideological assumptions of which even their authors often seem unaware. Part of the task of action research is to strip away the unexamined theoretical baggage that has accumulated around almost everything we do in schools. To do this, we must make the familiar seem strange, a task enhanced by both ethnographic and action research.

There Are Many Valid Ways to Do Action Research

Many practitioners have difficulty imagining themselves as researchers, because they have a particular image of research acquired from a research course they took during their undergraduate or graduate studies. This course work may have exposed them to both quantitative and qualitative research methodologies, but our experience indicates that quantitative research is more commonly required for virtually all graduate students. In this approach, representative samples, significance levels, and confounding variables were the order of the day, framing how quality research was considered. Only in recent years have introductory courses presented students with a fuller range of research traditions, and even in these cases, action research may or may not be included. It is hard for most practitioners to imagine doing quantitative, statistical research in their own settings. Although much research in education is of this kind, it represents only one of many options available to action researchers. Some questions may be best pursued with statistical research, and there are books available that address this approach to action research (e.g., Brause & Mayher, 1991; Myers, 1985; Rowntree, 1981). However, the emphasis in this book is on qualitative and narrative methodologies, which tend to be appropriated from anthropology, sociology, history, linguistics, and the humanities. Our current sense is that just as educators appropriated qualitative research from these various areas, we are now in the ongoing process of appropriating and adapting qualitative methods for use in the realities of action research.

By qualitative research, we mean anything from ethnographic methods to journals and essays. We have no interest in policing what "counts" as research and what does not. Our sense is that practitioners themselves are beginning to develop criteria for distinguishing rigor from sloppiness in action research. In Chapter 2, we discuss in more detail how action research challenges traditional criteria for the validity or trustworthiness of research studies.

Action Research Can Empower and Include a Greater Number of Voices

Action research has the potential for empowerment and the inclusion of a greater diversity of voices in educational policy and social change. We see action research as an opportunity to make the voices of those who work closest to the classroom heard. This includes not only those practitioners who work at school sites but also the students who study there and the people who live in the school's community. In Chapter 2, we refer to this as democratic validity/trustworthiness.

We see action research not merely as individual practitioners trying to improve their practice but as part of a larger social movement that challenges dominant research and development approaches that emphasize an outside-in, top-down approach to educational change. In other words, we believe that empowerment begins with a group of educational practitioners who view themselves not merely as consumers of someone else's knowledge but as knowledge creators in their own right. Unless educational practitioners who are committed to empowering themselves and their students insist on a greater voice in school reform movements, action research will be co-opted by those very movements, which are led by special interests more concerned with "national competitiveness" than with the welfare of children. Although these goals are not inherently incompatible, too many children are currently viewed as socially expendable from a purely economic perspective. We personally know and work with many practitioners with a commitment to social justice working at school sites. These practitioners, through their research, are beginning to challenge the mythologies and institutional and social arrangements that lead to school failure for a disproportionate number of poor and minority students.

Action Research Is Best Done Collaboratively

We believe that action research is best done as part of a collaborative effort. Ideally, collaboration is done with others who have a stake in the problem under study; however, it may also be done with a group of other practitioners who are also engaged in research. These other practitioners may or may not work at the same site, but they provide the action researcher with an emotional support group, a group of critical friends who can critique the researcher's work within a context of support.

Although we do not wish to discourage isolated practitioners—many of whom may have limited access to other action researchers—from engaging in research, the many advantages of collaboration are becoming increasingly apparent. In fact, many action research projects have emerged unexpectedly from teacher study and support groups (Saavedra,1994; Short et al.,1993).

THE MULTIPLE POSITIONALITIES OF THE RESEARCHER(S) IN ACTION RESEARCH

Most academic researchers assume that they are doing research *on* someone. That someone is generally referred to as the "subject," "informant," "interviewee," or "participant." What makes practitioner action research unique is that practitioners/researchers are their own subjects or informants. They are insiders, not outsiders, to the setting under study. "Insider" may seem self-explanatory, and one's position with regard to one's professional setting and relationships with colleagues, students, and community may, at first glance, seem straightforward. However, positionality often becomes a source of confusion for many practitioner action researchers.

Before practitioners began doing their own research, action researchers were seen exclusively as outside change agents who worked closely with their insider participants, often practitioners. We discuss the history and roots of action research in Chapter 2, but here, suffice it to observe that it was often assumed that action research was initiated by an outsider. The central issue for outsider action researchers was how to involve insiders in the research to a greater extent than was the case with traditional research. Much of this research was—and continues to be—contract or evaluation research and usually was funded to solve a particular problem or evaluate a particular program. Such research is still often undertaken in fields like international development, public health, and community psychology. At its most collaborative, it represents what Bartunek and Louis (1996) call insider/outsider teams.

In education, and increasingly in fields like nursing and social work, action research is more often done by organizational insiders, such as teachers, administrators, counselors, or school social workers and psychologists who see it as a way to deepen their own reflection on practice toward problem posing, problem solving, and professional development. In such cases the researcher and the practitioner are one and the same. The practitioner action researcher may be working alone on his or her research or as part of a larger team of people conducting the study. At the same time, it is not unusual to have university people in the schools guiding student teachers through action research projects (e.g., Green & Brown, 2006) or involved in study/inquiry groups with teachers that may also earn university credits (e.g., Luna et al., 2004). Or perhaps the school is a Professional Development School (PDS) site, and both university and school professionals are conducting action research about the professional development taking place on-site (e.g., Levin & Rock, 2003). As we think through who "owns" the research and how multiple players and positionalities impact the research process, the simple insider-outsider distinctions begin to blur.

While action research in education tends to be defined by its insider position vis-à-vis outsiders, issues of positionality don't end there. As an insider to the setting, the practitioner occupies a complex set of roles and relationships. Schools are hierarchical organizations. Administrators have formal power over teachers; teachers have formal power over students; more senior teachers may have formal or informal power over more junior teachers. Carefully thinking through one's positionality within an organization is important in understanding how it may impact the trustworthiness of the findings and the ethics of the research process.

If I am a principal doing action research to improve my professional development program for teachers, interviewing teachers to obtain data is problematic from a trustworthiness or validity standpoint and possibly from an ethical one as well. In terms of the trustworthiness of the findings, it is unlikely that teachers will be frank and honest when being interviewed by "the boss." Thus, the quality of the data will be questionable. From an ethical standpoint, teachers may feel coerced into participating, even if they are invited to volunteer (see Anderson & Jones, 2000, for more on this). There are ways around these problems, of course. Using anonymous surveys or having another teacher do the interviews might give a principal better-quality data, and making the research more participatory and collaborative might make coercion less of an issue as teachers see some benefit in participating in a process that is likely to improve their professional development. Many of these ethical problems are attenuated to the extent that the research is participatory from its inception.

We also occupy multiple positions related to our social class, race, ethnicity, gender, sexual orientation, age, ability/disability, religion, political beliefs, and so forth. Our position as male or female, Caucasian or African American, Jewish or Muslim influences what we see in our classrooms and what remains invisible to us. Even within our own school settings, we may be outsiders. The complexity of the notion of inside/outside is captured by Collins's (1990) discussion of being an "outsider-within." She suggests that one's location in an organization or community makes for varying vantage points and differing lenses of "reality." Some people are "outsiders-within," residing in the margins and observing "the contradictions between the dominant group's actions and ideologies" (p. 11). Collins maintains that outsiders-within offer a specialized, subjugated knowledge, a "peculiar marginality," that provides a unique standpoint on self and society. For example, nonwhites in a white-dominated organization may become expert observers of white culture as they navigate their day-to-day interactions with colleagues. Meanwhile, many white administrators and teachers may be totally unaware of this knowledge and in fact even deny that it exists. As we can see, being an action researcher requires not only reflecting on the research question at hand but also reflecting deeply about how our positionality becomes a lens through which we view reality.

"MEASURING UP" OR RECLAIMING OUR KNOWLEDGE?

The logistical problems that school practitioners face and the lack of a reward system for doing research in schools can make doing action research a daunting task. On the other hand, many educators claim that doing research in their own sites has changed their professional lives and has offered a welcome alternative to other imposed forms of professional development. We find that many educators, with a little practice, find learning the qualitative and ethnographic research methods described in Chapter 6 relatively easy. The real problem is adapting them to the realities of the real world of schools and classrooms.

Pearson (1993), one of our former students, was attempting to begin a study of classroom discipline. She confessed to us the following: "As I began my observations, I realized that I had not yet learned the 'tricks of the trade'" (p. 6). She described her harried day and her inability to take notes in class while she taught. Nor could she find the time to do sociograms or transcribe videotaped classroom data. She ended up blaming herself by internalizing her "failure" and concluded that trying "to solve this problem has given me a new insight into myself. I always thought of myself as organized. . . . I think there are levels of being organized, something like the levels of thinking skills. I'm still at the factual level. I'm obsessed with doing it, but haven't the understanding of it yet" (p. 6).

This tendency to blame oneself for not measuring up or for not learning the tricks of the trade is all too common among beginning practitioner action researchers. Part of the problem may be that practitioners are learning tricks for the wrong trade. Academic qualitative researchers do not have to juggle data gathering with teaching or administering a school. Juggling these multiple demanding roles will necessitate the ongoing development of user-friendly data-gathering methods.

One of the themes of this book is the gap between the call for teachers to be researchers in their schools and classrooms and the lack of discussion about how one manages to perform two full-time jobs simultaneously: the job of a practitioner with that of a researcher. This situation seems like a lose-lose situation for practitioners. To do the work as thoroughly as outsider research demands, they may have to sacrifice time with students or family, and yet if they do not do research like academic researchers, their work is labeled second class by the criteria of the university. Practitioners doing site-based dissertations may be willing to sacrifice for a year or two, but what about the practitioner who wants to do research as part of being a professional educator or to improve and problematize his or her own practice?

Few practitioners working in school settings currently get release time for research. Although this is a fairly standard perk in academe, it is seldom provided in elementary and secondary school settings. Writing, publishing, and gaining tenure reward a university scholar's desire to do research. Many school practitioners labor to do research despite the fact that it is seldom a part of their job description, although increasingly it can be included in professional development plans.

What do practitioners gain in adding a research component to their roles as educators that helps offset the demands in time and energy? How can qualitative methods be appropriated and adapted to work in the real world of practitioners and schools? In other words: Why do action research?

When coauthor Herr worked in a middle school, she often worked with teachers to improve their teaching. On one occasion, a teacher's chairperson, the teacher, and Herr sat in the teacher's classroom, reviewing her latest round of student evaluations. The results were devastating, and all three struggled to understand the negative feedback from the students. The teacher was a ready learner, eager for and quick to try suggestions that others offered. The hoped-for results still seemed out of reach.

The chairperson, a supportive ally in working with his department member, was visibly discouraged and worried. The teacher became teary and wondered whether she had what it took to succeed in this profession. Herr suggested that this teacher might be a good candidate to do some action research. The opportunity for the teacher to observe her own classroom in some systematic way might help her reflect and gain insight into her own practice. The chairperson, worrying about adding the burden of research to an already overburdened and discouraged teacher, wondered out loud if this might not be "too much" in addition to daily classroom preparations and other school obligations. The teacher replied that what was "too much" was the constant drain of living with unsolved practice problems. The thought of a systematic inquiry that might shed light on classroom problems felt like a lifeline, to which she eagerly grabbed hold.

There is no miracle end to the story. Now the teacher is embarking on her own inquiry of her classroom with the support of her chairperson and with consultation from Herr. The hope is that her self-discovery process will help unravel the mysteries of her teaching and improve her practice.

Accounts like Richards's (1987) in Chapter 3 also speak to the potential benefits of action research. Richards was discouraged by her underachieving eighth-grade class that she taught during the last period of the school day. The possibility of some insight and positive problem solving where "hopeless" practice issues are concerned can be a solid motivator for beginning some form of action research. Her action research transformed her hopelessness into an exciting adventure with her students.

Action research can also be a vehicle for sharing practices that work with other teachers. This happens when teachers are excited that through the trial and error of refining their own practices, they may have hit upon something that really works. In this case, the thought of systematizing informal observations of one's practice and then disseminating the results to a wider audience can be an attractive option. An example of this comes from Herr's (1993) experience in a school in which she worked as a counselor and teacher.

> I remember a conversation I had with a math teacher regarding a student I was concerned about; although academically able, the student was doing miserably in every class—except for math. I had approached the math teacher, hoping she could give me some insight into what "works" with this student. As we talked together, the teacher recounted that she had been doing some experimenting with her classroom setup, weaving more cooperative learning experiences into her math classes. She had noticed that her female students in particular seemed to enjoy the times the class worked in cooperative groupings; grades of the girls previously struggling seemed to be on their way up, and the teacher felt convinced that cooperative learning had something to do with it. As someone acquainted with the research literature showing that middle school is a particularly trying time for female adolescents, that self-esteem plummets, and grades, particularly

in math and science, drop, I can remember feeling exhilarated by this teacher's observations. I would be excited for her to consider doing some action research as a means to systematically record and test her hunch regarding what was happening in her classroom.

We need this teacher's findings as well as those of other practitioners as we work to understand how to create better learning environments for and with our students.

The importance of investigating and recording what works is particularly important in light of the difficult problems facing educators and the public discourse highlighting what does not work in our schools. As insiders in the system, practitioners have a unique vantage point from which to problem solve. In fact, in this age of mandating evidence-based practices, who better than school insiders to produce evidence about what works for diverse groups of students. And what better way to communicate this evidence than through educators narrating their findings through their research. The challenge is to create ways to do action research without overwhelming ourselves in the process, to make research an integral part of what we already do, rather than merely an add-on.

CONCLUSION

These are exciting times for action research. It has the potential to bring to light important theories about practice that have been too long discredited as informal theory or teacher lore. It can empower school practitioners by helping them discover their voices and resist attempts at deskilling. It can build collegiality and a common community of learning among practitioners, which in turn will provide a model of inquiry for students. On the other hand, it can also become one more teacher inservice scheme that can be packaged and taken on the road—another implementation strategy cooked up by management to build ownership in schools for the latest centrally mandated reform. Or perhaps it is one more requirement for education majors. It can become just one more expectation—one more thing teachers and prospective teachers are expected to do.

However, practitioners are beginning to build their own research networks. When they invite so-called experts to participate, it is increasingly on their own terms. While it remains to be seen whether this movement will lead to empowerment or be co-opted by a top-down reform movement, we remain convinced of its potential for individual as well as schoolwide growth and development.

CHAPTER TWO

Merging Educational Practice and Research

A New Paradigm

A BRIEF HISTORY OF ACTION RESEARCH

The Multiple Traditions of Action Research

Education tends to be an ahistorical field. We value the new and trendy and often fail to realize that the new is sometimes the old dressed up in new language. Action research has a long and varied tradition. It is important that both practitioners and academics understand that there is a diverse intellectual tradition of action research and that it is distinct from the academic research tradition in education.

Our purpose in describing the various action research traditions is to illustrate that action research is not new and is not monolithic. There are differing viewpoints among these traditions about why and how action research should be undertaken.

The notion of traditions is also important because what counts as valid research is what sociologists call a "social construction"

(Berger & Luckmann, 1967). At different times in different social contexts, what constitutes valid ways of creating knowledge will vary. It is not by accident, for example, that emancipatory, grass-roots approaches to research emerged from the oppressive social conditions of the third world. It is also not surprising that positivistic, quantitative methods emerged as dominant in the field of education in the United States during the early and mid-20th century and have reemerged in the current climate of the 21st century.

In this section we provide a condensed account of a variety of action research traditions. There is only space to whet the reader's appetite to explore further the work summarized here. We hope that practitioners, armed with knowledge of previous attempts to promote research by practitioners, will be in a better position to articulate the importance and legitimacy of their own work.

Beginnings of Action Research

The idea of educational practitioners doing research in schools goes back at least as far as the late 19th and early 20th century with the movement for the scientific study of education. Teachers were viewed as the front line of data gatherers for a massive research movement that saw teachers as researchers, working scientifically in their classroom laboratories (McKernan, 1988).

Although this vision of teachers as researchers never materialized, it is interesting to note that within this model, teachers were allocated the role of carrying out research in their classrooms that was designed by university researchers. This vision of teachers as researchers viewed teachers as mere gatherers of data that could be analyzed statistically.

As early as 1926, Buckingham (as cited in McKernan, 1988) recognized the potential of qualitative, case study research: "Among the many types of research work available to teachers, the making of case studies is by no means unimportant" (p. 176). The hierarchical relations between universities and schools reflected in most of this early work on action research continues to be a source of tension today.

Overlapping this scientific movement in education was the progressive movement inspired by John Dewey. In *Logic: The Theory of Inquiry*, Dewey argues that all inquiry involves both common sense and science. In a more direct reference to action research, Dewey (as cited in McKernan, 1988) states:

> Educational practices provide the data, the subject matter which form the problems of enquiry. . . . A constant flow of less formal reports on special school affairs and results is needed. . . . It seems to me that the contributions that might come from classroom teachers are a comparatively neglected field; or, to change the metaphor, an almost unworked mine. (p. 177)

Dewey's work is the inspiration of much of the current writing on the "reflective practitioner" (Schön, 1983), which has helped us better understand how school practitioners make sense of their experiences and engage in professional learning. (For a more complete discussion of action research and the Progressive era, see Schubert & Lopez-Shubert, 1997.)

The Action Research Tradition

Some see the origins of action research in the work of Kurt Lewin and the group dynamics movement of the 1940s. Although Lewin was not the first to use or advocate action research, he was the first to develop a theory of action research that made it somewhat respectable in the social sciences. Lewin believed that knowledge should be created from problem solving in real-life situations. Among the problems he studied were those related to production in factories and discrimination against minority groups (Lewin, 1946, 1948). Argyris and Schön (1991) briefly describe the goals and methods of the action research tradition:

> Action research takes its cues—its questions, puzzles, and problems—from the perceptions of practitioners within particular, local practice contexts. It bounds episodes of research according to the boundaries of the local context. It builds descriptions and theories within the practice context itself, and tests them there through intervention experiments—that is, through experiments that bear the double burden of testing hypotheses and effecting some (putatively) desired change in the situation. (p. 86)

The double burden that Argyris and Schön refer to is the concern with both action (improvement of practice, social change, and the like) and research (creating valid knowledge about practice). According to them, this sets up a conflict between the rigor and the relevance of the research—a conflict that has been viewed as both an advantage and a disadvantage by different commentators. Unlike traditional social science research that frowns on intervening in any way in the research setting, action research demands some form of intervention. For the action researcher, this intervention results in a spiral of action cycles in which one undertakes

1. To develop a plan of action to improve what is already happening

2. To act to implement the plan

3. To observe the effects of action in the context in which it occurs

4. To reflect on these effects as a basis for further planning and subsequent action through a succession of cycles (Kemmis, 1982, p. 7)

This cycle of activities forms an action research spiral in which each cycle increases the researcher's knowledge of the original question, puzzle, or problem and leads to its solution. In action research these are often referred to as plan-act-observe-reflect cycles, and all four moments of the cycle can occur during a single lesson or over a period of weeks or months. All competent practitioners engage informally in these cycles of reflective action, but action research makes such reflection more intentional and systematic.

Action Research in Education

During the early 1950s, action research was promoted in the field of education principally by Corey (1949, 1953, 1954) at Columbia Teachers College. Corey believed that teachers would likely find the results of their own research more useful than the results of the work of outsiders and thus would be more likely to question current curricular practices. Corey was the executive officer of the Horace Mann-Lincoln Institute of School Experimentation, which was founded at Teachers College. Under Corey's direction, members of the institute's staff collaborated on research with classroom teachers. In his 1953 book, Corey published several of these studies and a summary of what he called the "cooperative action research movement." Foshay (1993), a participant in the movement (Foshay & Wann, 1953), describes the rather sudden demise of action research in education:

> The chief limitation of cooperative action research, from the point of view of the educational researchers of the time, was that it was not possible to generalize from the examined population to others, because no attempt was made to see whether the examined population was representative of a larger population. In addition, since much of the research was designed and carried out by classroom teachers, who were not trained in research, the data often were flawed. For these reasons the movement was ridiculed in the publications of AERA, and it did not spread. It disappeared as the members of the Institute staff scattered with the passage of time. (p. 3)

It is not surprising, given the general hostility that educational researchers in the 1950s felt toward nonpositivist research of any kind, that action research was ridiculed and judged by positivist standards. By the end of the 1950s, action research had declined not only in the field of education but in the social sciences as well. In an article titled "Whatever Happened to Action Research?" Sanford (1970) suggested that funding agencies wanted more basic research and that an increasing split between science and practice led to the cult of the expert (Lindblom & Cohen, 1979) and the top-down, "social engineering" mentality of the period. In spite of its current popularity among teachers, action research is again under attack by a resurgence of positivism, social engineering, and "evidence-based" "teacher-proof" curricula.

Although action research never totally disappeared, interest in it waned during the 1960s—a decade in which adherence to the cult of social engineering reached its height. The late British researcher Lawrence Stenhouse is usually credited with renewing interest in action research in Britain during the 1970s.

The Teacher-as-Researcher
Movement in Great Britain

Although there had been much discussion throughout the 20th century of the idea of school practitioners doing research within their own sites, generally there had been more talk than action. With a teacher research movement that began in Great Britain during the late 1960s, this began to change. This movement is most often associated with the work of Stenhouse, who established the Center for Applied Research in Education (CARE) at East Anglia University, and with the later work of John Elliott and Clem Adelman of the Ford Teaching Project.

Elliott (1991) makes the case that teacher research began as a teacher-led curriculum reform movement that grew out of concern by teachers over the forced implementation of behavioral objectives in curriculum and Great Britain's tracked educational system. He describes his own participation in the teachers-as-researchers movement in Great Britain during the 1960s:

> Curriculum practices were not derived (by us) from curriculum theories generated and tested independently of that practice. They constituted means by which we generated and tested our own and each other's theories. Practices took on the status of hypotheses to be tested. So we collected empirical data about their effects, and used it as evidence in which to ground our theorizing with each other in the context of collegial accountability. We didn't call it research, let alone action research. This articulation came much later as the world of academia responded to change in schools. But the concept of teaching as reflexive practice and a form of educational inquiry was tacitly and intuitively grasped in our experience of the innovation process. Our research was by no means systematic. It occurred as a response to particular questions and issues as they arose. (p. 8)

The heyday of action research in Great Britain saw a teacher research movement develop in the schools as well as a series of large, state-funded collaborative action research projects. During the 1970s and 1980s, a lively debate took place in Great Britain over a number of issues in action research. Among them were a search for a guiding paradigm (Altricher & Posch, 1989), the political problems of promoting action research within institutions that do not want to look at themselves too closely (Holly, 1989), and the usefulness of more quantitative approaches to action research (Harwood, 1991). One of the most interesting critiques was that of feminist action researchers.

Feminist researchers involved in the Girls and Occupational Choice Project (Chisholm, 1990; Weiner, 1989) and Girls in Science and Technology (Whyte, 1987) argued that action research was being turned into a project in social engineering and was losing its "emancipatory" potential. German feminist action researcher Mies (as cited in Chisholm, 1990) argued that the radical potential of action research is lost when it is turned into a recipe and controlled by state agencies:

> [Early on] "action" was interpreted not as socially liberating and dynamic praxis, but rather, in a manner observable in many activist groupings where precise short-term goals are set, as a narrow pragmatism. The same would appear to be true for what is termed "action research," which typically comprises planned intervention in specific social contexts, mostly under the control and direction of state agencies and monitored by researchers—in other words, a sort of social engineering. (p. 255)

This concern with moving action research beyond narrow pragmatism and planned interventions by external agencies had been taken up earlier by a group of Australians led by Stephen Kemmis, who spent time with British action researchers at East Anglia (Tripp, 1990). Carr and Kemmis (1986) challenged older models of action research as essentially conservative and positivistic. In a later article, Carr (1989) reasserts that, "in theory, action research is only intelligible as an attempt to revive those forms of democratic dialogue and reflective theorizing which under the impact of positivism have been rendered marginal" (p. 89). He is concerned that as action research becomes more methodologically sophisticated and technically proficient, it will lose its critical edge.

Two booklets that had an important impact on teacher research in the 1980s were Kemmis and McTaggart's *The Action*

Research Planner (1982), a user-friendly introduction to the action research spiral, and Kemmis's *The Action Research Reader* (1982), a compilation of critical action research studies.

Participatory Research:
The Legacy of Paulo Freire

Long before feminists and critical theorists began their critique of the conservatism of traditional action research, a model of action research was taking hold in Latin America. After the Brazilian military coup of 1964, Paulo Freire, literacy worker and author of *Pedagogy of the Oppressed* (1970), was forced into exile in Chile. During the late 1960s and early 1970s, Freire and a group of Chilean literacy educators began a series of "thematic research" projects. Freire's (1970) notion of thematic research was a highly inductive process in which research was viewed as a form of social action. In this type of research, "generative themes," or issues of vital importance to community members, are identified, used as a basis for literacy instruction, and studied in a collaborative fashion. Such projects have a dual purpose: to help participants (usually adults) acquire literacy and to help them engage in social critique and social action. In other words, literacy involves learning to read the word and the world. This type of action research is called participatory research or participatory action research (PAR).

In 1976 the Participatory Research Group was created by the International Council of Adult Education in Toronto and its network centers around the world. During the last three decades, "participatory research" has been done all over Latin America and the rest of the developing world (Brown & Tandon, 1983; Fals Borda, 2001; Gaventa, 1988; Hall, 2002) and increasingly in the United States (Kelly, Mock, & Tandon, 2001). The first World Symposium of Action Research was held in Cartagena, Colombia, in 1977. This conference has since been held throughout the world and attracts thousands of attendees (Wallerstein & Duran, 2003). A North American example of a similar approach is the work in Appalachia of the Highlander Center, led by Miles Horton and more recently by John Gaventa (Gaventa & Horton, 1981).

Although methodological considerations depend on the context within which the study is undertaken, de Schutter and Yopo

(1981) describe the following as general characteristics of participatory research:

- The point of departure for participatory research is a vision of social events as contextualized by macro-level social forces.
- Social processes and structures are understood within a historical context.
- Theory and practice are integrated.
- The subject-object relationship is transformed into a subject-subject relationship through dialogue.
- Research and action (including education itself) become a single process.
- The community and researcher together produce critical knowledge aimed at social transformation.
- The results of research are immediately applied to a concrete situation. (p. 68)

In Freirian-inspired participatory research, the academic research model is challenged at almost every point. The dualisms of theory and practice, subject and object, and research and teaching are collapsed. This perspective also challenges many of the premises of more traditional models of action research. Many of the criticisms are similar to the feminist critique of action research discussed above. Brown and Tandon (1983) indicate that traditional action research tends to concentrate on an individual or group level of analysis of problems, whereas participatory research, with its more emancipatory emphasis, tends to focus on a broader societal analysis. Traditional action research tends to emphasize issues of efficiency and improvement of practices, whereas participatory research is concerned with equity/self-reliance/oppression problems.

Participatory research also operates out of a more politically sophisticated perspective and is viewed as taking place within a field of power relations in which conflicts of interest often create resistance to the research. Participatory researchers assume that they will be resisted from above (i.e., by powerful vested interests), whereas traditional action researchers are often consultants who are hired by the powerful. Herr's account of her action research in Chapter 4 is an example of action research that evolved into a participatory action research project as students took ownership of the research questions.

Action Science

Action science is largely associated with the work of Argyris (Argyris, Putnam, & Smith, 1985), who has been influenced by the action research tradition discussed above. More recently, he has incorporated aspects of critical theory into his work, particularly Habermas's (1979) theory of communication, which seeks to establish nondistorted communication in which the force of the better argument prevails, as judged in free and open discussion.

Argyris wishes to return the scientific dimension to action research, arguing that the problem-solving focus of action research has moved it too far away from the tasks of theory building and testing. The goal of an action science, according to Argyris (Argyris et al., 1985), is the generation of "knowledge that is useful, valid, descriptive of the world, and informative of how we might change it" (p. x). He has criticized some types of action research for adhering to traditional social science notions of "rigorous research," arguing that "to attain a certain level of rigor, the methodology may become so disconnected from the reality it is designed to understand that it is no longer useful" (p. x).

Drawing on the work of Dewey and Lewin, and often writing with Schön (Argyris & Schön, 1974), Argyris over the years has evolved an intervention strategy for changing the status quo that stresses organizational learning. According to Argyris et al. (1985),

[I]n social life, the status quo exists because the norms and rules learned through socialization have been internalized and are continually reinforced. Human beings learn which skills work within the status quo and which do not work. The more the skills work, the more they influence individuals' sense of competence. Individuals draw on such skills and justify their use by identifying the values embedded in them and adhering to these values. The interdependence among norms, rules, skills, and values creates a pattern called the status quo that becomes so omnipresent as to be taken for granted and to go unchallenged. Precisely because these patterns are taken for granted, precisely because these skills are automatic, precisely because values are internalized, the status quo and individuals' personal responsibility for maintaining it cannot be studied without confronting it. (p. xi)

Argyris's work is important for action researchers because it points out why many institutions may not be thrilled at the idea of close examination. It is also important because unless solutions to the classroom and school problems under study tap into the complex theories of action that underlie and maintain the status quo, problems will only be solved in a superficial and temporary manner.

Robinson (1993), a former student of Argyris, describes the need for problem-based methodology in educational research:

Much research has failed to influence educational problems because it has separated problematic practices from the pre-theorized problem-solving processes that gave rise to them and which render them sensible to those who engage in them. Once practice is understood in this way, the theorizing and reasoning of practitioners becomes a key to understanding what sustains problematic practice. Problem-based methodology provides a way of uncovering, evaluating and, if necessary, reconstructing these theories of action. (p. 256)

What Robinson's work implies is that action research should not simply promote practitioners' "practical theories" (Sanders & McCutcheon, 1986) in a nonproblematic way but should explore in self-reflective ways how some practical theories may be perpetuating the very problems practitioners identify for study.

The Teacher Researcher Movement in North America

Although the teacher researcher movement in North America occurred later than in Britain and Latin America, it was not derivative of either movement nor was it a reappropriation of the North American action research movement of the 1940s and 1950s. CARE and the work of Freire inspired many North American academics and some teachers, but the movement among North American teachers to do research began with a unique set of circumstances:

1. The dominance of the quantitative, positivist paradigm of research in education was challenged by qualitative, case study, narrative, and ethnographic research from the late 1960s on. Because qualitative forms of research more closely resemble the narrative forms already used by practitioners to communicate their knowledge, making these forms of research legitimate helped open the door for practitioners to experiment with more systematic qualitative approaches in studying their practice.

2. Research on successful school change efforts and schools as contexts for teachers' professional work began to report that school-based problem-solving approaches to change were more likely to be implemented successfully than large, federally funded, outside-in initiatives (Fullan, 1982; Lieberman & Miller, 1984). These findings spawned a large number of "collaborative" or "interactive" research and development efforts, in which educational practitioners were invited to work alongside R&D experts in implementing programs and improving practices. (For accounts of these collaborative research projects, see Griffin, Lieberman, & Jacullo-Noto, 1982; Oakes, Hare, & Sirotnik, 1986; Oja & Ham, 1984.)

3. The increased deskilling of teachers and the dissemination of teacher-proof curricula spawned an effort on the part of educational practitioners to reprofessionalize teaching and to reclaim teachers' knowledge about practice as valid. *The Reflective Practitioner,* by Donald Schön (1983), encourages practitioners to tap into their store of professional knowledge to make it explicit and share it with other practitioners. From the notion of "reflective practice," it was only a short step to that of action research, which became linked to an overall attempt by educational practitioners to reassert their professionalism. The report of the Boston Women's Teachers' Group titled *The Effect of Teaching on Teachers* (Freedman, Jackson, & Boles, 1986) described the structural conditions and isolation of teachers' work that makes professionalism difficult (see also Freedman, Jackson, & Boles, 1983). This report pointed out that teachers work "in an institution which supposedly prepares its clients for adulthood, but which views those entrusted with this task as incapable of mature judgment" (Freedman et al., 1986, p. 263). Liston and Zeichner (1991), in reviewing the group's work, point out that the research was used

to "combat the individualistic bias in the school reform movement of the 1980s, which served to direct teachers' sense of frustration with and anger about their work away from a critical analysis of schools as institutions to a preoccupation with their own individual failures" (p. 150).

These problems have increased in the wake of the omnibus No Child Left Behind educational reform legislation, signed by President George W. Bush on January 8, 2002, which gives these deskilling tendencies the force of law (McNeil, 2000). The social engineering tendencies in this legislation and its obsession with testing and narrow forms of accountability have decreased professional autonomy for teachers and administrators. Under the influence of such regimes, action research is captured almost exclusively by the technical knowledge interests described later in this chapter.

4. Encouraged by the pioneering work of Atwell (1982), Goswami and Stillman (1987), Graves (1981), Myers (1985), the Brookline Teacher Research Seminar (2003), and the Bay Area Writing Project, language arts teachers led the way in doing teacher research and writing about it from an "insider" perspective. They have not only used student writing as data but also written case studies of a variety of issues in the teaching of writing. Because of these teachers' own commitment to writing, they have tended to lead the way in writing and publishing accounts of their experiences as teacher researchers. (For examples, see Ballenger, 1993, 1998; Brookline Teacher Research Seminar, 2003; Gallas, 1993, 1997, 2003; Goswami & Schultz, 1993; Martin, 2001. See also our summary of Ballenger's [1993] research in Chapter 3.) The increasing importance of Vygotskian sociocultural approaches to literacy have also encouraged greater collaboration among researchers and practitioners (Lee, Smagorinsky, Pea, Brown, & Heath, 1999).

5. Many university teacher education programs and university/school collaborations began to emphasize teacher research. One of the best known efforts to incorporate teacher research into a teacher education program is that of Ken Zeichner and others at the University of Wisconsin (Caro-Bruce, Klehr, & Zeichner, 2007; Liston & Zeichner, 1991). Susan Noffke, Jennifer Gore, and Marie Brennan, all former university supervisors in the elementary teacher education program at the University of Wisconsin–Madison, have

documented the uses of action research in the preparation of teachers (Noffke & Brennan, 1991; Zeichner & Noffke, 2002). More recently, Mary Klehr, Ryan Flessner, Ann Schulte, and Julio Pereira have continued this work, and the Madison School District supports action research as a form of professional development and generation of knowledge.

A school district-initiated action research collaboration is led by Jackie Delong in Ontario, Canada. As superintendent of the Grand Erie School District, she helped found a partnership with the Elementary Teachers' Federation of Ontario, the Grand Erie District School Board, and Nipissing University. This has resulted in the use of action research for teacher training and development and a journal, *The Ontario Action Researcher*, through which they disseminate findings.

Programs of this kind are becoming more common in colleges of education and school districts and promise to have an important impact on moving teacher and administrative preparation programs toward a more reflective model. For accounts of other similar programs and discussions of the role of action research in teacher education and school-university collaborations, see Christman et al. (1995), Clift, Veal, Holland, Johnson, and McCarthy (1995), Gitlin et al. (1992), Johnson (2002), Moller (1998), Sirotnik (1988), and Smith-Maddox (1999).

6. The school restructuring movement of the 1980s began to propose restructuring schools to create conditions that nurture teacher inquiry and reflection. The Holmes Group's (1990) *Tomorrow's Schools* contains a chapter dedicated to schools as "centers for reflection and inquiry." This chapter covers themes first reported in Schaefer's 1967 book, *The School as a Center of Inquiry.* The notion of schools as communities of learners has grown over the past two decades (Rogoff, Turkanis, & Bartlett, 2001). Many independent collaborative efforts to restructure schools have included action research as an aspect of teacher empowerment. In Georgia, the League of Professional Schools has made action research a key component in the move to shared governance and school renewal (Glickman, 1993). The Coalition of Essential Schools is founded on the notion of ongoing inquiry and reflection and attempts to build these habits of mind in students. These types of reform movements have promise to make action research more legitimate.

Action Research as Self-Study and Autoethnography

While action research is best done in collaboration with others who have a stake in solving a problem, there is also an important place in action research for deep reflection that leads to individual professional growth. In fact, some writers on action research have criticized its tendency to privilege the group over the individual (Webb, 1996). Whitehead (as cited in Webb, 1996), for example, promotes action research as a self-reflective process focused on the individual.

> I believe that the incorporation of "I" as a living contradiction in explanations for the educational development of individuals has distinguished an original contribution to the Action Research movement. . . . I experience problems or concerns when some of my values are denied in my practice; I imagine ways of improving my practice and choose a course of action; I act and gather evidence which will enable me to make a judgment on the effectiveness of my actions; I evaluate the outcomes of my actions; I modify my concerns, ideas and action in the light of my evaluation. (p. 159)

(See also McNiff & Whitehead, 2000.)

This focus on the individual practitioner follows the lead of Schön (1983) in attempting to understand how practitioners learn their craft. A focus on one's own personal and professional selves is a form of action research usually called self-study (Bullough & Pinnegar, 2001) or autoethnography (Bochner & Ellis, 2002; Reed-Danahay, 1997).

Bullough and Pinnegar (2001) discuss quality criteria for self-study research, focusing primarily on research done by teacher educators in universities. However, viewing practitioner action research as self-study may be useful in providing a needed balance between the demands of "data gathering" and "self-reflection." They caution that self-study

> does not focus on the self per se but on the space between self and the practice engaged in. There is always a tension between those two elements, self and the arena of practice, between self in relation to practice and the others who share

the practice setting. Each self-study researcher must negotiate that balance, but it must be a balance—tipping too far toward the self side produces solipsism or a confessional, and tipping too far the other way turns self-study into traditional research. (p. 15)

Practitioner action researchers are seldom studying a problem in their classroom or school divorced from their own personal and professional beliefs and actions. The gaze of the teachers studying their own classrooms or principals studying their own schools must be directed both outward and inward.

Practitioner Action Research: From Academic Tradition to Social Movement

Older traditions of action research were generally associated with academics, mostly social scientists who were virtually all men, such as Dewey, Lewin, Corey, Stenhouse, Elliott, Argyris, Schön, Freire, and Kemmis. As school practitioners become more active in sharing their work and action research becomes a broad-based movement, it has the potential to reject the dualistic hierarchies of university and school, knowledge and action, theory and practice. It has the potential to become a truly grassroots, democratic movement of knowledge production and educational and social change. Winter (1987) elaborates on how action research challenges current conceptions of social inquiry:

Action research addresses "head on" social inquiry's fundamental problems—the relation between theory and practice, between the general and the particular, between common sense and academic expertise, between mundane action and critical reflection, and hence—ultimately between ideology and understanding. (p. viii)

However, few commentators on action research go into detail about what "critical" reflection looks like or how it is accomplished. Too often, it is assumed that a paradigm shift to action research will automatically provide a critique of the status quo grounded in practitioners' realities. Kincheloe (1991) presents an alternative possibility:

When the critical dimension of teacher research is negated, the teacher-as-researcher movement can become quite a trivial enterprise. Uncritical educational action research seeks direct applications of information gleaned to specific situations—a cookbook style of technical thinking is encouraged. . . . Such thinking does not allow for complex reconceptualizations of knowledge and as a result fails to understand the ambiguities and the ideological structures of the classroom. [In this way] teacher research is co-opted, its democratic edge is blunted. It becomes a popular grassroots movement that can be supported by the power hierarchy—it does not threaten, nor is it threatened. Asking trivial questions, the movement presents no radical challenge or offers no transformative vision of educational purpose, as it acts in ignorance of deep structures of schooling. (p. 83)

In a similar vein, Miller (1990) recounts how she and a group of teachers in a research study group struggled with this very issue of expanding the focus of action research so as to become "challengers" of nonresponsive educational institutions. One teacher researcher in the group asks the following question:

Do you think that we could just turn into another form, an acceptable professional form of empowerment? Well, what I mean is that nothing would please some administrators I know more than to think that we were doing "research" in their terms. That's what scares me about the phrase "teacher-as-researcher" these days—too packaged. People buy back into the very system that shuts them down. That immediately eliminates the critical perspectives that we're working on, I'm afraid. But I'm still convinced that if enough people do this, we could get to a point of seeing at least a bigger clearing for us. (p. 114)

As Schön (1983) points out, social institutions are characterized by dynamic conservatism. This conservatism is dynamic in that it constantly pulls practitioners back to a status quo that, as noted by Argyris et al. (1985), consists of norms, rules, skills, and values that become so omnipresent as to be taken for granted and to go unchallenged. Either practitioner action research can reproduce those norms, rules, skills, and values, or it can challenge them. However, practitioners intuitively know that when they challenge the norms, the institution's dynamic conservatism will respond in a defensive, self-protective manner.

A survey conducted in 1999 of institutions affiliated with AACTE (American Association of Colleges for Teacher Education) indicated that almost half required teacher education candidates to participate in action research (Henderson, Hunt, & Wester, 1999, as cited in Green & Brown, 2006). But as Green and Brown (2006) point out, there does not seem to be a clear-cut concept or unified set of procedures that is agreed upon for these experiences. While it is increasingly popular to include some form of action research in teacher preparation, these efforts do not necessarily link teacher research with larger issues of equity in educational systems.

If the practitioner action research movement is to break out of the dynamic conservatism of schools and school systems, then these institutional issues must be addressed by action researchers. As Miller (1990) indicates, this may be best done in the context of action research study groups.

A teacher in Miller's (1990) group wonders whether, as teachers find their voices through critical forms of action research, their schools will welcome their voices or view them as troublemakers:

> What's bothering me still is what's beneath the apparent. What's bothering me is not really the idea of no copy machine for teachers to use, or mice in the school, or the lack of supplies. I've finally realized that teaching is a political thing. Its politics remain under the table. I know that I have deliberately and consciously avoided this for many years. I can honestly say that I was aware of it but chose to remain removed, naive, and ill-informed. When I started in 1977, I told myself that I'd never be involved. So I taught each and every class with exactly what I was given, did exactly what I was told. I never questioned class size, supply procedures, curriculum requirements or extracurricular demands. I volunteered for everything from spring concert, to participating in Gym night, to working in three schools with no time for a scheduled lunch period. But, now I'm no longer willing to do all of that, or at least I now ask "why?" I know that I'm different now than I used to be as a teacher, I know I'm thinking differently, I *know* that I'm involved, because teaching *is* involvement! I know

my involvement, my becoming vocal, has been noticed. And I
don't think they like it! But I can no longer be the teacher who
just teaches what others have thought up and given name to.
I'm running things now. What about me as an *educator?* Can
there be such a thing, can I exist? (p. 140)

Practitioners must make their peace with how much of a chal-
lenger of the status quo they wish to be. Some are more skillful and
in stronger positions to take stands on issues than others. We need
more accounts of those who do decide to challenge the status quo
through their action research and the complexities they encounter
in these efforts (Herr, 1999b). However, if action research is not
done with a critical spirit, it runs the risk of legitimating what may
be—from the perspective of equity considerations—unacceptable
social arrangements.

ACTION RESEARCH: EPISTEMOLOGY

Quality Criteria for Practitioner Action Research

Terms like *validity* and *trustworthiness* are used to describe
quality criteria for quantitative and qualitative academic research.
Validity is a term favored by quantitative researchers, and *trustworthiness* is favored by qualitative researchers. The choice of language for quality criteria for action research is important, because
to use either term risks being evaluated by inappropriate criteria.
Some have suggested the term *workability* as a term more appropriate to action research. However, we find this notion of "what
works" to be too utilitarian. Eventually, action researchers will
develop a language system more appropriate to the particular
dilemmas involved in action research, but for the purposes of this
book, we use *validity* and *trustworthiness*, with the caveat that neither is a particularly good fit.

In a general sense, *internal validity* or *trustworthiness* refers to
the trustworthiness of inferences drawn from data. Quantitative
researchers tend to use statistical analyses to make these inferences, whereas qualitative researchers tend to use qualitative
data. *External validity* refers to how well these inferences general-
ize to a larger population or are transferable to other contexts.

Because academic educational researchers are part of a positivistic tradition inherited from the natural sciences via the discipline of psychology, they consider the notion of statistical validity to be of utmost importance in educational research. The influence of ethnography and qualitative case study methods tempered this tendency for a while, but in recent years there seems to be a return, at least in the federal government, to an emphasis on positivist, statistical research methods. Because qualitative researchers have developed their own set of rules about the validity, which they call "trustworthiness," of qualitative research findings, we will review these rules before proposing new ones for practitioner action research.

Although qualitative researchers are not in total agreement, they generally reject the claims of positivism that research is fundamentally about pursuing truth value (internal validity) by demonstrating that causes and their effects have been isolated. Lincoln and Guba (1985) propose that the comparable standard of "trustworthiness" is more appropriate for naturalistic (i.e., qualitative) inquiry. A study's trustworthiness involves the demonstration that the researcher's interpretations of the data are credible or ring true to those who provided the data and that multiple data sources have been compared or "triangulated."

Although the standards for qualitative or ethnographic inquiry are different from those used by quantitative researchers, they may not be appropriate for action researchers. This is partly because qualitative researchers tend to be outsiders studying settings in which they are not true participants; practitioner action researchers, on the other hand, are insiders studying their own setting. Most qualitative or ethnographic researchers want to study a phenomenon in its *natural* setting—thus the term often used to describe this approach, *naturalistic inquiry.* To the extent that researchers act within or change a setting through their presence, they "contaminate" the setting. Though somewhat overstated, a qualitative researcher wants to be a fly on the wall, observing a social setting as it develops independently of the researcher. While it is true that traditional ethnographers often lived in the communities they studied, had key informants, and interacted with participants in order to gain access to the setting and to gain their trust, the basic position of "outsider" is intentionally maintained.

In many ways, the two groups have opposite dilemmas. Academic researchers (outsiders) want to understand what it is like to be an insider without "going native" and losing the outsider's perspective. Practitioners (insiders) already know what it is like to be an insider, but because they are "native" to the setting, they must work to see the taken-for-granted aspects of their practice from an outsider's perspective. This is further complicated by the fact that many academic researchers have, in fact, been school practitioners (as well as having experienced schools as a student) and are, therefore, in some sense both insiders and outsiders. Moreover, many school practitioners have been socialized into academic research through graduate study and have internalized many outsider social categories. Therefore, the distance between university researchers/ practitioners and school practitioners/researchers is sometimes not as great as we make it out to be in theory.

Furthermore, qualitative researchers do not always agree among themselves about the purposes of research and the criteria for validity. For example, some qualitative researchers, often called critical or feminist ethnographers, prefer a more interventionist, emancipatory approach to qualitative research. Because of the more traditional qualitative researchers' fly-on-the-wall approach to school and classroom observation, some critical and feminist researchers claim that qualitative research is mired in positivism, in that it "affirms a social world that is meant to be gazed upon but not challenged or transformed" (Roman, 1992, p. 573).

In spite of some common experiences with schooling and an expressed openness to collaboration, the culture of the university research community and that of school practitioners are characterized by very different purposes, norms, views of valid knowledge, and work conditions. For instance, the purposes of academic qualitative research and practitioner action research are fundamentally different. Qualitative research belongs to the knowledge creation/ dissemination/utilization model of applied knowledge in which knowledge is generated by university researchers and disseminated to practitioners, who apply it in their settings. By contrast, most action research is utilized in the same setting in which it is created.

Furthermore, many qualitative researchers (and most action researchers) still see the social sciences as the model for what they consider "data" or "evidence" for assertions. This usually involves some form of observation, interview, survey, or archival/document analysis methods. More narrative types of qualitative and action research drawing from the humanities are often viewed with suspicion. While we have addressed these humanities-oriented approaches to some extent throughout this book, we recommend further reading in this area if you think such an approach will better capture your findings. (See Barone, 2000; Connelly & Clandinin, 1990; Eisner, 1997; Evans, 1995.)

An intense debate has taken place between defenders of action research and those who largely dismiss it as serious research. For example, Huberman (1996) criticizes Cochran-Smith and Lytle (1993), Miller (1990), Gallas (1993), and others who defend action research done by teachers as guilty of hubris because of what he considers exaggerated claims for action research. For many academics, the acceptance of action research is given only on the condition that a separate category of knowledge be created for it. This is usually expressed as some variation on "formal (created in universities) knowledge" versus "practical (created in schools) knowledge" and a strict separation of research from practice (Fenstermacher, 1994; Hammack, 1997; Huberman, 1996; Richardson, 1994; Wong, 1995a, 1995b). For example, Richardson (1994) defines action research as "practical inquiry" that focuses on the "improvement of practice" and then uses her own definition to relegate it to secondary status when compared with formal research. Fenstermacher (1994) declares that practical knowledge results from participating in and reflecting on action and experience, is bounded by the situation or context in which it arises, may or may not be capable of immediate expression in speech or writing, and deals with "how to do things, the right place and time to do them, or how to see and interpret events related to one's actions" (p. 12).

In response, Cochran-Smith and Lytle (1998) reject the formal/practical knowledge dualism as unhelpful and see it as greatly limiting the very nature of teaching and action research, which they claim is more about

> how teachers' actions are infused with complex and multi-layered understandings of learners, culture, class, gender, literacy, social issues, institutions, communities, materials, texts, and curricula. It is about how teachers work together to develop and alter their questions and interpretive frameworks

informed not only by thoughtful consideration of the immediate situation and the particular students they teach and have taught but also by the multiple contexts—social, political, historical, and cultural—within which they work. (p. 24)

Clandinin and Connelly (1995) have further argued that outsider knowledge is often experienced by teachers as a "rhetoric of conclusions," which enters the practitioners' professional landscape through informational conduits that funnel propositional and theoretical knowledge to them with little understanding that their landscape is personal, contextual, subjective, temporal, historical, and relational among people. Clearly the formal/practical knowledge debate is about more than research; it is about the very nature of educational practice itself.

We think this dialogue among academic gatekeepers and practitioners is a healthy one and hope that practitioner action researchers will soon be accepted into it as equals. Nevertheless, action researchers are well advised to think through the epistemological implications of insider research in which knowledge utilization and creation alternate as action informs theory and theory informs action, with the goal of understanding and changing practice. In this type of research, academic conceptions of validity, whether quantitative or qualitative, are of limited use to the action researcher.

If action researchers are to be accepted in a larger dialogue about education, they must develop some inquiry criteria for their research. This is not to say that they need to justify themselves by the same inquiry criteria as for academic research, but rather that they must make the case for a different conception of validity. This conception of validity should respond to the purposes and conditions of practitioner action research and the uniqueness of its contribution to the dialogue.

The very condition of being a teacher requires a certain appreciation for the differences between rigorous and sloppy work, between analysis and mere opinion. Educational practitioners routinely apply these criteria to their students' work, and there is no reason to believe they would resist applying them to their own and each other's work. In fact, as we discuss below, the project of defining inquiry criteria for action research is currently under way.

Criteria for "Validity" or "Trustworthiness" in Practitioner Action Research

As we mentioned in Chapter 1, practitioners do research in their sites for different reasons. If the purpose of action research is to produce knowledge for dissemination in fairly traditional channels (e.g., dissertations, journals), then the criteria for a "valid" or "trustworthy" study may be different from the criteria of practitioners who organize their research around specific problems within an action context and recycle the knowledge back into that context.

Furthermore, whereas social science research often fetishizes method, action research is less dependent on research method for its trustworthiness criteria. Less dependence on social science methods causes what Greene (1992) identifies as "a blurring of the boundaries between ways of knowing offered by social science and by literature and other humanities" (p. 41).

The following criteria are tentative, and they are best applied to action research that is transformative in nature (i.e., research that is linked to some kind of action to change educational and/or institutional practices).

Outcome Validity/Trustworthiness

One test of the validity or trustworthiness of practitioner action research is the extent to which actions occur that lead to a resolution of the problem or a deeper understanding of the problem and how to go about resolving it in the future. The assumption here is that problem solving takes place in the context of the site and is "solved" or "understood" within those parameters, possibilities, and limitations. We have called this *outcome validity* or *trustworthiness*. Watkins (1991) points out that "many action research studies abort at the stage of diagnosis of a problem or the implementation of a single solution strategy, irrespective of whether or not it resolves the presenting problem" (p. 8). Thus, outcome validity is synonymous with the "successful" outcome of the research project. This, of course, begs the question raised below under democratic validity, that is, successful for whom? Outcome validity also acknowledges the fact that rigorous action research, rather than solving a problem simply, forces the researcher to reframe the problem in a more complex way, often leading to a new set of questions/problems. This ongoing reframing of problems leads to the spiraling dynamic that characterizes the process of most action research over a sustained period of inquiry.

Process Validity/Trustworthiness

Process validity or trustworthiness asks to what extent problems are framed and solved in a manner that permits ongoing learning of the individual or system. In this sense, outcome validity is dependent on process validity in that if the process is superficial or flawed, the outcome will reflect it. Are the "findings" a result of a series of reflective cycles that include the ongoing problematization of the practices or problems under study? Such a process of reflection should include looping back to reexamine underlying assumptions behind problem definition (Argyris et al., 1985). Process validity must also deal with the much-debated problem of what counts as "evidence" to sustain assertions.

Here some criteria might be borrowed from naturalistic inquiry, depending on how "evidence" is defined. The notion of triangulation, or the inclusion of multiple perspectives, guards against viewing events in a simplistic or self-serving way. Triangulation also can refer to using a variety of methods, for example, observations, journaling, and interviews, so that one is not limited to only one kind of data source. "Process" is not, however, limited to method. In narrative and self-study forms of inquiry, there are distinct criteria for what makes a good empirical narrative (as opposed to fiction). Connelly and Clandinin (1990) warn that "not only may one 'fake the data' and write a fiction but one may also use the data to tell a deception as easily as a truth" (p. 10). (See Connelly & Clandinin, 1990, for an elaboration of validity criteria for narrative research.)

Democratic Validity/Trustworthiness

Democratic validity or trustworthiness refers to the extent to which research is done in collaboration with all parties who have a stake in the problem under investigation. If not done collaboratively, how are multiple perspectives and material interests taken into account in the study? For example, are teachers or administrators, through action research, finding solutions to problems that benefit them at the expense of other stakeholders? Are students and their parents seen as part of the insider community that undertakes this type of research, or are they viewed as outsiders by action researchers? While process validity depends on the inclusion of multiple voices for triangulation, democratic validity views it as an ethical and social justice issue.

While "collaborative" and "participatory" are sometimes used interchangeably, it is possible for teachers, administrators, and counselors to collaborate in doing action research to solve school problems such as student attendance or attainment. The research becomes participatory when the research "subjects" or "informants," that is, the students themselves, are brought into the research as coresearchers. Making students coresearchers not only is more democratic; it also benefits both students and the study in other ways. (See Monica Richards's study in Chapter 3 and Herr's study in Chapter 4 for examples of how making an action research study more participatory can energize all participants and result in better data.)

Another version of democratic validity is what Cunningham (1983) calls "local" validity, in which the problems emerge from a particular context and in which solutions are appropriate to that context. Watkins (1991) calls this "relevancy" or "applicability" criteria for validity: that is, "How do we determine the relevance of findings to the needs of the problem context?" (p. 15).

Catalytic Validity/Trustworthiness

Catalytic validity or trustworthiness is "the degree to which the research process reorients, focuses, and energizes participants toward knowing reality in order to transform it" (Lather, 1986, p. 272). In the case of action research, not only the participants but the action researchers themselves must be open to reorienting their view of reality as well as their view of their practitioner roles. All involved in the research should deepen their understanding of the social reality under study and should be moved to some action to change it (or to reaffirm their support of it). The most powerful action research studies are those in which the practitioners recount a spiraling change in their own and their participants' understandings. This reinforces the importance of keeping a research journal in which action researchers can monitor their own change process and consequent changes in the dynamics of the setting. While this criterion overlaps with process and democratic validity, it highlights the transformative potential of action

research, which makes it so appealing to many critical peda-
gogues, staff developers, and school reformers.

Dialogic Validity/Trustworthiness

In academic research the "goodness" of research is monitored
through a form of peer review. Research reports must pass
through the process of review by other researchers in order to
be disseminated through academic journals. Many academic
journals even provide opportunities for researchers to engage in
point/counterpoint debates about research. A similar form of peer
review is beginning to develop within and among practitioner
action research communities. Many action research groups are
forming throughout North America, as practitioners seek dialogue with peers.

"Bias" and subjectivity are a part of action research (and all
research, for that matter); that is, the assumption is that practitioner action researchers have experiences and beliefs that come
into play as they think about the issues or problems under study.
The key is that these experiences and beliefs need to be critically
examined rather than ignored. To do this, mechanisms may need
to be put in place to ensure that they do not have a distorting effect
on outcomes. Lomax, Woodward, and Parker (1996) establish the
importance of validation meetings in which ongoing findings
are defended before one or more critical friends. Bone (1996)
describes a validation meeting:

> I asked three people to act as critical friends; one was my
> deputy [principal], one was a member of staff, and the other
> was from outside the school, a friend who was also a business
> consultant. I selected my critical friends in order to get a
> range of different responses to my work. They helped me
> reflect on my practice and validate my research claims. (p. 23)

In order to promote both democratic and dialogic validity,
some have insisted that practitioner action research should only
be done as collaborative inquiry (Carr & Kemmis, 1986; Torbert,
1981). Others simply suggest that action researchers participate
in critical and reflective dialogue with other action researchers
(Martin, 1987) or work with a critical friend who is familiar
with the setting and can serve as devil's advocate for alternative

explanations of research data. When the dialogic nature of practitioner inquiry is stressed, then studies can achieve what Myers (1985) calls "goodness-of-fit with the intuitions of the teacher community, both in its definition of problems and in its findings" (p. 5).

All of the above validity/trustworthiness criteria for action research are tentative and in flux. We agree with Connelly and Clandinin (1990), who, in discussing validity criteria for narrative inquiry, state:

> We think a variety of criteria, some appropriate to some circumstances and some to others, will eventually be the agreed-upon norm. It is currently the case that each inquirer must search for, and defend, the criteria that best apply to his or her work. (p. 7)

Are the Findings of Action Research Generalizable?

There are many ways to approach the question of how results of action research are "generalized" or transferred to other settings (often referred to as external validity), but we suggest one taken from the work of Robert Stake (1986) on *naturalistic generalization*. Although Stake developed this approach to generalization in the context of qualitative, responsive evaluation research, we feel it has powerful implications for action researchers. Stake's concept of naturalistic generalization is similar in many ways to Lincoln and Guba's (1985) notion of "transferability," in which findings are not generalized but rather transferred from a sending context to a receiving context. According to Lincoln and Guba,

> [I]f there is to be transferability, the burden of proof lies less with the original investigator than with the person seeking to make an application elsewhere. The original inquirer cannot know the sites to which transferability might be sought, but the appliers can and do. The best advice to give to anyone seeking to make a transfer is to accumulate empirical evidence about contextual similarity; the responsibility of the original investigator ends in providing sufficient descriptive data to make such similarity judgments possible. (p. 298)

Greenwood and Levin (1998) discuss this notion under the term "transcontextual credibility." Although similar to the notion of "transferability," Stake's elaboration of naturalistic generalization is more closely tied to *action* and therefore will serve our purposes here better. After years of well-documented failure by outside experts to bring about planned change in schools, Stake (1986) argues that it is time to rediscover the lessons about change that John Dewey taught us:

> Almost absent from mention in the "change literature" is the common way in which improvement is accomplished, a way followed intuitively by the greatest, and the least, of our thinkers. It is the experiential way, an evolutionary way, recognized particularly by John Dewey. One may change practice when *new experience* causes re-examination of problems: Intuitively we start thinking of alternative solutions. (p. 90)

Besides Dewey, Stake cites the work of Polanyi (1958) and Schön (1983), who argue that practice is guided less by formal knowledge than by personal knowledge based on personal or vicarious experience. They also argue that resistance to change is often a form of personal protection.

Stake's argument stipulates that action or changes in practice usually occur as a result of either some kind of external demand or coercion or the conviction on the part of practitioners that an action or change is necessary. We have seen time and again how coercion is successfully resisted by practitioners and how most lasting change takes place through *internal conviction*, or to use a more popular term, *ownership*.

A further premise is that a practitioner's internal conviction is influenced by a mixture of understanding and faith (voluntarism). Understanding, a primary goal of action research, is arrived at through dialogue and reflection drawing on two kinds of knowledge: experiential and propositional. These two kinds of knowledge, according to Stake (1986), are tied to two kinds of generalization: formalistic and naturalistic. "Continuing the analysis, we might say that theory and codified data are the main constituents of our formal, verbalized generalizations—whereas experience, real and vicarious, is the main constituent of the naturalistic generalizations" (p. 97).

Figure 2.1 summarizes this highly condensed chain of influence, in which *action* is influenced by *internal conviction,* which comes from voluntarism and *personal understanding.* This, in turn, is achieved by both formal and *naturalistic generalization,* the latter being the result of direct and *vicarious experience.* In other words, practitioners tend to find traditional research, which is based on formalistic generalizations, less useful than narrative accounts from schools and classrooms that provide them with vicarious experience. Stake (1986) describes how naturalistic generalization is different from more traditional, formalistic generalization:

> The intention of most educational research is to provide formalistic generalization. A typical research report might highlight the correlation between time spent on team projects *and* gain in scores on an achievement test. The report might identify personality, affective and demographic variables. Even with little emphasis on causation this report is part of the grand explanation of student learning. It provides one way of knowing about educational practice.
>
> A more naturalistic research report might deal with the same topic, perhaps with the same teachers and pupils,

Figure 2.1   Robert Stake's Evolutionary View of Change

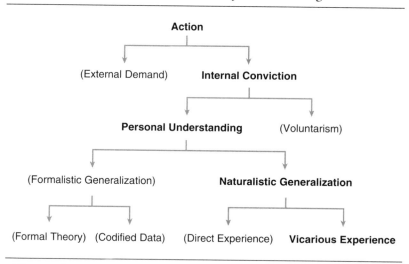

SOURCE: Adapted from Stake (1986).

yet reflecting a different epistemology. The naturalistic data would describe the actual interactions within student teams. The report would probably report project work—conveying style, context, and evolution. A person would be described as an individual, with uniqueness not just in deviance scores, but as a key to understanding the interactions. A reader senses the experience of teamwork in this particular situation. It is a *unique* situation in some respects, but ordinary in other respects. Readers recognize similarities with situations of their own. Perhaps they are stimulated to think of old problems in a new way. (pp. 98–99)

This type of research fits well with current practitioner culture, where, although less systematic, stories are shared daily among practitioners as part of an oral craft tradition. Likewise, Mishler (1986) suggests that the structure of the story is built into the human mind much like deep structures of grammar, and it is largely through narratives that humans make sense of and express their understanding of events and experiences.

We have limited our discussion to certain issues relating to what positivists call the internal and external validity of action research. There are many other issues, issues like how action research generates, tests, or extends social theory or to what extent action research studies can and should be "replicated" by other researchers. There are also other ways to think about and justify a study's external validity. We have provided Stake's approach because we find it a compelling way to think about how action research is taken up by other practitioners and researchers.

ACTION RESEARCH: POLITICS

The Politics of Knowledge, Institutional Change, and Professionalism

One of the underlying assumptions of this book is that action research is best viewed as a vehicle for the empowerment of practitioners, students, and communities toward a goal of institutional and social change from the inside. We feel that the vision of action research as a packaged inservice promoted by external reformers or as the activities of isolated individual practitioners pursuing minor research questions sells the possibilities of action research short. Action research, perhaps more than other innovations, must challenge the sociopolitical status quo of the setting. In fact, we do not really think there are "safe" action research questions unless the researcher contains the exploration of the problem or question so as to divorce it from the larger sociopolitical context in which it takes place. "Solutions" derived from this kind of exploration rarely meet the validity criteria described above.

For practitioners to resist falling into "sanitized" forms of action research, we must explore both the ways in which schools are themselves political and the functions that schools serve in a broader sociopolitical context. We do this not to discourage practitioners from engaging in research but to help them understand the resistance they may encounter from some subordinates and peers. When action research is done skillfully and with the welfare of students at the center of the research, tremendous benefits are likely to accrue to all involved.

What Do We Mean by "Politics"?

When we talk about the "politics" of action research, we mean several things. First, as action research moves beyond the four walls of the classroom, there is a need to understand the institutional micropolitical forces that practitioners will encounter. This institutional aspect of action research has been generally glossed over in most of the literature.

Second, as school practitioners begin to redefine their roles as professional educators, they must critique the narrowness of current definitions of their roles. The work of educational practitioners is becoming more fragmented, more supervised, more assessed, and consequently more controlled from the outside. The attempt to gain control over and redefine one's profession is an essentially political move.

Third, the question of who creates knowledge about teaching, administering, and counseling is a political question. We frequently hear how inaccessible and irrelevant most of the knowledge created by outside researchers is for educational practitioners. Much of what practitioners know about their practice is "subjugated knowledge" (Foucault, 1980) or knowledge that is not viewed as valid by those who create knowledge in universities and those who make educational policy.

We live in a time when subjugated knowledge is being brought to light. Women's studies programs and various ethnic studies programs have successfully demanded legitimacy for diverse cultural and gendered ways of knowing. The knowledge of school practitioners and their students is a form of subjugated knowledge because it is not given legitimacy by those who make educational policy.

Fourth, underlying all these political aspects of action research is the ultimate need to problematize many of the purposes or "functions" of various educational practices and of schooling as a social institution. We discuss each of these issues in greater detail in the remainder of this section.

Institutional Micropolitics

When teachers or principals say that their school or district is "political," they are usually talking about what we refer to here as "micropolitics." Micropolitics includes behind-the-scenes negotiations over material resources, vested interests, and ideological commitments. The micropolitical struggles in many schools are over such issues as inclusion of special education students, varying views on reading instruction, academic tracking, and bilingual and multicultural education. Frequently, micropolitical struggles are over such things as professional jealousy, student class placements, parent-teacher relations, office or classroom space, hall duty, and gender and racial politics. Micropolitics is what gets talked about in private among teachers; it is also what never gets talked about because it is too "political." Micropolitics often exists within the silences created in educational institutions. It is as much about what does not get said as it is about what does.

Because of the essentially political nature of life in schools (and school districts), educational practitioners who are engaged in research in their schools are not necessarily welcomed with open arms by colleagues and administrators. Often they may feel threatened by potential side effects of action research. Given its potential for moving beyond the study site and challenging power relations, action research should not be undertaken ingenuously.

Often these side effects occur even when the research has been carefully contained within the four walls of the classroom. One middle school teacher found that when she began interviewing her students and engaged them in a collaborative study of their own classroom, the students started asking similar questions of teachers in other classrooms. This caught other teachers off guard, and they correctly attributed it to the teacher's research project. Action research, like all good qualitative research, has a natural tendency to spill over into areas one had not expected to study. For example, practitioners should expect that pursuing questions about one's classroom will inevitably lead to questions about the institutional context within which classrooms are embedded. Questions raised at the level of the school site will inevitably lead to questions about school district policies and central office politics. Qualitative research is by nature holistic, and therefore it cannot easily be used to study a phenomenon independent of the various layers of its social context.

The institutional politics of action research rub up against what Schön (1971, as cited in Holly, 1989) calls the "dynamic conservatism" of social institutions. According to Schön,

> A social system is a complex of individuals which tends to maintain its boundaries and its patterns of internal relationships. But given internal tendencies towards increasing disorder, and external threats to stability, energy must be expended if the patterns of the system are to be held stable. Social systems are self-reinforcing systems which strive to remain in something like equilibrium. . . . Social systems resist change with an energy roughly proportional to the radicalness of the change that is threatened. (p. 80)

Action researchers who work in schools are often ill-prepared for resistance (sometimes in the form of indifference) to their efforts. They encounter a school and district culture that values individual effort, professional isolation, and conformity.

Hutchinson and Whitehouse (1986) describe the encounter between the action researcher and institutional politics in the following terms:

> While action research fosters collegiality, informality, openness, and collaboration, action researchers have to contend with educational institutions that are structured hierarchically with formal asymmetrical relations of power and responsibility. These, seen as polar tendencies, contribute to

the struggle between two "political" realities where, usually, the action research project is . . . emasculated, neutralized, cut down to size by and within the institution. (p. 85)

Hutchinson and Whitehouse (1986) argue that practitioners who engage in research must deal not only with institutional politics but also with how their research contradicts the ways in which most practitioners define "professional competence." Referring to teachers, they state:

Confined to the narrow social context of the classroom, a teacher's professional experience and her notions of professional competence are defined by the immediate curricular responsibilities and the practical matters of teaching and learning. . . . The action researcher has to reassess reality and commit herself to the notion that social reality is culturally created and contains contradictions of truth and value. In accepting this, and in attempting to involve others in a critique of practice (and all that this implies), she soon encounters resistance from those who understand their professional competence to be a positive and direct outcome of the social reality that is confined to the classroom but cut off from the wider social and political contexts. (p. 93)

Teachers, in particular, live in a fishbowl. Their professional competence is constantly vulnerable to question from parents, students, principals, and fellow teachers. They are understandably defensive about what they may perceive as attacks on their professional competence. Once action researchers have conquered their own fears about engaging in a social and cultural critique of their own practices, they should expect many of their fellow practitioners to view such a critique as a threat to their own vulnerable sense of professional competence. This broadening through inquiry into one's own practice of what it means to be "competent" leads us to also rethink what it means to be a professional.

The Politics of Redefining Professionalism

Action research has been suggested as a way to reprofessionalize educational practice, particularly teaching, in the face of increasing attempts to standardize and deskill teachers' work (Cochran-Smith & Lytle, 1993). We will briefly explore what it has meant historically for educational practitioners to gain professional status and what it might mean today for practitioners to rethink what it means to be a professional.

There are many excellent historical accounts of how educational practitioners gained professional status. Gitlin et al. (1992), in an attempt to condense much of this literature, demonstrate how the move to gain professional legitimation has actually intensified the divisions between educational research and practice. As normal schools and teachers' colleges were abandoned in favor of university status, colleges of education increasingly adopted the arts and sciences definitions of valid knowledge over those of educational practitioners. According to Gitlin et al.,

> Challenges to the normal school were based on both their practice emphasis and the inclusion of women in those institutions. To achieve professional status required not only a move away from practice toward scientific research, but also a move to differentiate the work of teachers, commonly seen as women's work, from the educational leadership positions held mostly by men. (p. 80)

The quest for professionalization also created a hierarchy between universities and public schools. Academics were viewed as creating valid knowledge about education, and so these "experts" were allotted time for research. They were also able to institute a system of peer governance in which questions of tenure, retention, and promotion were decided by colleagues.

The role of action research in the politics of redefining professionalism is a continuation of this history. It is encouraging to see academic journals and the Holmes Group (1990) calling for "schools as centers of inquiry" and "teachers as communities of learners." However, until academics are willing to address the material conditions of teachers' work and help bring these worlds closer together, their promotion of action research will sound hollow.

Ironically, the renewed interest in the professionalization of teachers has arrived at a time of a crisis of confidence in the professions generally. According to Schön (1983),

[W]hen leading professionals write or speak about their own crisis of confidence, they tend to focus on the mismatch of traditional patterns of practice and knowledge to features of the practice situation—complexity, uncertainty, instability, uniqueness, and value conflict—of whose importance they are becoming increasingly aware. (p. 18)

This crisis of confidence comes, in part, from trying to force a definition of professionalism that values problem solving over problem framing, scientific knowledge over personal knowledge, and facts over values onto an educational reality that is messy, intuitive, anecdotal, and value laden. Unfortunately, as Cochran-Smith and Lytle (1999) pointed out, even before No Child Left Behind made it federal policy, a growing standards and high-stakes testing movement had made an action research approach to professionalism even more difficult:

As pressures for school and classroom accountability inten-sify, research-based, whole school improvement models become increasingly widespread, the concept of best practice guides discussions about student achievement and teacher education, and the authoritative role of outsiders in school improvement becomes the rule rather than the exception. Part of what these developments have in common is a set of underlying assumptions about school change that de-emphasizes differences in local contexts, de-emphasizes the construction of local knowledge in and by school communi-ties, and de-emphasizes the role of the teacher as decision maker and change agent. (p. 22)

In other words, these policy changes de-emphasize many of the most basic tenets of action research. However, research or evi-dence-based practices like Success for All or Open Court reading programs are evidence-based according to a one-size-fits-all approach to research that shows little understanding of nuanced teacher knowledge or student variation. Evans, Lomax, and Morgan (2000) call for evidence-based practices based on the establishment of a community of teacher researchers whose inves-tigations provide the evidence upon which they make decisions to improve their teaching. Here "evidence" is local and is generated and applied in the same setting, which does not preclude teachers using traditional research as a further source of "evidence."

Finally, some educational practitioners have attempted to broaden the notion of "professional" to include more of an advocacy stance toward social issues related to education. This is really an old debate begun by "social reconstructionists" like Counts (1932), who argues that because democracy has to be re-created by each new generation, it is the task of educators to help young people reconstruct society rather than adapt to it. An example of teachers taking a strong advocacy position is the creation by Rita Tenorio and Bob Peterson (as cited in Diegmueller, 1992) of *Rethinking Schools*, a widely read newspaper developed to "shake up every teacher in the system, including the union leadership . . . by offering a vision of what we think should take place in the public schools" (p. 26). Although not all attempts at social transformation are as ambitious or as successful, the tendency of educators to view themselves as apolitical often keeps them from thinking—even at the classroom level—in ways that challenge the status quo.

The Politics of Educational Knowledge

Who creates knowledge about education, how it is created, and who uses it for what purposes are all political questions (Anderson & Herr, 1999). Many see action research as a social movement in which practitioners are attempting to assert their own ways of knowing educational and organizational processes as valid knowledge. In postmodern terms, the knowledge of educational practitioners, along with the knowledge of other marginalized groups like women, the poor, and some ethnic and racial groups, is subjugated knowledge. The problems of educational practice have always been framed by those who do not work in schools. Educational practitioners have traditionally been portrayed in the literature on educational reform as childlike creatures who foolishly resist attempts to bring about changes based on research done in universities and research and development centers. For example, the current federal guidelines tie Title I funding to the use of "scientifically proven" curriculum materials. As discussed in the previous section, this amounts to a de facto endorsement and imposition of scripted programs such as Success for All or Open Court reading programs (Allington, 2002).

Educational planners think in terms of knowledge created outside of schools and disseminated or diffused into schools, where it is implemented or utilized by practitioners. Planners hope this process will result in the institutionalization of their research-backed innovations. Ironically, action research and teacher learning communities are promoted at the same time that teacher autonomy is being drastically reduced, particularly in districts with large Title I programs. Part of the current school reform strategy is to provide pressure and punishment from above while creating limited autonomy for decision making at the school level. Particularly in low-income schools, this autonomy is so limited as to be merely symbolic. Teacher knowledge is devalued when reforms are forced on them. Action research can be a way for teachers to push back on outside-in reforms and to expand the limited autonomy they still have.

However, as educational practitioners move to reassert their professional prerogatives, they must be sensitive to others, such as parents, who are in their own way "experts" about their children, and students themselves, who are also "experts" about their own experiences and needs. Although educational practitioners may rightly feel oppressed in their work conditions, the most oppressed groups are students, who are relatively powerless organizational members, and poor and minority parents, whose children live in marginalized communities.

For this reason, practitioners are advised to include students and parents in their research whenever possible and to be willing to submit their own cherished beliefs (even "progressive" ones) to examination when their students and communities question them. For example, Delpit (1993) found, through critical reflection on her experience as a classroom teacher, that proponents of a whole-language approach to the teaching of reading have in many cases done a disservice to poor, African American children, who, she argues, may benefit from a skills-based approach. Delpit does not endorse "teacherproof," scripted curricula but rather a more nuanced and unbiased assessment of the needs of each child and greater dialogue with communities teachers may not understand. One of the lessons of qualitative research is that all educational practices are context bound and that what might be effective or appropriate in one context might be ineffective or inappropriate in another.

Furthermore, if teachers are going to successfully resist current reforms that deskill them and provide narrow scripted curricula for students, it will have to be in alliance with the low-income communities whose children are falling further behind, despite the No Child Left Behind rhetoric of the current reform. There is growing evidence that when principals and teachers build alliances with community organizations, rather than see them as threats, they increase—not decrease—their power to effect change (Mediratta, Lewis, & Fruchter, 2002; Shirley, 1997).

The Politics of Schooling as a Social Institution

As practitioners generate questions for inquiry, these questions will not only spill over the boundaries of their classrooms into other classrooms and the school as a whole; they will also generate questions that reflect broader social issues. It is difficult to ask questions about ability grouping, for example, without asking to what extent one might be participating in a social tracking system and the ethics of one's complicity in structures that seem beyond one's control. Most of the dilemmas that educators encounter in their schools and classrooms reflect broader social dilemmas and conflicting aims of schooling in American society. This should be self-evident, since schools are social institutions in the sense that they are created by and reflective of the society in which they are embedded, but most educational practitioners have been socialized not to think in this way. As social institutions, schools are stages on which many of our social dramas—from racial integration to occupational sorting (tracking)—are acted out. Some types of questions may seem more political than others, but any question we ask about educational practices in schools is necessarily political. We often attempt to frame questions about schools as if they were not social institutions that reflect a wide variety of vested interests and ideological commitments.

This is due to a long history of depoliticizing schools and universities. While we are not suggesting that teachers should politically indoctrinate students, we are suggesting that teachers and university professors not shy away from asking critical questions concerning how socially just classroom and school practices are. Noffke (1997), in her discussion of the personal, professional, and political dimensions of action research, quotes from an address by Martin Luther King Jr. (1966, as cited in Noffke, 1997) to the attendees of the Conference on Social Change and the Role of Behavioral Sciences:

> We do not ask you to march by our side, although as citizens, you are free and welcome to do so. Rather we ask you to focus on the fresh social issues of our day; to move from observing operant learning, the psychology of risk . . . to the test tubes of Watts, Harlem, Selma, and Bogalusa. We ask you to make society's problems your laboratory. We ask you to translate your data into direction—direction for action. (p. 305)

King's plea is similar to that of some 20th-century social scientists, such as Kurt Lewin, C. Wright Mills, and W. E. B. Dubois, who have challenged the ways that "disinterested" research tends to collude in sustaining an unjust status quo. As educators—whether teachers, teacher educators, school administrators, or university researchers—we are all collectively responsible for what is done for and to children in our name. We are not merely "following orders" as agents of the state or doing "disinterested" research in universities. We act upon the world, and our actions work for or against certain groups. We cannot escape the webs of vested interest that are embedded in our schools and universities. Where we see injustice, we have an obligation to name it and to make it a focus of our reflection and research.

Beginning action researchers with an interest in issues of equity may want to begin with Ruth Johnson's (2002) *Using Data to Close the Achievement Gap: How to Measure Equity in Our Schools.* While the book relies heavily on surveys, it is an excellent way to surface equity issues in schools in a way that provides data for the incredulous. From who has access to computers to who gets counseled out of going to college, it provides an array of places to begin in studying equity issues in your classroom or school and does so in a relatively nonthreatening way.

CONCLUSION

This chapter may have raised the anxiety levels of budding action researchers. We hope, however, that it may head off any unrealistic expectations of doing neat and tidy studies in a political vacuum. We also hope it has freed practitioners from the burden of having to follow rigid research procedures encountered in universities. As Greene (1992) points out, the real issue for practitioners is less "getting it right" than "making it meaningful" (p. 39). In other words, action research is about deepening our understanding of school life in the service of students. This is the goal of many critical thinking practitioners. Action research can be a vehicle toward that end.

In Chapters 3 and 4, we provide examples of practitioners struggling with the various issues raised in this chapter. In Chapter 3, we attempt to give the reader a sense of the diversity of research that practitioners have undertaken. We have chosen studies that we feel exemplify the inquiry criteria discussed above. In Chapter 4, we provide a case study of coauthor Herr's research to illustrate the complexities of teacher research with a goal of student empowerment.

CHAPTER THREE

What Does Practitioner Action Research Look Like?

One of the best ways to learn the possibilities of practitioner action research is through reading accounts of their work. We are fortunate that in the last two decades an increasing number of excellent examples have found their way into print. This, in part, reflects a growing openness of some academic journals to this genre of research, the creation of some journals that explicitly showcase action research, and books like the Practitioner Inquiry Series edited by Marilyn Cochran-Smith and Susan Lytle for Teachers College Press.

When reviewing examples of practitioner action research, it becomes readily apparent that approaches are wide ranging, from informal observations to highly formalized research projects; in short, there is no one "right" way to approach the issue of studying one's own self and one's own practice site. Chism, Sanders, and Zitlow (1989) suggest that practitioners are constantly engaged informally in practice-centered inquiry:

> We recognized that teachers naturally do seem to use a
> form of inquiry to help deal with the problematic realities of

teaching. It is a process that has not often been articulated but is familiar in the experience of many. In a given situation, effective teachers often: (a) Consider the situation based on the information available to them as participants in this particular teaching-learning process and select some action (a practice) tentatively based on their understanding of what is educationally desirable in that situation, feasible and likely to be effective in the sense of resulting in desired outcomes; (b) Try out the practice and observe its results; and (c) Revise the practice if necessary, correct for flaws observed and try it again. (p. 2)

Practitioner action research translates this type of informal questioning of practice to one of more intentional and systematic inquiry that lends itself to problem solving as well as possible dissemination to a larger audience.

The following examples should not be perceived as exhaustive in terms of the action research currently being done by insiders in their own sites. Although more accounts by practitioners are appearing in print, action researchers often enter the research process as a means of solving their own practice dilemmas or questions rather than necessarily to contribute to the field of education as a whole. They may never consider writing a professional paper, and the rewards of publication may be outweighed for educators by the time and energy required to prepare their research for the publication process. At the same time, there is much to be learned through the accounts of action researchers as they pursue research in their own sites. Methodologically, there are many variations on insider action research as well as many epistemological complexities that can best be addressed by those working within these genres of research. We are also in an age of top-down school reforms and innovations; our own sense is that these are best offset by the expert knowledge of practitioner researchers who can supply evidence regarding their own practices. The practice and dissemination of practitioner action research, then, has implications for individual educators and offers the possibility of impacting the larger field of educational theory and practice.

As educators begin to research their own practices and sites, they often read academic research with new eyes. They not only gather ideas for their own practices and research but also find that their own research pushes back some on what is "known," or expert knowledge. We are also seeing higher education academics begin not only to teach action research but also to carry it out in their own university classrooms (Hyland & Noffke, 2005; Price & Valli, 2005). These developments offer a kind of dynamic interaction that has the potential to strengthen practitioner action research as well as that done by academics.

The examples in this chapter illustrate a wide range of current practitioner action research. The example of Hermann-Wilmarth's (2005) work illustrates self-study research conducted from the perspective of improving her "walk and talk," her intentions as an instructor coupled with the feedback of a challenging student. Richards's (1987) research will resonate with many practitioners: What do I do with this class when it looks like nothing I do is effective? While initially investigating her own classroom practices, Richards crosses hierarchical lines and invites her students to be coinvestigators in discovering what might help them become more successful students. Russell (1992) provides an illustration of the potential for practitioner action research to broaden into empowering practice. In Russell's case, other professionals became involved in the process and eventually spoke out on a district level. Ballenger's (1993) work is a striking example of the power of the insider's lens brought to bear on research data. Only through her tacit knowledge of the children's relationships could Ballenger have come to the insights that allowed her to push the edges theoretically.

The examples from both the Denbigh Action Research Group (Evans et al., 2000) and the principals' group (Christman et al., 1995) demonstrate the use of the group process to support the conceptualization and implementation of research. Both groups function as sounding boards, providing the opportunity for professional dialogue, which is often difficult to build into the school day.

Methodologies in these studies vary. A number of the researchers (Ballenger, 1993; Christman et al., 1995; Richards, 1987) utilize journal writing as a way to capture their day-to-day reflections and encounters; the principals' group (Christman et al., 1995) used journals as a way to bring the reality of their school days and decision making to the group as a whole. The researchers in the Denbigh group (Evans et al., 2000) used story writing as a way to initiate dialogue about pressing professional concerns. Hermann-Wilmarth (2005) responded to an extensive e-mail from a student, using it to create a self-reflective dialogue with his critiques of her teaching.

A number of the researchers (Christman et al., 1995; Evans et al., 2000; Russell, 1992) relied on relationships with colleagues as part of the research process, critical friends with whom they could have sustained dialogues regarding their findings and methodologies. Both Richards (1987) and Morgan (Evans et al., 2000) moved students into the roles of collaborators in their research processes.

Observations, whether of their own classroom environment and student interactions with materials (Ballenger, 1993; Russell, 1992) or the shadowing of students as they went through their school day (Richards, 1987), were used to contextualize and understand the students' experiences of the school day. Audiotaping class activities and transcribing the tapes for analysis (Ballenger, 1993; Richards, 1987) were used in a similar way. Teachers seemed to see taping as a way to capture the unfolding of the day-to-day educational process and to be able to analyze it later. These and other methodologies for practitioner research are discussed in depth in Chapter 6.

These examples of practitioner action research touch on a range of possibilities. There are examples of university-school collaborations; research across authority lines such as students and teachers; research as part of professional development; and seasoned as well as new teachers studying their own classrooms, exploring the theoretical implications of their studies. The hope is that research possibilities pertinent to the reader's own practice site will begin to crystallize through reading the research accounts offered here.

SELF-STUDY ACTION RESEARCH: JILL M. HERMANN-WILMARTH AND "THE CASE OF A DISRUPTIVE PRESERVICE TEACHER"

As described in Chapter 2, the value of self-study research is increasingly being recognized; the focus is not "on the self per se but on the space between self and the practice engaged in"

(Bullough & Pinnegar, 2001, p. 15). Bullough and Pinnegar warn that self-study is a balancing act: veer too far in either direction and the researcher risks creating a "confessional"; turn it too far outward and it becomes "a traditional study." Hyland and Noffke (2005) make the distinction, in their own study, that while they gather student data from the courses they teach, the focus is to "inform questions about our own practice" (p. 368). Self-study researchers have the option of working alone or in collaboration with each other (McIntyre & Cole, 2001) with a focus on an ongoing understanding and improvement of one's own practice.

In the following example, we highlight the work of Jill M. Hermann-Wilmarth (2005), a teacher educator, as she works to critically engage her own pedagogy through self-reflection and response to one "disruptive preservice teacher," Anthony. Based on their struggles together the previous semester—several unpleasant confrontations, classroom outbursts by him, and many conferences that ultimately resulted in Anthony seemingly genuinely excited about his learning—Hermann-Wilmarth admits to feeling "slightly apprehensive about another semester of balancing my desire to live my pedagogy in my teaching and the unpredictability of Anthony's response to me as his teacher, but I was hopeful" (p. 472).

Her hopeful stance was quickly challenged. She describes her class of preservice teachers alive with discussion. On this particular day they are in smaller discussion groups, and the room "seems to buzz" (p. 471) with students actively engaged.

Sitting in the midst of what I, as a classroom facilitator, hope is impassioned learning and growing around the issues of language arts exploration is Anthony. His laptop is open, and as he stares intently at the screen, he occasionally stabs at the keys before furiously deleting whatever it is that he has just written. When I ask him if he would like to add to his group's discussion, he gruffly answers, "Oh, I didn't read," and turns back to his computer. Students in his group roll their eyes, shake their heads, and awkwardly attempt to invite him into the dialogue, with little success. Their history with this classmate, I know from anonymous notes in my mailbox, is full of confrontation. Several students have repeatedly reported that not only does he not complete his assignments, but he makes belittling comments and judgments toward their own work. (pp. 471–472)

Beyond this, Anthony typically arrived to class late, "if at all." Once in class, he wandered in and out during discussion time, often leaving for long periods at a time.

But they continue to lurch through the semester together, and while Anthony does not particularly engage with the other students, he seems to connect with Hermann-Wilmarth, albeit often outside of class. Her own impression is that she is gaining some ground with him, but what has appeared to be progress is soon called into question. Hermann-Wilmarth offers:

I felt that at least with me, Anthony had found a space in which to explore his ideas about teaching. When near the end of the semester, Anthony sent me an email that informed me that this indeed was not the case, I was shocked. With his email, Anthony effectively sent me into a reevaluation of my classroom and my pedagogy. He forced me to acknowledge that although I profess to teach from a liberatory stance, my approach can be oppressive. The challenge for me was to read and respond to Anthony's email from a dialoging place. . . . I was afraid that if I did not measure each word, I would silence Anthony even more than I already had. (p. 474)

Part of Anthony's long e-mail letter to her expressed the following:

Not necessarily for any reason that you could control, but I just do not feel comfortable talking to you about my feelings, and because of that I have withdrawn my efforts. It is not that I do not care about the work; I am just nervous to turn it in. I do not feel like my work is good enough, nor do I feel that when I do work to my highest ability that it is recognized as such. I only feel like you tell me that I am not doing a good job. I do realize that this is perception on my part, and I do not think it unflawed—but it is the way I perceive the matter at hand. (p. 474)

His long letter continues in this vein, documenting the grievances of his time in Hermann-Wilmarth's class.

In the spirit of self-study, she decides on the following strategy:

> In the hours following my initial reading of Anthony's letter, I struggled with how to reply. Ultimately, I decided that the best way to do this would be to respond to chunks of his letter in the body of his own text. As I continue to assess myself as a teacher, I want to reenter this teacher-student dialogue as a third, reflective voice. (p. 474)

This echoes what Bullough and Pinnegar (2001) suggest whereby the focus is not on the self but rather on the space between self and the engaged practice. Hermann-Wilmarth uses the "data" offered by Anthony—his long correspondence via e-mail—but with a focus in the analysis toward informing questions about her own practice (Hyland & Noffke, 2005). She "chunks" Anthony's offered writing, responding in bits and pieces, working to "hear" the lessons suggested in his comments.

We highlight below Hermann-Wilmarth's (2005) thinking regarding entering into this kind of action research and why she decided to explore and probe what she terms her own "stumblings."

> This self-study . . . focuses on how I tried to bring together the goals of my teaching and research, which are guided by Freire's (1970) call for praxis: "reflection and action upon the world in order to transform it" (p. 33). These two semesters were also my first two as a full-time graduate student, fresh from the elementary school classroom. I learned both from this study and from Anthony, the student at the center of the study, that teaching and pedagogical practice is always, as Ellsworth (1997) wrote, a paradox "that can never be settled and resolved once and for all" (p. 8). Although I attempted to teach my students guided by the theories about the dialogue of Freire (1970) and hooks (1994) in particular, I stumbled regularly. Anthony pointed out my stumblings, and this study is my attempt to answer hooks's (1994) call to remain engaged with my teaching and students and to examine how I use my power in the classroom. (p. 472)

Hermann-Wilmarth grapples with her multiple positionalities as she makes her way as the instructor of the class and uses her awareness of the complexity of these positions as a starting point for her self-study:

> Each time I enter a classroom community, I grapple with my position as a person steeped in both privilege—through race, class, and education, I am a member of the dominant culture—and oppression—as a lesbian I belong to a socially marginalized and sometimes feared group. Although more sure of my safety and position in the university than I was as an elementary school teacher, I continually debate my own self-disclosure as a lesbian to enhance the discussion of self-justice and issues of security and vulnerability to which that self-disclosure would expose me. (p. 472)

Added to the mix just described was her newness to the role of university instructor and her youth (she was 25 at the time she was teaching this class, and Anthony, the preservice teacher, was 21). Her very lack of experience in this teaching role made it a particularly productive time to do a self-study, which provided her with a way to get her bearings and learn as she went, but also added to her vulnerability—how unsettling it can be to bring into focus one's first attempts at teaching in a particular context and then share the learning derived from this self-study with others! Hermann-Wilmarth held herself to a high standard in this regard, observing that

> [t]he process of self-reflection is central to critically engaged pedagogy. Edelsky (1999) demanded that teachers and students question "whose interests" (p. 15) are served by status quo classroom practice. . . . If I refuse to listen to the critique of students who cannot find a liberatory space within the framework of the class, I privilege my classroom for those who can find accessibility there. . . . My student Anthony provided a critique that not only frustrated and challenged me—he clearly didn't buy into my definition of a liberatory classroom—but required that I engage with my own reflection in meaningful ways so that I didn't constantly reproduce an oppressive classroom. (p. 473)

As she made her way as a graduate student now teaching prospective elementary school teachers, the critiques that Anthony offered her, in the form of his behaviors and a lengthy e-mail, could easily have put her on the defensive. Instead, Hermann-Wilmarth utilized self-study to reframe his critiques as a learning opportunity for herself and make it a fruitful experience. In this regard, she is setting the tone for her future as a teacher, one who takes the path toward self-study, even in the midst of critique. She moved toward and into a tense teaching situation and invited her own learning.

Hermann-Wilmarth concludes:

> My reflective analysis of who I was both in my relationship with Anthony and as a teacher in a supposed liberatory class occurred in the writing of this article. The significance of this postreflection is that it provides a future challenge. I have acknowledged that although painful, the teaching that Anthony provided through his email is both powerful and vital to my own process of becoming a more fully liberatory educator. He pointed to my shortcomings in a way that I hope will influence me when I meet my next class. (p. 478)

It is this focus on the ongoing understanding and improvement of one's own practice that is the strength of self-study action research.

ACTION RESEARCH IN THE CLASSROOM: MONICA RICHARDS AND THE "BUMS" OF 8H*

We offer one of the earlier pieces of teacher research to be published, Monica Richards's (1987) account of her classroom research, for several reasons. Beyond the fact that the questions Richards poses for herself will feel familiar to many educators, this example also shows how her questions shifted as she interrogated what was—or wasn't—happening in her classroom. In terms of her own growth, Richards documents how she moved from relying on the expertise of "published researchers" to trusting her own research process. She continues to actively read and seek out pertinent professional literature but adds her own research expertise to the problem-solving mix. While she specifically added various

*From Richards, M., "A teacher's action research study," in *Peabody Journal of Education*, 64(2), pp. 65–79. Reprinted with permission.

types of data gathering, she also incorporated things she was already doing and used them as data; for example, a daily journal that she routinely kept became an important running record of her reflections on the classroom.

In her narrative account of the self-dubbed "bums" of 8H, Richards, a middle school language arts teacher, sets the scene for her research by letting the reader in on what motivated her to undertake her study in the first place:

> Every year I ask myself the same question, "How am I going to motivate a group of students who do not want to learn?" I employ many strategies, trying a new one or two every now and then, but none has ever been so effective that other teachers came knocking at my door for the "answer."
>
> In the past I had relied on suggestions by published researchers and educators or techniques recommended by my colleagues, but nothing came close to affecting my sixth period class, the self-styled "bums" from 8H. (p. 65)

Motivated by the kind of desperation that can occur when teachers are faced with a class where "nothing works," Richards broadened her original question about how to motivate students who do not want to learn to include questions related to teacher behavior:

> What behavior must I exhibit/model to elicit an interested response at the onset of the class; how can I maintain that interest; and finally how can I get students to self-initiate verbal or written performance? What mode of interaction best facilitates motivation to achieve objectives? And what is it that occurs in highly motivational situations? I wanted to determine what environmental factors in the classroom might influence motivation, and what types of rewards are effective. (p. 66)

Richards used a methodology that included a daily journal. She had previously intentionally left the "bums" of 8H out of her journal "because the thoughts and words to describe what had happened in 50 minutes with them were so horrendous that I could not bring myself to write about them" (p. 66). She also used tape recordings of class activities and student interviews and questionnaires. To launch her study, she shadowed 8H as it proceeded through its day, and although she was not surprised by what she saw, the cumulative impact of her observations was staggering. Here was a group making its way through the school day with little success or affirmation of the learning process; the "bums" of 8H were obviously used to failure.

In what she terms "beginning again" with the group, Richards read the students her research proposal, enlisting their help to communicate with her and to work together on the research process:

> I began reading my proposal for research to them. They all listened attentively. Even George, who usually cannot resist laying his head down for a short snooze, remained alert. "If we agree to work together, you will have to communicate with me." They all agreed to do so.
>
> I had no idea 8H could be so serious, so understanding. Reading my proposal had been the first step in working together. I knew my perceptions of them were accurate, and they knew how I really felt about them and their neglect of the learning process. (p. 70)

By inviting her students into the problem-solving process, and by proposing to look at the impact of teacher behaviors as well as those of the students, Richards forged a partnership with her students that began to set a new tone for the classroom.

Crossing the hierarchical lines that separate students and teachers is risky business. In being vulnerable to the students by asking for feedback, Richards invited the honest communication that was crucial to the study. She also invited her students into a reflective process that helped them demystify their own lack of success in the educational arena. This mutual vulnerability and reflexivity, with implications for change on the part of both the teacher and the students, set the stage for all to strategize together on what might best help them improve the learning process.

Richards began to try some interventions in her classroom. In her journal she writes about an experiment in sending notes home to parents and the risks she felt in trying this:

> About seven people had completed their homework. They read their compositions aloud. As I praised each one, I handed

them a positive note to take home to their parents rewarding their good work in Language Arts today. Norman was especially happy about his. Proudly he showed it to the person in front of him—comparing notes possibly. Or was he laughing, making fun of it? This was my fear. Is Norman (and others like him in 8H) too cool, too macho to get a positive note from the teacher? I'll talk to them about this tomorrow. (p. 69)

Searching for other positive motivators for her class, Richards mounted a motivational bulletin board, with a horse on a race track, illustrating the progress the class was making in attendance, homework, and participation. She also devised a list of extrinsic motivators and tried to prioritize them in the way she thought her students would; for example, Number 1 on her list was a bonus point system.

In keeping with the spirit of partnership in the problem-solving process, she shared the list with the class and asked the class to prioritize it as well. Richards writes about their process and her own as she gained new information about the class:

I discussed the priority of items on the checklist. I had assumed the number one item would be a bonus point system where the class earning the most bonus points in one six-week period would choose their own reward. 8H rated it number ten, and after a little discussion decided it didn't even need to be on the list. They rated teaching resources number one. How wrong I was about them! I was also wrong about the positive notes home. I shared my fear about them being too "cool" for a positive note. Norman, Scott and Dawn all said that's not true. They said they took their notes home and showed them. Norman was serious. Dawn and Kim rated them especially high on their list—about second, with verbal praise a close third. . . .

I was not only working with 8H to reorganize each strategy and develop classroom incentives, but I was valuing their ideas. They cooperated fully, taking the activity seriously. Everyone contributed ideas. . . .

Clearly, I had wasted many days assuming 8H was incapable of deep reasoning. I was guilty of letting their outer appearance and low academic ability sway my attitude. I had underestimated them; I found that they were capable of mature thoughts. I soon came to realize that they not only needed but also appreciated a teacher who was knowledgeable and caring. (p. 71)

At the same time, Richards was allowing her own problem solving to be informed through her reading of the literature on motivation, and her outside reading helped her frame her next intervention in the classroom. She reflects that it

helped clarify and put into perspective my focus on motivating students who do not want to learn. It also provided a framework, a definition, and an organizational pattern for discussing motivation and study skills on a more personal level. I not only wanted to get in touch with 8H, I wanted 8H to get in touch with themselves. (p. 72)

In thinking about the success of the unit that she had planned and the high level of student participation, Richards observes that the positive student behavior was due in part to the content of the lesson but also due to the change in teacher behavior:

I expected everyone to be successful and productive. They had vowed to communicate and work together with me. We had common expectations.

In a tape-recorded session of 8H discussing a previous day's work, I discovered that retention was excellent. I asked them to restate, in order, their four largest inhibitors of motivation. These were (a) " . . . comparing me with another student in class," (b) "Picking out a certain group of students as pets," (c) "Lack of trust in students," and (d) "A teacher always 'cuts you down.'"

A positive dimension of dealing with these inhibitors or "coping" devices were then restated: (a) get advice from a counselor, (b) talk privately with the individual with whom you have a conflict, (c) students' actions speak louder than words, and (d) have a cooperative attitude. (p. 73)

Documenting many positive changes in the day-to-day interaction and learning in her class, Richards and the class looked forward to report card day. In a study unit that they had done on motivation, students had voted that getting good grades was the first source of motivation. (Second to this, in the students' perception, was having parents care, followed by having a bright, caring teacher.) In Richards's own class, only 4 students out of 26 had lower grades than in the last marking period. In looking at their grades overall, though, 5 students' grades were up, 9 students maintained their previous performance, and 12 students had grades that were lower. Richards writes:

> I was not pleased with the results. When asked why so many grades dropped or remained the same, the students placed the blame on the teachers for the most part. Remarks like "He don't like us," or "She doesn't know how to teach. All she does is pass out worksheets," had been said before and were now being repeated. (p. 75)

Trying to understand why, when the students had put so much emphasis on getting good grades, there was not more improvement in this area, Richards, in keeping with the spirit of the research, asked herself questions about the behaviors of both students and teachers. She wondered whether the other teachers accepted the students as they were. Had they tried to find out where the students were? How did they grade? She wondered whether the students had fulfilled their end of the obligations. While puzzling over these issues in the larger realm of the students' experience in school, she was able to identify why things had improved in her own classroom:

> I can, however, explain why the students' grades in my classroom improved in four weeks. We had a common understanding that getting good grades was important; we were interested in the content of the lesson; we valued each other's ideas; we were working and learning together. This interchange of teaching and learning was the most valuable lesson to be learned.
>
> I also believe that what will be remembered in the minds of the students of 8H will not be a letter grade received in a class, but rather the memories of having experienced success and praise for achieving, regardless of how small the achievements.

I had been mistaken about the students' potential because of their appearance. . . . Spending time discussing self-image and attitudes had proven beneficial. Until we openly shared our feelings about each other, there was a vacancy in my learning and in their learning. (pp. 75–76)

Richards ends her study with an increased awareness of her role as a teacher, as well as a greater sense of her students and what motivates them. She also got the results she was looking for, that is, a class that performed at a higher level, as measured in their grades.

Although "ending" her research on this note, it seems that, considering the spirals of action research, Richards is well poised to begin the next round of questions, perhaps in a broader realm. She could pursue answers to some of her own queries as to why the students did not perform better in other classes. One suspects, based on Richards's research, that the necessary ingredients involve not only increasing the motivation of the students but also increasing reflexivity on the part of teachers and students as to what they contribute to the dynamic of failure. If Richards were to continue the research spiral, perhaps she would have the opportunity to share her own learning and classroom results in a larger arena, working with other educators in her school. This kind of dissemination of her research could have an impact beyond her classroom in the larger environment of the school, potentially creating a new context for learning for the "bums" of 8H.

THE SPILL OF INDIVIDUAL RESEARCH TO "THE SYSTEM": ROBYN RUSSELL

Russell's (1992) account of her practitioner research has as its starting point her own struggle with silence and voice. It grows to encompass an analysis of many layers of her school and larger professional issues in education. Russell's work is an example of how one individual's reflections and questions can become a powerful catalyst for the development of a multilevel approach to intervention in a school. In this summary of her work, we trace the development of Russell's research from her individual reflections to her institutional analysis. The research process helps Russell find her own voice, and as the research proceeds, she increasingly finds ways to use it.

A teacher in the Utah public school system, Russell was a participant in a graduate program, known as the Educative Research Project, offered through the University of Utah. The program works to explicitly challenge the hierarchical differences between teachers and academics (Gitlin et al., 1992). Believing such hierarchy silences teachers' voices and their input into educational reform, participants from the university and teaching communities work together to broaden the base on which such expertise is based. Linking understanding of the educational world with their ability to act in it, participants are encouraged to reflect on, examine, and remake schooling (Gitlin et al., 1992).

In her initial self-reflection, Russell contextualizes the ways that women are silenced in current society, linking that observation to her choice of the teaching profession. Looking at the profession historically, she discovers that teachers have rarely had an active voice in educational theory and research. As a master's degree student, Russell writes an account of her school's history that moves her into an analysis of the ways that school structures silence teachers. She analyzes the architecture of her classroom, the mandated curriculum, and the required textbooks and juxtaposes these observations with the readings she was doing as part of the graduate program. Russell writes:

> These readings . . . released me from the guilt of what I could not change, and gave me permission to change all I could. I gained confidence in my teaching. I began to speak out and not hide behind my "closed classroom door." This signified a major shift in my relation to the system. (pp. 91–92)

As part of her graduate program, Russell was paired with another teacher for ongoing dialogue, described as the Horizontal Evaluation Method. They were to analyze collaboratively the relationship between their teaching intentions and their practices, identifying the mismatches or thinking through why they wanted to achieve a particular end (Gitlin et al., 1992, p. 52). In this process, Russell came to the realization that teachers in general do not have a voice in educational reform. She observed that school structures, such as the teaching schedule, teacher isolation, and the historical feminization of teaching contributed to this silence. At the same time, Russell was observing a change in herself and formulating her research question.

> The simple act of talking about these issues began to change my professional life. I was beginning to gain a sense of empowerment. . . . These changes in my perception of the teacher role caused me to look at how others could also benefit from dialogue. A recurrent question began to appear in my thoughts and writing. How might our school, or even our profession, change if discussion and reflection were made available and encouraged? (p. 93)

This linking of her own experiences to the teaching profession in general, the larger institutional context, and the experiences of other teachers led Russell to look for a way to establish a consistent block of time in her school for conducting dialogue among teachers about educational issues. She reasoned that if teachers could have time to talk among themselves, they might become more willing to express their ideas in a wider forum. Drawing on her own experience and having learned to express her thoughts as her trust with her dialogue partner grew, Russell hypothesized that the same would be true for teachers if they were offered a safe place to discuss their ideas:

> Somehow, I felt that the development of teacher voice was a key to membership in the historically exclusive club of educational decision making. Without a firm concept of what exactly I wanted to express, change or become empowered to do, I leaped into my research. All I knew with any certainty was that I wanted us to start talking to each other. (pp. 93–94)

She adds:

> I saw it as one possible avenue toward the restructuring of the educational hierarchy, of making some impact on the invisibility and silence that Thorne (1984) argues is an inherent

part of a gendered profession. . . . I yearned for new ways of making myself visible and heard, while bringing with me a chorus of other teachers. (p. 94)

Moving from a personal realm, her own struggles with being silenced and working to find her voice, Russell began to contextualize her own concerns and became aware of the larger forces that colluded to silence not only her but her professional peers as well. This kind of linking led to a different design for possible intervention. It was a move from the privatizing of a problem or issue (i.e., "this is my struggle") to "this is my issue but many teachers struggle in this way because of the design of educational institutions." The design of Russell's research moved her to intervene in a way that might encourage teacher voice, with the larger agenda of impacting educational theory and reform. Russell designed her research with the goal of restructuring the educational hierarchy and affecting silencing.

She first surveyed the other teachers in her building regarding their attitudes about professional dialogue on educational issues. She asked how many would be interested in dialogue sessions should they be offered. Based on this information gathering, which indicated a positive interest in the opportunity to talk with other teachers, Russell organized voluntary teacher dialogue sessions, open to any faculty in the school. The research continued over a period of two years, during which time Russell reflected on and made changes in the process of teachers conversing together.

Russell and her partner in Horizontal Evaluation continued to meet during this time, providing a second source of data. They met following each of the teacher dialogue sessions "to compare the intentions of the meetings with the realities of what actually transpired" (p. 95). The pair explored Russell's assumptions about each meeting and planned for the next one. Russell analyzed transcripts of each meeting with her partner to ascertain how the process of Horizontal Evaluation was influencing the dialogue sessions.

In writing about her two years of research, Russell explores themes that reflect her own questions. For example, she asks how much to structure and lead the dialogue groups, how to move them from "Robyn's meetings" to one of shared ownership. She reflects on themes that are common to many educational settings, such as how to create time in busy teachers' schedules for the dialogue groups or how to obtain compensation for the extra time if the groups are held outside of the regular school day. She puzzles over how to enlist administrative support and sanction. Interventions designed to solve some of the issues that arose then could vary from a reflection on her particular roles and changing her style of leadership in the meetings to working to convince administrators that allowing time for teacher-generated dialogue could result in positive results for education.

In the second year of the research, the teachers named their meetings Professional Dialogue Sessions, worked out a regular schedule to meet on the third Friday of each month for lunch, and generated a list of topics to be discussed during the school year. Finding a collective voice, the Professional Dialogue Session group decided to work on a specific project. They proposed a computer lab for the school despite the refusal of an earlier request by the administration. This type of empowered effort among teachers had been previously unheard of in the school. Russell attributed it to the organizational power of the dialogue group.

As is often the case in the life of researchers, intentional actions coincided with serendipitous events. In this case, the school district offered the possibility of piloting one of three computer systems. Members of the Professional Dialogue Session became part of a larger computer committee asked to investigate and decide on a computer system. The committee was given a weekend to decide which one they wanted and then to recommend it at a faculty meeting the following Monday. Committee members, feeling that it was a mistake to make such a costly decision with so little time to investigate the options, reported that view to the larger faculty meeting:

> Our faculty meeting became a forum for discussing the assumptions behind the administration's practice of giving us choice among limited options, and very little time for making informed, well-investigated decisions. The Professional Dialogue Session group that had decided to present a proposal to the faculty for a computer lab recommended the rejection of the option to pilot any of the three systems on the premise that the district's procedure of limiting our choices was not a

choice. The faculty enthusiastically approved. . . . Our faculty recognized and examined common parameters to the educational choice usually given teachers, such as choosing between a limited number of alternatives, and found them unacceptable. (p. 108)

The Professional Dialogue Session group invited the district superintendent to its next group meeting. He accepted the invitation, which resulted in a working session. As often happens when dialogue is opened up, new information was gathered and perceptions were changed. The distribution of power was rearranged as teachers empowered through dialogue became a collective force, working together toward an agreed-upon end.

Reflecting on her two years of research, Russell was able to document changes occurring in herself, the teachers, and the administration. The Professional Dialogue Sessions continued in the next school year. Russell conceptualizes the next step in this process of uncovering and encouraging voice:

The personal and professional ramifications of this study expand in all directions for me as I see the broader implications of dialogue and educational empowerment. Parents and students have been even more discouraged from speaking than teachers. Eventually, I must find ways to include their voices as well. My hope is that I can encourage my students' voices while providing them with a receptive audience. This is what I have wished for myself. My personal journey to develop my teacher voice has taken me further down the path to the doors of more partners in silence than I imagined to be possible. (p. 115)

EXPANDING THEORY THROUGH TEACHER RESEARCH: CYNTHIA BALLENGER*

A prolific teacher researcher, Cynthia Ballenger (1993, 1996, 1998, 2004; Ballenger & Rosebery, 2003) brings a sense of overwhelming respect to her read of the world of children. Much of her work documents what she learns from the children in her

*Note: Reprinted with permission.

classroom as she enters their worlds, often as a cultural outsider. In the following example, she offers a bottom-up view of what transpires in her preschool classroom to push on and expand what it is we know about literacy learning.

Ballenger (1993), at the time a preschool teacher in a Haitian community in Dorchester, Massachusetts, studied how the preschoolers in her classroom approached learning about print and found herself identifying inadequacies in models of literacy learning. Her observations and reflections of her students did not seem to fit with accepted explanations of ways students acquire literacy knowledge. Ballenger's work is an example of practitioner action research that informs and expands existing theory.

In this bilingual preschool, which serves mainly the children of Haitian immigrants, Ballenger and the children fluidly move between Haitian Creole and English. Ballenger's teacher's aide was at one point not rehired due to budget cuts. Here Ballenger (1993) writes of the impact of this on her teaching:

> Without an aide, I found myself in the position of observer much more than I otherwise would have been. I became increasingly aware of the extraordinary ability these children had to take care of themselves. They took each other to the bathroom, helped each other with jackets, knew when it was the right moment to invite an angry child back into the group, even reprimanded each other when it was appropriate. I taught these children—but I also sat back more than usual and watched them run their own small community. (p. 10)

Through the processes of writing journals and transcribing audiotapes of her classroom, Ballenger documented her students' unique approach to literacy learning. She began to define a "shadow curriculum," the students' curriculum that supported their learning and ran parallel to the curriculum designed by Ballenger. Reflecting on her own curriculum for the preschool classroom, Ballenger (1993) saw as part of her job exposing children to print and letting them experience its many functions. She expected them to generate hypotheses about what print is and is not:

> I expect that these hypotheses will be continually reanalyzed and corrected by the child in light of his/her continuing experience with print. I see my job as making sure that the

experiences are there. I do this both by explicit teaching of facts ("No, that is not your name yet. You need a Y at the end"); by drawing their attention to contradictions in their theories ("Only girls can have S's? What about Steve? And here's an S in Rubenson"); and by doing lots of reading and writing. At the same time I really value the kind of thinking that goes on in these hypotheses, right or wrong. I see it as logical thinking, as analysis. (p. 11)

Ballenger (1993) soon realized that the children did not experience print in the same way. Her journals and transcriptions reveal the children's meaning-making of letters, what Ballenger eventually called their "shadow curriculum, events which involved print, but which were outside my plans and expectations" (p. 13). Following are some of her examples of this.

Note 1:   Marc calls Sora to show her whenever he finds an *S* among the letters. "Sora, your *S*." She obediently goes to him each time she is called and looks at the letter he is indicating, then returns to whatever she is playing.

Note 2:   Mackson spells his name: *M* for Mackson, *A* for Andy, *C* for Carl, *K* for Kellie, *S* for Sora—and then he stops; he cannot go further since he knows no one whose name begins with *O* or with *N*.

Note 3:   Tiny Tatie, not yet three years old, never says a word and never comes to circle where we read the names and talk a little about letters. I am amazed to discover that she has been walking around all morning with two fingers in the shape of a *T*. When asked what she's doing, she says, "It's me," and continues silently to parade her *T* around the classroom. . . .

Note 6:   Giles is just four years old. He had learned to write his whole name. This day Giles is making his *G*, announcing it as he goes. "Cindy, I make my *G*." He cuts the paper on which he has written, carefully avoiding the *G*, and parades around the classroom saying, "I no cut my *G*." He repeats the process, making more *G*'s and not cutting them many times this morning, each time announcing to me and the world, "Cindy, I no cut my

G." Finally I find myself saying to him, "No, Giles, I see. You take good care of your *G*" as if he were carrying a doll around instead of a letter. Giles later appears with a *P* for Paul and an *R* for Rafi, his two best buddies. He doesn't cut them either, as he tells us all. Next he makes an *S* for Steven, whom he does not like. "I cut Steven's *S*," he announces in a dire tone.

Working to understand this shadow curriculum, Ballenger moves from looking at individual children's responses to print to a more general view. In making meaning of observations of individuals, Ballenger (1993) writes:

Marc: What is Marc doing in field note 1? He and Sora are playing together. The activity is keeping track of Sora's *S*'s. There is another girl whose name begins with *S*, as Marc well knows, but she and Marc are not particularly close, so it is Sora that he calls to him each time he can find an *S*. Print is part of being friends with Sora, and being friends with Sora is a way to use print.

Mackson: The way Mackson spells, using everyone's name, becomes typical for the classroom. All the children who can, identify the letters of their name in this way. I initially try to break them of the habit, assuming that they have the mistaken impression that you can own letters, that your letter is yours and yours alone. I am therefore always telling them that it is not really Tatie's *T*, for example. Other children and other words also have *T*'s. We always observe when more than one child's name begins with the same letter. The children accept what I say and learn that turtle begins with *T* and that stop has a *T*. However, nothing breaks them of this way of spelling, and finally I become charmed by it myself. Again, print and friendship proceed together.

Tatie: Tatie, the youngest in the class, tries to keep all the *T*'s—coloring papers, magnetic *T*'s, and cut-out letters—in her cubby. She knows that she shares *T* at least with Teo, another child in the classroom. She is a very silent child, although obviously aware. In note 4 Tatie has used the *S* and her *T* to greet, to make some sort of social connection with Sora's mother at a point where she is still not willing to talk.

Giles: Giles places his own letter on the public stage by announcing it and his care for it. He then includes his two friends in the circle of his care, and acts out his opposite feeling for another member of the group. He uses letters to comment upon his connections with, and feelings for, his friends. He is acting on a stage of his own creation when he cuts Steve's *S*. . . . Giles . . . keeps repeating that he hasn't cut his *G*. He does not appear satisfied until I finally say, "Yes, Giles, I see. You take good care of your *G*." At that point he goes on to make other letters and act upon them. What is behind such persistence?

The final response is from a completely different area of a teacher's repertoire.

"You take good care of your *G*" is the sort of response I make when children are playing in the house corner with babies. In my particular case, it is intended to be a comment on separation. It refers to the care that children receive at home and the ability they have to carry that care with them as they go to school. Giles had moved us into the symbolic drama of everyday life. I was not consciously aware of this move. When I heard my response on the tape, I recognized it and its source, although I never decided consciously to respond to him in this way. Something in his tone must have prompted my response. Having received it, Giles went on to develop his drama. (pp. 15–16)

In moving to the offerings of theory to understand her children's creations with print, Ballenger finds them lacking. Generally seeing children's acquisition of print as a precursor to understanding the logic of reading and writing, the existing models seem to imply that children learn print when they are motivated by the acquisition of scientific or technical knowledge. Ballenger (1993) critiques these models as part of the world of "literalness" and states that "this model is not adequate for the approach taken by my children" (p. 17). She sees her children using print as representative of their social network, an observation that pushes existing theory. It is important to note that without Ballenger's tacit knowledge of the existing relationships among her children, her meaning-making of what she was seeing and hearing could have taken her in extremely different directions. The framing of the data in relational terms pushed her toward theory questioning and expansion.

GROUP COLLABORATION ACROSS SITES: THE PRINCIPALS' GROUP

Perhaps because practitioners do not necessarily find encouragement in their own school sites to see themselves as researchers, and perhaps because of the isolation many educators face in their day-to-day practice, the formation of wide-reaching groups outside the school site for the support and feedback of reflective practitioners as researchers is highly appealing to many of us. For those who are currently the sole researchers in their sites, the groups act as a forum for research development and critical thinking about data gathered. Although many of us would prefer to be part of a site-based "community of inquiry" within our own schools, a group of educators outside our sites may be an alternate source of support and encouragement when the former is not available. As the following example illustrates, there is room for much fruitful collaboration when practitioners isolated in roles at their own schools find and work with their counterparts in other sites.

This example is drawn from the work of five female elementary and middle school principals and an educational ethnographer who are part of a principals' journal group (Christman et al., 1995). They work in a large urban school district. The presentation of their journal writings for themselves and each other twice a month has become a catalyst for action in their individual work sites. Although each practices as a lone administrator during the workweek, each has the benefit of the thoughts of others in similar positions during their meetings. The principals see the journal group as a feminist activity where they work to understand their

experiences as "the other" in a profession that is still male domi-
nated. They ask themselves and each other whether they can be
feminist principals and whether they can exercise the authority of
their positions in ways that are relational and caring. Following
the premises of action research, working through the spiral of
problem posing, reflection, action, and observation, the journal
group is a forum for the conceptualization of these steps.

One of the principals in the group, Arlene Holtz, wrote about
what she termed the most significant journal entry she shared
with the group in their first year of meeting. It involved an
incident in the middle school in which she is principal, a school
desegregated by busing African American students. An African
American female student, Takia, was brusquely brought to Holtz's
office by one of the male teaching assistants who had caught her
on the playground with a six-inch knife. Holtz (Christman et al.,
1995) recorded the incident in her journal for her own reflection
as well as for the group:

> Takia Richards entered my office on Thursday shouting a
> stream of threats and profanity at Mr. O'Connor, the red-
> faced assistant who threw her into a chair. He told her, "Shut
> up!" which had no effect on her, and he handed me a six-inch
> florentined brass object.
>
> "It's a butterfly knife," he told me. "Open it up."
>
> Gingerly I released the catch and pulled back on the brass
> casing. A six-inch blade, sharpened on both sides, emerged.
>
> "She was carrying it open beside her thigh in the yard,"
> he said. (p. 218)

Holtz recounts that the assistant explained that once Takia
realized he had seen her with the knife, she threw it into her girlfriend's purse. He produced a small black shoulder bag, with the
thin strap broken. He explained that her girlfriend wouldn't
release the bag, "so I ripped it off her shoulder" (p. 218). Holtz
reports that "[t]hroughout this explanation Takia continued to
shout a stream of invectives at everyone until I told her 'Shut up!'"
(p. 218). Kneesha, the girl who owns the purse, enters the office,
crying. The teacher she enters with explained that Kneesha was
innocent. This sets off Mr. O'Connor, and he and Kneesha began
shouting at each other, each disputing the other's account of

what occurred. Holtz reflects that by this point in the episode, she felt "no particular care or concern for either of the girls" (p. 218).

She later reflected:

> As I write this now, I wonder what I was thinking as it all unfolded. I'm a principal, an educator. This was police work. I have no stomach for it. For crying out loud, my strengths were supposedly language arts, curriculum, and middle-school organization. This was as far from all that as I could get. (p. 218)

Kneesha's teacher again reiterated that she was innocent. "She's an honor roll student. She's very upset." This caught Holtz's attention and she moved to reassure the student:

> I saw a frightened child, not a criminal. I realized that she was afraid of *me*. Her fate lay in my hands. I looked at her. I *really* looked at her. Four feet, five inches, dark-skinned, well-dressed, frightened. A child. At first I missed the child. I reached out and touched her shoulder. "Trust me, Kneesha. I'll protect you." Had I made a promise I couldn't keep? I wondered. I felt like crying. That's the wrong emotion, I thought. Shut it off. (p. 218)

Eventually, Takia admits that Kneesha had nothing to do with the incident, that she had indeed put the knife in Kneesha's purse. She extracts a promise from Holtz that she will not allow anything to happen to Kneesha. When Holtz agrees, more of the story comes tumbling out—that Takia had brought the knife to school for her own protection because some girls had been bothering her on the way home from school. Throughout this exchange, Holtz finds herself shifting:

> Despite my authoritarian demeanor with this child, I managed to see something in her character that I value: she was loyal to her friend. What is more, for reasons unknown to me, she was willing to trust me, with her trust based on my word, my promise. (p. 219)

Holtz called both girls' mothers and then the police. Two white officers arrived.

"So what do you want?" the cop asked. "I guess we'll take both girls." "No," I said. "Not both. Just one."

He looked at me. "Look, we'll let J.A.D. sort it out."

"No," I said. "You either take one, or no one."

"You tryin' to tell me my business?"

"No," I said. "I'm the principal and I'm reporting that we confiscated a knife from this student." I point to Takia. "She threw it into this girl's pocketbook. She had nothing to do with it." I sat beside Kneesha and put my arm around her tightly. "You can't take her. If you do, I'll withdraw everything." (p. 220)

Eventually, the police led Takia away in handcuffs. Shortly after this, Kneesha's mother arrived. Holtz journals the following account of their exchange:

"I'm glad you're here," I told her.

Before I could speak further, she interrupted me. "What do you plan to do about this pocketbook?"

I looked at it. "I think it can be easily repaired," I said. "Mr. O'Connor's first concern was to get the knife out of harm's way."

"He could have asked politely."

"Well, I think he did ask her, but she clutched the bag and wouldn't give it to him."

"Then he could have gotten someone else to speak to her."

"There was an open knife in the pocketbook," I said. "He secured it for safety reasons."

"You can tell my lawyer that."

"What?"

"Oh, I intend to sue you."

"Me, what for?"

"Did you reprimand Mr. O'Connor?"

"Reprimand him? No. Mr. O'Connor, I think, did his best. It was an unfortunate—"

"Oh, I'm sick of listening to you. Tell it to my lawyer. You have no appreciation for our children's feelings."

I felt slapped across the face. What was this whole day about?

"Tell your lawyer to call our lawyer," I said. "I don't talk to lawyers." (p. 221)

Holtz's journal is her central source of data for the processing of her role as principal. She does this through her own meaning-making of what she has written as well as through the input of the group. As a beautifully written example of journal writing, it serves as her group's lens into her school situation. The group is not on-site together, so in order to share knowledge of each other's workplace, they depend on the data the journals offer for their meaning-making. Bringing fresh eyes to what is a familiar setting for Holtz, the group analyzed the incident in ways that were not immediately apparent to Holtz herself. In this example, the group introduced race as a factor in the dynamics of the exchange.

Holtz first worked to make sense of the incident herself, reflecting on the turn of events and how she handled them. She used the process of journal writing to gain further insight into her job as principal. Reflecting on the incident, she writes about what she sees as "the myths of the principalship":

> I entered the principalship with the idea that what mattered most was what happened inside classrooms. I was dedicated to improving the teaching/learning in our school. I considered all this other stuff as extraneous and unimportant. I saw the problems associated with discipline as roadblocks I had to negotiate in order to get on with the important work such as improving instruction. The events in this journal forced me to reconsider this attitude. By the end of the journal Takia really matters to me. I move from her punisher to her protector. I assume my rightful role of teacher who cares about what happens to her in the future. I entered the principalship with the mistaken notion that I could delegate this kind of work to someone else. I can't. I shouldn't. What happens to Takia is as important as what happens to the honor student. Each child matters. It all matters. (pp. 221–222)

Holtz went on to reflect on her own role in the incident. She felt that while she encouraged Takia to get through the ordeal with a shred of dignity, the attitude and behavior of the police— one of contempt and meanness—made her feel that she did not do enough, that somehow she had betrayed Takia as well.

It was only in our journal group that I began to feel forgiveness for how I handled the matter. Holly (another principal in the group) said, "Arlene is trying to choose in the moment what is best for the children, and all in all, doing a good job, but still feeling so bad, so bitter, somehow off the mark. It reminds me of situational ethics. The importance of understanding the context, the situation, in order to understand the decisions we make." It is only in our group that I find acceptance and safety in which I can explore events such as those I described. (p. 221)

What is important in this example is the function of the group in expanding Holtz's vision of her practice and her analysis of her data, offered in the journal account. Although Holtz did not initially name race as a factor in the incident, when group members named it for her, she acknowledged their insight. The group allowed for an honest reflection and acceptance of feedback because of the level of trust they had built. In this way, the group mirrors the cycle of action research: they present their practice puzzles, they reflect together, those reflections potentially impact their practice, and then they continue to bring their observations to the group to begin the cycle again.

SCHOOL-UNIVERSITY PARTNERSHIPS: THE DENBIGH ACTION RESEARCH GROUP

We highlight the work of the Denbigh Action Research Group for a number of reasons, but one important one is the cutting-edge approach they are taking to the current context in which many of us as educators find ourselves. As members of the group, Moyra Evans, Pam Lomax, and Helen Morgan (2000) observe, we are in an age calling for evidence-based practice. Ironically, this coincides with the incredible growth of teacher action research, yet this is not seen as a contribution to the "evidence" that is demanded. They note that this omission persists despite many more published accounts of action research, many of which deal explicitly with the improvement of teaching and learning. Noting that action research too rarely reaches the public domain or is ignored when it does, the Denbigh Action Research Group came into being, in part, to address some of these concerns. The use of narratives as a vehicle for professional development evolved from Moyra Evans's dissertation research.

Grounded in Winter's (1991) narrative methodology and Whitehead's (1989) living theory approach, Evans's (1995) dissertation uses what she calls "memory work" to help her gain distance from her own taken-for-granted understandings of her practice. She forms her interview and observation data into fictional stories that serve to ensure both anonymity and sufficient distance to theorize her data. The stories help her identify patterns in her data, and the stories are read back to the participants for validation. Not only was story used to contribute to the theorization of her data, but it was also used as a way to facilitate professional learning with her staff. She suggests that as administrators begin to experience the contradictions between their values and their actions, their need to resolve these contradictions drives their research.

> I believe that my values lead my actions in moving towards a more fulfilling and satisfying way of life for me, and for those with whom I work. I am driven to change my practices because I recognize that they do not reflect fully my values, and I therefore feel ill at ease with myself. I take steps to change my actions and the way in which I see and think about my actions. . . . I believe that this is a value-laden, educational process—that I am taking part in an educational enquiry to get in touch with and live more fully my values about being a deputy head and supporting teaching and learning. It is educational because I act to change myself according to the values to which I am committed. (p. 40)

Evans is quick to add, however, that she cannot do this alone. She states that she needs a group of people to challenge her thinking, to provide alternative points of view, to point out inconsistencies in her thinking, to make problematic the assumptions she has taken for granted.

The Denbigh Action Research Group took up many of these issues and expanded them to create a multifaceted project with the goal of using action research both for professional development and to inform the larger fields of teaching and administration. They write:

> In this paper we set out to describe a particular initiative in school-university partnership and to show how a form of

research that took root in a community of teacher researchers was transferred to the classroom with benefit for the teacher and the students. An aim of this paper is to close the circle: from university to school, from teacher to school, from knowledge creation to publication, from publication to the practice and policy of teacher education and back. (Evans et al., 2000, p. 407)

Evans, a deputy principal who headed up professional development in the school, invited teachers to volunteer to be part of an action research group. Drawing on her own experience as an action researcher, Evans (Evans et al., 2000) suggested forming a group in which each member

writes a story about a pressing professional concern and this is offered to the group for discussion. By the end of the discussion there is plenty of food for thought and each teacher can go away to reflect upon the experience. Writing the story enables the teachers to get in touch with aspects of their work which are of particular concern to them. They are helped to discover where they are not living out their professional values and so are uncomfortable with their current practice. The story method enables teachers to gain the confidence to share vulnerable aspects of their practice. Once this confidence is demonstrated they are encouraged to ask each other more probing questions, to share ideas and feelings about their professional experiences and to try out alternative ways of doing things. (pp. 407–408)

Evans was able to get the meetings on the school calendar, formally recognizing the investment of time in research. In addition, the members could gain university credit toward a new postgraduate diploma in action research offered by Kingston University. The understanding was that teachers would select their own area of study for their action research and they would work in collaboration with colleagues in the development of reflective practices. For the university, "the radical element" was twofold: the new diploma was almost wholly school based and the instruction was handled by staff within the school.

The teachers who registered for the Diploma were supported by the school financially, through an 85% contribution towards the fees; in terms of time through planned meetings on the school calendar; in the School Development Plan through being part of the short- and long-term objectives. The initiative was supported by Kingston University: through discounted fees which were laid out in a memorandum of cooperation; through provision of a university-based internal examiner who also acted as a critical friend; in the accreditation procedures. There was a clear understanding of the supportive partnership between school and university by the people involved in accrediting the scheme: Pam Lomas supported Moyra Evans, Moyra Evans supported the teachers and the teachers' practice changed so that the pupils benefited. Action research was to be the means through which this supportive partnership was to operate. (p. 410)

In the group, teachers investigated their own practices, read relevant educational literature, and used the group to discuss their own research in relation to the work of others. Helen Morgan, one of the teachers in the group, reflects:

This learning environment has provided not only academic stimulation but also a great deal of emotional support. . . . The support has been a very valuable factor to all members of the group. . . . I believe that my practice has greatly improved as a result of being part of this culture and as a result of the reflective practices that it encouraged from teachers. (p. 410)

Morgan (Evans et al., 2000) went on to set up an action research group for a small number of her students around the same principles as those established with the teachers: "group support, reflection in action and action research" (p. 411). Morgan's aim was "to enable students to explore and discuss their thinking about themselves in relation to their school lives so that they could become more successful students" (p. 411). The students surprised Morgan by focusing their initial discussions on "motivation and how this was affected by the quality of their learning" (p. 411). Drawing from her experience in the teachers' action research group, Morgan introduced the students to the story writing method to clarify their concerns. And as in the teachers' group, the stories were presented to their peers for discussion and further clarification. One student, Denise, volunteered this observation of the process:

Because I wrote a story from a kitchen appliance's point of view it meant that the personal element of the experience was hidden and people could discuss the issue more freely as they knew I would take any criticism less personally. This also allowed more people to take part because the description was more general and not limited to my own circumstances and they could relate to my story in different ways. (p. 414)

Through facilitating the student action research group, Morgan gained a better sense of the issues affecting her students' learning and made changes in her own teaching. Beyond this, she took the information she gained from her own inquiry with the students to the school at large. Ideas and suggestions that came from this information were incorporated into school structures.

Accounts like those of the Denbigh Action Research Group potentially address gaps in our current knowledge base. Lytle and Cochran-Smith (1994, as cited in Evans et al., 2000) point out that the voices of teachers, the questions they ask, and the interpretive frames they use to understand and improve classroom practices are missing from the field of research on teaching. Zeichner (1994, as cited in Evans et al., 2000) picks up this same criticism and "adds to it the worry that although many university courses encourage teachers to construct their own knowledge about teaching, these accounts are usually put on the shelves and largely ignored" (p. 416). To address these gaps,

teachers from schools need courage to share their ideas in scholarly forums and to stand firm in their criticism of what they see as inappropriate ways of addressing school knowledge and teacher educators from academia need courage to engage in research and writing that counts less than other research given present forms of academic censorship and their consequences. . . . The potential of teacher research has been recognized . . . but is not necessarily welcomed by the educational establishment. (p. 416; all excerpts from Evans et al., 2000, are reprinted by permission of the publisher, Taylor & Francis Ltd, http://www.tandf.co.uk/journals)

The hope of the Denbigh Action Research Group is that work like theirs can help close "the circle, particularly between research and its implementation in practice and policy" (p. 416) and that in going public and through publications, the work of teacher researchers can provide the evidence needed to inform policies and practices upon which to base school reforms that benefit students.

FINAL THOUGHTS

A reason for compiling this chapter of examples is to convey the exciting and important work currently being done by practitioners in their education sites. The puzzles that form the basis for the initial research are often "personal," that is, educators wondering how to improve what it is educators do. The evolution of the research process often takes them beyond the bounds of their own classrooms and into broader realms of educational issues. Typically, this broader involvement comes out of the spiral of action and intervention that flows from the researchers' data gathering and meaning-making.

As practitioners gain their voices, self-consciously observing and recording their day-to-day activities and using tacit knowledge to inform their data further, the implications for the field of education—from improving practice to rethinking research methodologies to expanding theory bases—are varied and exciting. The courage to follow the research process and take ongoing actions based on it is part of what is noteworthy here. It is also what can put practitioner action research in the vanguard of educational change.

CHAPTER FOUR

Empowerment and Practitioner Action Research

An Example

To illustrate the research being done by practitioners at their own sites, we offer the following lengthy case example of work done by Herr (see also Herr & Anderson, 1993; Anderson & Herr, 1999; Herr, 1999a, 1999b, 1999c) in her school setting. This is a window into what was an ongoing process, a work that was still unfolding even as we were writing about it. We capture here a piece of a larger practitioner action research study that spanned several years. It was conducted and written during the time that Herr was a middle school teacher and counselor in an independent school.

GETTING STARTED

For the independent school I work in, April is often a make-or-break time. Students not doing well academically or who are having major difficulties with the discipline system run the risk of not being reenrolled for the next school year. The students in the school are all of high ability academically, having had to gain entrance to the school through a difficult admissions process. Several years ago, I mentally went through the list of students with whom I, as a middle school counselor and teacher, had worked intensely. Many were students of color or of socioeconomic backgrounds lower than the norm for the school. Some were students that the school had recruited as part of a goal to diversify the school racially and socioeconomically. I concluded that a fair number of them were hanging by a thread. The end of the school year could find some of them gone, or it could bring the possibility of another year of struggle. Either way, I was discouraged, feeling that somehow I should know how to do all of this better, how to help them be more successful.

I found myself mentally rehearsing the stories the students told me of their day-to-day experiences in the school. Although it once had a wealthy, all-male, student body that was predominately Anglo, the school had actively worked in the past few years to diversify its student population. Now coed, it boasted one of the larger populations of students of color in independent schools. Through a solid endowment, the school was able to offer a great deal of financial aid to provide opportunities to talented students who could not afford the tuition. But while this active recruitment and financial aid made it possible for a diversity of students to come to the school, it was not enough to retain them. Particularly at risk were the students of color who were also of a lower socioeconomic background; the combination of risk factors seemed to put them in particular jeopardy. I was also aware that, despite working vehemently on their behalf, my own intervention as a school counselor and teacher was not enough. I was concerned about what appeared to be a growing sentiment among some at the school: a blaming of the students if they did not appear to be able to take advantage of the educational "opportunity" being offered them through admittance to the school. There was also a quiet groundswell questioning whether the school had lowered its admission standards in admitting these students in the first place.

I was looking for ways to improve my own practice, but I was also aware that the stories I was hearing in the confines of my counseling office had broader implications as the school grappled with what it meant to be a truly diverse institution. I was looking for a way to bring the students' stories into the public domain so that the institution could hear the same voices I heard in my counseling sessions and factor them into the change equation of the school. Ethically, I did not feel I could privatize their stories or pretend that the only site for intervention rested with the students themselves. I was trained in social work, and my framework suggested that the resolution to problems was in the interaction between the students and their school environment. I wanted to understand better the lack of fit between the students and the institution, and although I wanted to continue to work with the students, I wanted to understand the ways that we as an institution needed to grow as well.

It was out of this frustration that the "stories of students of color" research was born. Feeling vulnerable to blind spots in my status as an Anglo woman, I joined two other colleagues in the school to conceptualize the stories project. Working with a Hispanic administrator and an African American teacher, we agreed to attempt to raise the students' stories to a level of public awareness in the school. The African American teacher and I would do the interviewing.

One goal of this study was to broaden the definition of legitimate discourse in the school by explicitly asking students to reflect on and verbalize, in the interview process, their experiences as minority students in the school. The "grand tour" question was: "Tell me what it's like being a student of color here." The wording of the question was deliberate. Through asking directly about their experiences as students of color, we were attempting to offer a legitimating voice, that is, we were recognizing and expecting that their experiences were different from those of the majority. The goal was to convey an acknowledgment of the belief that there is power in the social construction and meaning attached to race and ethnicity (as well as gender, age, sexual orientation, etc.).

We ended the school year with a few interviews completed. I had asked a few middle school students whom I knew well to participate in the study. My fellow teacher researcher had targeted a few graduating seniors, wanting to get their reflections as students who had been in the school for a period of years and had, apparently, navigated the experience successfully. We had the taped interviews transcribed and then traded interview stories. We were buoyed by the richness of the stories that the students were sharing. A taste of listening to their experiences convinced us that we were on a path that had much to teach us. We committed to continuing the project into the next school year.

We are now three years into the study. The focus of this chapter is on the issues presented for researchers studying their own site, particularly when the research critiques some of the institution's practices and when the research effort is part of an empowering process for the participants involved. What began as a fairly typical research interview study grew into more of a collaborative, action-oriented effort involving the students, my fellow research colleague, and me.

Although the interviews provided a wealth of information regarding the lived experiences of students of color in the school, just as important was the impact of the interview process itself on the students. In their research with adolescent girls, Brown and Gilligan (1992) discuss the power of placing girls in the position of being "experts" on their own lives, coupled with adults wanting to hear student voices and soliciting their stories. Rose (1990) suggests that one of the roles for the practitioner involved in empowering practice is the development of a dialogue with the client, assisting the client in expressing, elaborating, externalizing, and critically reflecting upon feelings and understandings of daily life events. As students named their reality in terms other than personal failure, that is, analyzed and critiqued the school environment in which they were expected to function, they sought ways to change the very composition of the institution. The research questioning served as a catalyst to begin the change effort.

THE PROCESS OF EMPOWERMENT

My research colleague and I asked an African American male high school student to gather a small group of his friends for a group interview. He was a student I had known since his days as a sixth grader in the school. Experiencing his own ups and downs through the years, he was a freshman when these interviews began. As a full-time teacher and a school counselor/teacher doing this research in our "spare" time, we chose to use a group interview format for expediency as well as in the name of methodological experimentation. We hoped to gather a broader sample of stories than our individual interview format had yielded and to speed up the research process. We were also curious about the effect on the students of hearing about each other's experiences in the same school. We wondered whether hearing each other would act as a catalyst in drawing out further reflections from the students. Our hunch was that students of color in our school rarely had the chance to trade stories, and we were curious as to what would evolve if such an opportunity were provided.

We were also interested in experimenting with joint interviewing. For example, I had previously interviewed a female African American student and then my colleague interviewed her as well. We both then reviewed the data to ascertain whether there were differences in the data when gathered by a female interviewer with a female interviewee and an African American interviewer with an African American. Our experiments with interview formats were leading us across racial and gender lines and now from a one-on-one interview to a joint interview format with a group of students.

The original premise of the research was that my colleague and I would gather the students' stories and figure out a way to present their experiences to a larger audience in the school. Originally, the thought was that we would offer anonymity to the students, shielding them from risks in offering their reflections on their school experience. We envisioned asking for the opportunity to read excerpts of the interviews at faculty meetings or working with the Faculty and Staff Diversity Committee. We thought the interviews might bring to light data that the committee would need as it worked on diversity issues. In general, the idea was that the students would tell us their stories and we would lift up their voices to be heard.

Six boys, 9th and 10th graders, gathered with us for our lunchtime interview. What started as a neat, orderly interview quickly evolved into an untidy, dynamic process of its own. Over pizza, we asked our lead-off question: "Tell us what it's like to be a student of color here." We then turned on the tape recorder and listened for 45 minutes as the students talked openly, teased, laughed, and interrupted each other. As the first meeting drew to a close, dictated by the time allotted for lunch in the school, the students wanted to know when we would meet again. We set a date for the next week. This quickly evolved into a routine—an ongoing lunchtime meeting that met biweekly.

The number of boys participating ebbed and flowed, from 5 to 12, but with a core group of 8. The boys invited other students they thought might be interested; we left it to their discretion as to whom would be included. The group at different points included Jews, Hispanics, and Asians, who, along with the original African Americans, were concerned with diversity issues and the experiences of students of color in the school.

The following vignettes are drawn from the recordings of the lunchtime groups. They illustrate the steps to empowerment that the group helped foster and the process of moving from a strictly interview study to a more collaborative effort with the students.

IS THIS RACISM?

One of the earliest uses of the group involved comparing incidents and the group members discussing among themselves and with us what was and was not racism. Working to make sense of the world they were expected to function in daily, the students raised stories to analyze, sometimes deciding an incident was an intentional act of racism, at other times deciding it was an innocent misunderstanding. Often they would pool their information about the person involved and check if there was a track record of remarks that could seem racist. Conversely, they would also swap information that would let them conclude that an incident was probably a misunderstanding of some sort.

In this defining process, the boys also raised the question of what they could expect from the school administrators in dealing with racist incidents when they happened. The question the boys seemed to be asking was: "Will you hear us when we tell you that a racist incident has occurred?" Because the administrative staff was overwhelmingly Anglo, the boys had to cross racial and hierarchical lines to be heard. The following excerpt gives a flavor of this struggle.

The incident under discussion was that several of the boys had been called "nigger" by Craig, a student of Hispanic/Native American/Anglo origins. The boys spoke with Craig, and when he did not stop the name-calling, they spoke with a grade dean about it. One of the boys recounted the story.

When the grade dean was talking to me, he said he had talked to Craig and Craig said he hadn't meant anything derogatory by it.

But I don't understand that part because even after we told Craig how we felt about it, he continued to call us niggers. So I'm not sure he didn't mean it to be derogatory. The grade dean also said that Craig was a new kid and just wanted attention.

I talked to the grade dean about three times. I retold it for him like three times just so he could get straight what happened. The grade dean said that he didn't believe that Craig meant anything by it. If that's the case, then Craig is either lying or really stupid, because we told him how we felt about this. We made it very forcibly clear, but he continued, so I'm not sure that the grade dean is correct.

It may be something unconscious on the grade dean's part. Would you want to say, "Yeah, some of the kids I'm responsible for, well, they're a little racist and they tend to hate people other than themselves, but you know, they're not bad." Would you want to say that? . . . He didn't do this like consciously, but I think his main point was to try and suppress it, to try and keep everybody from like—well—just kind of like blowing it off and hoping that it wouldn't happen again.

In raising the incident in the group, the boys were setting forth the contradictions in the legitimated explanation of the incident: if Craig really did not mean to be derogatory, then he must be "stupid," since he did not change his behavior after being confronted by the boys. If he was lying and the grade dean accepted his explanation, it was in lieu of facing the fact that some of the students in his domain might be racist. In their persistence in bringing up the incident with the group, the boys seemed to be asking if their perceptions of racism were correct and to be seeking support in learning how to deal with them. It was also a signal of a probable departure from the version of reality portrayed to them by the adult authority structure of the school. With the support of the group as a whole, they were holding on to their own sense of reality about what is or is not racism, even when their views were not legitimated by the school administration. They were becoming the experts on their own experiences.

They also seemed to be testing us as researchers and as other adults working in the school. Would we feel that we had to back the party line, or was criticism of administrative decisions allowed? As adult participants in the school structure, and with prior relationships with at least some of the boys, we were known as faculty versed in and committed to diversity issues. The boys had every right to expect a sympathetic hearing from us. Our willingness to be angry along with them or to hear them when they did not feel heard in other parts of the school was a further step toward validating and encouraging their voices.

Linked with a growing understanding of racism was an increased awareness of themselves as minorities. A sense of being singled out for their race brought them together as well as heightened their own growing sense of their racial identities.

Boy 1: There's like one major good thing that's come out of this [the incident with Craig], and that's like the minorities within—I know in the freshman and sophomore class, there's more unity. They seem to care what happens like to the other ones. Whereas before, like when I was down in the middle school, if something like this would happen, I can't honestly say that my brothers would have come down and like helped me out.

Boy 2: That's true, that's true.

Boy 1: But I think that this has provided more unity, not just within the Afro-American—

Boy 3: [Interrupting]—But with everyone.

Boy 1: But with everyone. I mean the Asian brothers and the Hispanic brothers.

Boy 4: I don't think there's that much racial tension in the middle school. I mean, I remember all through sixth to eighth grades I saw everyone as just like—just one human race. Humans, that's all I saw. In high school I still viewed everyone as human, but it just happened that the people who were nice to me were other minorities and the people who I'm still friends with—well, some white people, but they just happened to be just a little less nice to me.

Teacher Researcher: What I'm trying to understand is if there is something about the high school climate that precipitates this kind of awareness, whether it is

	negative or positive. What we need to understand is what is it about this environment that brings about this sort of consciousness, this awareness that I'm different, and I'm different because, and why?
Boy 5:	I really don't know what it is; it just snaps. I don't know what happened over the summer between eighth and ninth grade; I started snapping, you know, looked in the mirror and said, "Hey, I'm Asian!"
Boy 1:	I'm Asian and I'm proud!
Boy 5:	Exactly!
Boy 2:	Asian power!
Boy 3:	Well, it seems like, it seems like to me the more black you get, the more flack you get. [Loud laughter from the group]

RESPONDING TO THEIR WORLD

The name-calling incident was a catalyst for ongoing group discussion. By continuing to raise the incident for discussion, the boys signaled that although the administrator involved might consider the case closed, from their point of view it still needed to be acknowledged. The repercussions of the initial exchange with the grade dean on this matter were made explicit in a conversation in the group about a month later.

> I mean right now, I mean, like there are only a few people, probably the people in this room that I would feel comfortable coming to with like the issue of diversity. . . . If my diversity is being threatened, then I wouldn't—I wouldn't feel comfortable going to just any faculty member. I wouldn't feel comfortable going to that dean just because of like the way that he handled the last thing, just kind of like "forget it." I mean, I wouldn't feel comfortable going to him.

Working with the idea that at least some of the administrators were not willing to deal with racist incidents, the boys used the group to discuss possible responses to the original incident with

Craig and to brainstorm should something like the name-calling incident occur again. They spent a lot of time speculating that if Craig repeated his offense, there would be violence and they could not take further insults sitting down. When they first raised the idea of beating up Craig, I remember having a sick feeling in my stomach, thinking that what had started as a fairly innocent research group could be accused of fanning trouble in the school. At the same time, I felt like we had to stay with the process and let the boys hash it out and make their own decisions. What we as adults involved in the group tried to do was push the perimeters of their decision making so that they would consider any possible repercussions to their actions while it was all still hypothetical.

Initially, the boys felt that because their actions would be justified, for example, Craig "deserved" to be beaten up, the consequences for them would be minimal. They believed that the school would perhaps slap their wrists; at most they speculated they would be put on probation. Working to link our research questions to a larger, sociohistorical context, we were gathering information but also providing the boys with a framework for decision making. At this point, with us pushing, the boys began to connect their potential actions to the larger sociocultural frame.

Teacher Researcher:	So I hear you saying that your hands would probably be slapped but there wouldn't be any more consequences to you if you did that.
Boy 2:	I think there's something a little more important than our personal consequences, like whether each one of us is put on probation. If that [beating up Craig] happened, it would damage—
Boy 1:	[Interrupting]—It's going to look like a black gang took this kid out . . .
Boy 2:	Yeah.
Boy 1:	. . . and kicked his butt.
Teacher Researcher:	So you lose either way?
Boy 1:	Yeah, it sets a precedent.
Teacher Researcher:	Yeah, that's just what I'm asking. So what are the consequences of that—let's say if it was a black

	gang that beat up this kid. Do you think that there would be reaction aside from the faculty? I mean, do you see where the community would react?
Boy 3:	Yeah, some people that were borderline before would, I assume, say "Well, I don't mind Negroes so much," but if all of a sudden a gang of Negroes went out and beat Craig up, they'd probably be pushing, saying, "Look, they're trying to take over the campus," you know?
Teacher Researcher:	See, I want you guys to really think about the consequences if you really beat him up because here is an "insignificant incident," and yet, the first reflex response of you guys, you beat up a kid like that. There's going to be a whole, almost archetypal, reflex response about this incident. You guys said you would be just slapped a little bit, or given probation. Do you think that you could be expelled?
Boy 4:	Well, I don't even think that the most rational thing to do is to just beat him. I don't think that it is.

There was also a growing awareness on the part of the boys that the norms of the school culture were distinct from those represented in other parts of the larger community. Much of their work focused on this awareness, coupled with the sense that, while they tried to defend the school culture to those outside of it, their presence within the school was not without contradictions. While struggling to function in a school environment that felt in many ways like a foreign culture, their very existence in the school and their attempt to abide by its norms meant that they were moving away from support and solidarity offered by groups outside the school. In this example, they were also moving away from one portrayal of what it means to be "really black." Caught between at least two worlds and conflicting senses of what it means to be a person of color, the boys struggled to decide in what direction to move.

| *Boy 1:* | These guys that are members of the NAACP, they like talk to me. They're all, "Why haven't you beat him down yet?" And I have to try and explain like |

the whole concept of like the administration, like the consequences and everything, and they, they say something to me like, "Oh, if you were really black—you just let him get away with that." That really upsets me.

Teacher Researcher:	So you get it at both ends.
Boy 2:	There's like people within our own school, like within my class even that—they say, "Why do you guys have to act so black; why do you have to like, always stand around together, like in the stairwells, and always just talk to each other?"
Boy 3:	Why do they have to act so white? [Laughter]
Boy 4:	Well, if we're all hanging out together, that means that they're hanging out together, doesn't it?
Teacher Researcher:	Well, what about the climate that allows for this? What in the school climate has caused you guys to just hang out together?

Rejecting the various alternatives they have thought of or have had offered to them, the boys entered a reflective period, working to center themselves and think through what felt right to them in their unique circumstances. They struggled with the tenets of "freedom of expression," wondering if they had the right to act at all, even in the face of racism. The group moved to a discussion of everyone having the right to believe whatever they wanted versus being free to act on that belief. That is, people could be prejudiced, but discrimination, the action connected to it, was an infringement on their rights. The boys were questioning the acts of the perpetrators in this incident as well as what they themselves would allow themselves in terms of a response. The following excerpt summarizes the group's conclusions on this point.

I don't agree with what he believes, but I think everyone has the freedom to believe whatever they want to believe, even if it's wrong. But there's a fine line between what you believe and offending other people. I mean, sensitivity is the bottom line here. If you believe it and you express it frequently and it offends other people, that's just unacceptable. He has the freedom to believe whatever he wants, but he can't just go around offending people. I mean, you have to be sensitive to other people's feelings.

This is the standard the boys worked to implement toward their own planning and actions, that is, how to believe what it is they believe as it relates to diversity issues while being sensitive members of the community. They saw themselves as part of the school. With that membership came certain rights and obligations. This led them directly to the plan they finally decided on: working to change others' beliefs. They concluded that racist actions are based on "ignorance" and that one of their goals was to see how that kind of ignorance could be replaced with knowledge.

Boy 4:   I figure it's our school; it's our time to learn. It's our time to educate ourselves; it's our turn to educate each other. . . . I feel that this school is just wrong in general because they say this school is supposed to prepare us for the outside world and they don't; they don't teach about other people's history. I mean if you're going to grow up and work in this country, you're going to have to know about other people's ethnicity because you're going to work with them when you're older. I don't think they sufficiently prepare us. See, everything is like ignorance. What Craig said is out of ignorance. Everyone is just ignorant about each other's backgrounds, and they don't understand like—

Boy 3:   [Interrupting]—they were saying like Malcolm X was un-American.

Boy 4:   Well I'm sure they weren't even reading anything about him. I mean, he grew up in a time—he was living in a time that was full of racial strife; there was a lot of tension. See, that's what people need, awareness about other people's ethnicity and why they're the way they are, and I mean the school. It teaches about certain types of history but not the history that directly affects us.

Boy 2:   Are we going to ever have any opportunity to have like black history courses and like Asian history courses?

Boy 3:   If they do have them, it won't be while we're here.

Boy 2:   I mean, like I get offended when people come up to me and say "What does that X on your hat mean? Ten? X-rated?" or something like that. I mean, I get offended kind of.

The boys had moved to a critique of the school culture as represented in the curriculum. They were linking the racist name-calling with an environment that left a void where informing, enlightening knowledge should provide a safeguard from "ignorant" attacks. The lack of awareness of a school community that did not seem to connect the *X*'s on their T-shirts and hats to Malcolm X was read by the boys as a symbol of the ignorance they referred to as the root of the racist name-calling and other incidents in the school. Not seeing themselves represented in the curriculum, they conceived the plan of beginning to ask for a more inclusive course of studies that represented a diversity of histories.

They also looked for ways to take the lead in the process of educating themselves and others. That search led them to the founding of the Minority Awareness Committee (MAC) on campus. The school had, in the past, attempted to foster a Student Diversity Committee, an organization that would work with the equivalent committee of adults in the school on diversity issues. The conclusion of the boys was that "the diversity committee just doesn't get anything done," and that was why a new, more proactive group needed to be formed, initiated by students rather than administrators and other adults in the school. After wrangling to get a vision of what the new student group should be, they drew up a proposal to have the MAC formally incorporated as a recognized organization in the school.

Boy 1:   One thing that epitomized the whole reason I wanted to start the MAC was—I was passing this [petition to support the recognition of the MAC] around in history class and someone grabbed this, and they were all reading it, trying to decide if they were going to sign, right? And you know Sandy Hanes, she's all, "We're already aware of this stuff;

we know you're minorities—what else do you want?" That totally epitomizes why I want this.

Boy 3:   I think we should just like focus on educating people who are ignorant. . . . This doesn't necessarily like stereotype white people and this doesn't exclude minorities—but just target people who are ignorant—

Boy 2:   [Interrupting]—Yeah, of minorities, their own culture or other cultures.

Boy 4:   I think we should just unite; that's the point.

Boy 1:   By becoming an officially recognized organization, we can apply to have a forum [a student-led assembly for the whole school]. We can apply for a forum to educate—tell people what we are and what our point is. Because there's a lot of people, like Evan Schneider (an Anglo student) started this whole rumor about how the whole purpose of the MAC was to get rid of all the white males at school, and there were like people who were just jumping on the bandwagon of that. He threatened to start a proposal that this group was going to be controversial and should not be allowed.

Boy 3:   He thinks we're militants.

Boy 5:   People are feeling that this is just going to be like a minority-only thing. I think that's the biggest problem.

Boy 6:   I don't see what the problem with minority only is.

Boy 2:   One thing we need to emphasize from Mr. F.'s [the activities director] view is we need to allow Caucasians into it.

Boy 4:   No!

Boy 5:   But we do!

Boy 4:   I don't see what the problem with minority only is.

Boy 6:   Well, I think what we should do is include anyone who wants to learn about other people's cultures.

Teacher   Why are the white students saying that if you
Researcher: have a group of minority students together, it's
               divisive—whatever term they will use—it will cre-
               ate trouble and so on and so forth, which is a very
               historical response to any kind of organizing effort
               on the part of minorities. It's very important what's
               behind that, okay? Don't just respond to their
               response—then you just have emotions going on.
               Try to understand what their feelings are, what
               their fears are, what their motives are. What does it
               relate to historically?

The birth of the MAC brought a new era to the research
process. As a friendship group, the boys got together often at
lunchtime and continued discussions of the themes raised in the
group. The tape recording of the lunchtime group represented just
one slice of the multiple, ongoing discussions taking place among
the boys. The lunchtime discussions became strategy sessions as
the boys planned the development of the MAC. They came with
typed agendas and a sense of the work they needed to accomplish
to become a functioning, recognized group on campus.

Based on the work of Gutièrrez (1990), empowerment in the
context of this research refers to the concept of individuals contextualizing their experiences, critically reflecting on and reformulat-
ing their worldview, and gaining a sense of personal power to join
with others in changing the social order. The students in this study,
hearing on an ongoing basis that they were the experts of their own
experience, that their voices needed to be heard in larger arenas of
the school, used the group created for data gathering as an arena for
contextualizing and critiquing their experiences. They became
agents for change on their own behalf and for the institution at
large. The research process served, in part, as a catalyst for the
students' empowerment and ownership of the change process.

POLITICAL AND METHODOLOGICAL
IMPLICATIONS OF EMPOWERMENT

The notion of empowerment includes a sense of ownership of the
process. As the energy and vision of the student group grew

beyond the bounds of the lunchtime meetings, there was not even the guise that we, the adult researchers, were "in charge" of the change process. Rather, the effort became one where the adult researchers and the students were joined in the process of institutional change. They became collaborators producing critical knowledge aimed at concrete applications within the school. As the boys increasingly found their own way, as the MAC gained momentum and credibility within the institution, the struggle for us as researchers was one of methodologically capturing the change effort—a dynamic, fluid process that was taking place in a number of settings within the school with a variety of actors. As adults seasoned in the change process, it also meant anticipating the backlash that was a usual part of that process. Last, we had to work to not squelch the rush of energy released in the enthusiasm of the students' first efforts at organized institutional change—a bit worrisome to two adults feeling "responsible" for the actions, protection, and safety of a young and politically naive group of change agents.

The worry spoke to a sense of collaboration with the students while the unavoidable awareness of a hierarchy of adult/adolescent, faculty/student relationships persisted. We were also aware of a movement beyond our control in the sense that we, as the researchers, did not get to call the shots. Although that sense of empowered students felt "right," there were no road maps that we were aware of to learn how to cooperate in that empowerment across adult/student lines. The patronizing plan of us "telling their stories" was far behind us, yet there seemed to be no clear guidelines for the territory we had moved into once those subject/object lines had been blurred. How much was the initial research effort a catalyst for this sense of movement among the boys? What was our responsibility to them and to the work for change? How could we help them be wise in their efforts? What was our role, if any, with the MAC?

We were also struggling to conceptualize our own work in the change effort. The boys had formed a student organization that was publicly raising issues of diversity. If we were to collaborate in the change effort, we needed to conceptualize more clearly the adult part of that and lend our efforts to the overall work for diversity. Our original idea, that of raising the students' voices so their experiences could help inform the diversity process, was well on its way; the students had become their own spokespeople. We struggled to bring into focus our next part of the work.

THE NEGOTIATION OF MULTIPLE ROLES AND MULTIPLE LEVELS OF REALITY

As a practitioner doing research in my own work site, obviously the role of the researcher was not the only one I assumed within the school. In fact, as far as the school was concerned, the stories project was an addition to my regular responsibilities, something that was "allowed" as long as I could keep up with it and my other responsibilities. What was becoming a vital part of my awareness was something that only my research colleague and I had access to: an ongoing dialogue with the boys. I felt a growing dissonance in trying to match the boys' reality, as they portrayed it, with other dialogues going on in the school. Diversity issues were addressed without taking into account the student perspective.

In the research group, we worked hard to assure the students that they were the experts on their own experiences and that we needed to hear their views to be able to work effectively for change. However, this did not necessarily translate to the way the institution as a whole went about decision making. Adults, myself among them, invested with the charge to help create policy recommendations, were not necessarily tapping into the student reality when trying to frame decisions. Yet the richness of the students' stories kept playing in my mind as I went about the rest of my work. I began to feel like I was functioning in two worlds, because there seemed to be such a gap between the students' voices and the discourse in the adult domain of the school. I was feeling more connected and safer in the student group than I was feeling in the school as a whole. This was disquieting for an adult to feel, yet somehow, on a subjective level, I knew I was encountering "real" dialogue in the student group that was not necessarily a part of my adult discussions.

I felt caught between the reality of the boys' storytelling and the sanctioned discourse of the school. Although as an institution we were endorsing the movement toward multiculturalism, I was not sure that what the school had in mind encompassed my read of what that movement toward diversity would mean. I was seeing diversity as a challenge to a hierarchical structure in the school, where we would grow to a place of shared decision making based on the voices of the real "experts," those whose lives were impacted by our policies. Because I was hearing very little in the public discourse of the school that seemed to be equating the diversity movement with power sharing, I was all too aware that I risked being marginalized from the rest of the school community if I expressed my own conclusions. But I was also aware that there was no going back, that the boys' stories framed what I was hearing in the public discourse and helped create a sense of dissonance for me. My choice seemed to be either to discount the boys' stories or to confront some of the taboo areas in the school; neither alternative looked appealing.

Just as the students had times when they were meeting without either of the researchers being involved, both my research colleague and I were involved in other activities in the school that directly touched on issues of diversity. When did our researcher hats come off and our roles as practitioners emerge? Was it possible to separate the two?

I remember sitting in a meeting with some of the parents of children of color who were proposing some policy changes for the school handbook that identified and responded to racist attitudes and incidents in the school. The dialogue involved representatives from the school administration and the Faculty and Staff Diversity Committee. As an intense dialogue flowed back and forth, I found myself jotting down the equivalent of field notes, trying to capture the sense of the conversation on paper. I instinctively did this, thinking it would inform some of my thinking about how an institution creates an environment where all can thrive.

Ultimately, I stopped trying to take notes during the meetings because I found it distracting to my role of participant. It was hard for me to engage in the dialogue fully while trying to record it on paper. Although not a part of my formal research, the dialogue that the field notes recorded was part of the larger contextualization of the boys' stories, outlining in broader strokes the school's work regarding diversity issues. I struggled with whether these field notes were "usable" data, because I did not feel that I had "permission" for such note taking. I was very aware that the others in the group saw me as a participant, as a member of the Faculty and Staff Diversity Committee, rather than a researcher. It felt like one thing to record a student group and another thing to cast the lens of inquiry onto a group process that potentially portrayed representatives of the school administration in a less than favorable light.

A number of the boys' parents were directly involved in these parents' groups. In the boys' group, we began to recognize a flow of information to the students as parents processed the meetings at home. Because the school and the parent community were struggling to be allies over issues of diversity rather than ending up as divided and warring factions, it was particularly tricky in the group to decide, as adults, just how open to be. Our own emotions and spirits ebbed and flowed, dependent on our perceptions of how much "progress" we were making, how much was possible, and how much of our concern should be shared with students. These questions caused us to wonder how to collaborate with students, how to work across hierarchical lines of adults/ adolescents and teachers/students, and how to be representatives of the school while critiquing it.

Both my research colleague and I had been appointed to the Faculty and Staff Diversity Committee charged to bring some leadership to the school on multicultural issues. It was within this smaller arena that I began to take some risks, to deepen the dialogue regarding movement toward a truly multicultural organization. With a knot in my stomach, I tried, at meetings, to be as real as I could while simultaneously assessing the level of risk to me. Aware that the boys' stories were taking place in an environment that I interacted with on a daily basis, I wondered how to use their stories to inform the committee process. I also wondered how, through the decisions we recommended to the school administration, the diversity committee might work toward making the environment one where all students, as well as those in our boys' group, would thrive. The dilemma methodologically was how to use the data that we were collecting to inform the decision making that was simultaneously occurring in other arenas in the school.

We had been recording all the lunchtime groups, and I had hired someone to transcribe them, but there was no time to pore over the transcripts systematically and to make sense of all the themes, much less to use computer software to code them. If I wanted to be in the larger dialogue already occurring in the school, I had to take what opportunities presented themselves, whether I was "ready" or not. Our first round of data analysis consisted mostly of the quick debriefing my colleague and I went through immediately following the lunch groups—the same time frame that ended the group and took the students back to class imposed itself on us as well. This sense of snatching time for research in the midst of an already busy schedule was an ever-present struggle. We compared a sense of what we had heard, what meanings we could make out of it, and what plans we would make next. Although I wished for a leisurely hour for this debriefing and meaning-making, in reality we had about 20 minutes.

It felt overwhelming to be working to make sense of all that I was hearing from the students, "the data," while simultaneously needing that burgeoning understanding to inform courses of possible action being proposed in other avenues in the school. I had a longing for some order, a sense of wanting to finish one area (i.e., data gathering and analysis) before I needed to use it. I had not anticipated that moving into an action research framework would feel so uncomfortable, that I would need to speak in the forums offered to me while feeling that I myself only had partial knowledge. I longed for the mythology of a cleaner research project, where I would speak from a safe, distant place about my data, and the change effort would carefully flow in a systematic way, informed by the power of the research results. I had not expected the reality to be so much messier than the research I had done in other sites where, as an outsider, I entered a research site and studied it but was not intimately involved in it.

For me, as a school employee, this kind of intimate involvement with my research site raised issues of vulnerability as I struggled with how to be honest to my own perceptions, increasingly informed by the student stories, while not sounding so dissenting at school meetings that I would be discounted or face negative sanctions. I felt accountable to the students, in the face of their terrible honesty, to be true to the reality they were portraying, although I was also aware that it was not easy to be real in many settings in the institution. I was being changed in the process of listening to the students, aware that I had an opportunity that others in the school did not have at that time, but I also felt that my growing awareness was creating a gap between myself and other adults in the school.

Doing this type of research with another colleague was critical. Our relationship provided one space in the school where my worlds could come together, where I could be real with another adult without risk. It was a safe space where I could process and integrate the data, allow it to impact me, and feel the support of another adult in the same school community. Sometimes I felt exhilarated by doing this research; at other times it felt like an "add-on," something else to tackle in the midst of too many other demands. At times I found myself wondering why I had ever gotten myself into it. Looking back on it now, I can say it changed my life.

TRANSFORMATION BECOMES A KIND OF WAR

Schön's (1971, as cited in Holly, 1989) concept of dynamic conservatism leads to the expectation that, as a group within an institution works for change, there will be an equal force working to maintain the status quo. "Because it sees every effort at transformation as an attack, transformation becomes a kind of war" (p. 80).

In mid-December, my research colleague received a death threat via the computerized communication system of the school. Explicitly racist in its content, the threat was signed, "Sincerely, KKK." By January, the MAC had received a similar threat, signed by the "Aryan Control Committee." The school struggled not to make the incidents public in hopes of increasing the chances of apprehending the perpetrators. Eventually, local and federal investigators were called to investigate. Phones were tapped when members of the boys' group and my research colleague started receiving threatening phone calls at home. Headlines spilled across the local newspaper, giving daily updates of the events. Television crews came to campus, shoving microphones in the faces of the boys from the group.

The headmaster addressed the school community in an all-school assembly, reassuring students and faculty alike that all that could be done was being done. He reiterated that the school stood behind its efforts to continue working on diversity issues. A middle school student, a Hispanic girl, discovered a threatening note in her locker. The contents were similar to notes delivered to the MAC. We organized a vigil, a candlelight show of support for those threatened, along with an open microphone for students, faculty, and staff to voice their fears, disappointments, and outrage. Parent meetings were held to discuss the incidents, the increased security, and the climate that might allow such a thing to happen.

The ranks of the MAC swelled, and it held its own public forums to let students speak not only of the current, blatant incidents but also of what life was like on a day-to-day basis for students of color in the school. Parents of the boys in the group called me, worried and sleepless, living with tapped telephones and hoping to stave off further threats to their children. Emotionally torn and exhausted, my research colleague took a short leave of absence from the school. The investigators found nothing conclusive. We tried to resume school in a somewhat normal fashion. That spring, two bomb threats led to the evacuation of the campus, and we made the newspapers once again. Were these threats related to the earlier threatening notes? No one knew. Did the bomb threats contribute to a feeling of danger? Definitely. We grimly worked to get to the end of the school year.

EPILOGUE

The following school year was quiet. The MAC was reconfigured and changed its name to the Humanity Interaction Team (HIT). A few of the original members were still a part of it. Others were lobbying for a black student union on campus to continue defining what it means to be an African American in a predominately Anglo environment.

My research colleague, originally on leave from the public schools, left at the end of our eventful school year. As part of a parents' group, he continues a dialogue on race issues with the headmaster. His presence and model of how to be authentic and vulnerable are missed on campus.

The student coordinators of the HIT have asked me to work with them on a weekend retreat, helping them talk across racial lines. The work goes on. I continue to interview and try to understand the movement of diversifying in a school context.

I spent a lot of time thinking through how much the organizing of a group of students of color contributed to a tumultuous school year and how much was just the reality of living in a racist society. I wondered how much I put students at risk just by asking the question, "Tell me what it's like being a student of color here."

There is no real way to ever know. What we do know is that as we work to raise voices, others work to silence them. As we make the invisible visible, others resist seeing. As we learn to work together, collaboratively, we are a threat; that threat does not go unnoticed. When the racist threats occurred, the fledgling MAC was in a position to respond. As an already organized entity, it linked with others in the school and worked to use the threats as an educational tool. This is not the kind of research that measures cause and effect, but it is the kind of research that points to possibilities.

DISCUSSION

The scenario outlined here by Herr is an extreme example of the spillover effect referred to earlier in this chapter. Practitioner action research takes place in a large, institutional context and is not necessarily containable to one corner of the practitioner's world. Following the vagaries of action research, the researcher, at best, can prepare to follow where the sense of empowerment is leading—often out of the corners and into the larger institution.

Although the original research was conceptualized to improve practice, that is, to help create a more nurturing environment for diverse students, its actual evolution, including the sense of empowerment of the students, expanded the research agenda to one where research and action became a single process. Rather than the change effort following a linear equation where the data are gathered and then are applied to problem solving, the research question acted as a catalyst, generating a theme—racism—for further exploration and education. The results of this kind of exploration were immediately applied to the students' situation: they felt that racist name-calling reflected an ignorance of diverse histories, an ignorance supported by the narrow range of the school's current curriculum. They decided to work to educate the ignorant. The course of action came from a critical look at the world in which they functioned and a linking of their situation to a larger, sociohistorical context (i.e., the historical interaction between the dominant culture and people of color and an examination of their reflex responses to racist incidents in the light of this sociohistorical view). The courses of action eventually chosen resulted from this analysis, coupled with a sense of the students' own empowerment—"It's our school; it's our time to learn."

The researcher's challenge is to become just another participant, rather than one of the ones in charge of the change effort. By encouraging a sense of empowering participation, researchers relinquish a sense of control of the research/action and are committed instead to shared decision making, with their voice being just one in the chorus calling for change.

BUT IS IT RESEARCH?

Some might say this has been a compelling narrative of the possibilities and risks of empowerment, but how does it speak to a larger community, whether of practitioners or academics or others? What are the "findings"? Where is the theory? Is this research? Imagine the comments a reviewer of an academic educational journal might make!

Most practitioners who work in schools like the one described will find these questions humorous. They will see them as a spoof on how academics, even qualitative ones, think about research. Practitioners bring to narratives a wealth of tacit knowledge and a set of similar preoccupations that resonate with many of the situations and insights described. Only another practitioner can know how it feels to be in the situation described. This narrative will be received by practitioners with an empathy and poignancy lacking in the hard-nosed questions about findings, theory, and method. As practitioners read narratives like this, they are actively engaged in the process of naturalistic generalization described in Chapter 2.

Drawing on our categories from Chapter 2, the internal validity of the study is established in the account. The democratic validity of the study, or the inclusion of multiple voices or perspectives, was achieved through the inclusion of the perspective of the students of color. Although not included in the above account, data from school committees and the administration were also gathered.

Outcome validity was established through the continual rethinking of the dilemmas presented, which ultimately resulted in a permanent student diversity organization. Questions of diversity were not "solved," but a mechanism for dealing with diversity issues from the students' perspective was a concrete result of the study.

Process validity was established as Herr discussed her ongoing decision making about methods. In practitioner action research, process validity refers to finding methodological adaptations that fit the contingencies of the setting and the flow of action. Ongoing learning was established through the continuation of the HIT, which indicates that the learning will continue. This type of validity has not been achieved at the institutional level, although real organizational learning is probably beyond the purview of a single action research project.

Catalytic validity resulted in an increased level of consciousness both in the students of color and in other students in the school, as well as, although to a lesser extent, in some teachers and administrators.

Finally, dialogic validity was achieved through the collaboration between colleagues. The two colleagues were able to check each other's perceptions. Because the collaboration was interracial, some degree of perception check was provided for the white Anglo researcher.

However, in spite of the external validity of the naturalistic generalizations and the internal validity gauged from the above criteria, it is still fair to ask if there is any generation or testing of theory in Herr's study. Although perhaps not generating new theory, the study does confirm and extend work that identifies the problems of change residing in disjunctions between discursive and "deep" levels of organizational functioning (Argyris et al., 1985; Robinson, 1993).

This study shows that the politics of practitioner action research, and of change generally, are internal and external, complex and multilayered. The relationship between these levels is significant. Once one has tapped into the deep or real level of an organization, the discursive level becomes more and more transparent. Of course, one could argue that neither level is real in that both are social constructions; however, they are constructed socially for different purposes. As Anderson (1990) suggests, the discursive level is constructed in such a way as to support the status quo and legitimate the organization to its environment. The deep level, in this case the students' worldview, is constructed out of the students' experiences in a racist society. These different constructions also exist within a context of hierarchical and unequal distributions of power.

This organizational duality often leads to alienation (or worse) for both students and practitioners who attempt to point out the disjunctions between levels. Students may end up communicating their sense of dissonance by "acting out" behavior, leading to sanctions and possible expulsion from the institution. Proactive practitioners are often silenced through labeling (e.g., "negative," "troublemaker," "feminist," "angry," "abrasive") and other forms of marginalization. In this way, the deep level of organizational life is kept invisible to the rest of the institution, thwarting any meaningful change. As practitioners, we need to keep asking ourselves what is worth the risks involved and how committed we are to our institutions. Deeply valuing ourselves and our educational settings means a willingness to keep risking raising our voices and working to help them be heard.

CHAPTER FIVE

The Research Question, Ethical Considerations, and Research Design

T his chapter addresses areas that practitioner action researchers need to think through as they anticipate beginning research projects in their own sites. There is often a sense, for insiders to the action research process, that there is not a clear-cut beginning or, for that matter, end to the research. Sometimes a beginning or an end is imposed, as in the beginning of a university course or the end of employment in a setting. We are not usually starting as blank slates; that is, it is not that we have not given thought to some of the issues we want to explore, but rather that they continue to puzzle us. Or perhaps in professional readings we have become intrigued by unique approaches or ideas and wonder what it would be like to try to apply them in our own settings. The idea here is that our professional dilemmas and puzzles, our frustrations, or what we learn from others' writings are all fruitful grounds for action research.

Each researcher should assume there are a number of questions that could be relevant and interesting to pursue in her or his site. Practitioner action research takes place in local contexts at given points in time amid various vested interests. It is worth researchers considering the potential risks they may be taking in asking particular questions, to take into account the politics of the local context and whom—including themselves—they may place at risk through their inquiry.

It is good to consider these issues, because once the action research spiral is set in motion, researchers should not assume its spiraling is totally under their control. It is impossible to completely anticipate the directions the inquiry will take or the kinds of interests it will attract or threaten. One unique aspect of doing insider action research is that we are initiating research in a setting where we may already have relationships. It may also be a place where we intend to stay for a long period of time, even if the research ends. Given these realities, insider researchers may ask themselves what research question they want to take on and what feels too politically volatile to tackle at a given point in time. This problem is somewhat lessened when research is done collaboratively with other teachers or stakeholders or is done around research questions of interest to the whole school.

We are not suggesting here that the "right" research question is always the one that makes us feel "safe." Rather we are suggesting that institutional realities factor into the decision to pursue one research question over another as the researcher assesses possible tradeoffs and complexities. Depending on the context, a researcher may make the choice to deliberately put a question on the back burner for a while, perhaps to be considered at another time. Or conversely, an issue may strike at the core of a researcher's ethics, or bottom line, and from that vantage point it may feel impossible not to pursue. In this case, the researcher may decide to pursue a question because it is ethically difficult not to, even if it seems risky for the researcher professionally or personally.

Practitioner action research is deliberately set in motion to bring about changes, to ourselves and our practices and perhaps our school institutions. In this sense, it is a *disturbing* form of research, in that it has the potential to interrupt the status quo. If, as the researchers, we have set these possible changes in motion, we may welcome the insights that come with the data-gathering process and even happily anticipate changes. Others in the site may feel differently and may see the inquiry as a threat or an imposition, something *done to them* rather than chosen. We pointed out in Chapter 2 that when institutional interests are disturbed—or are anticipating being disturbed—they rally to maintain institutional equilibrium. Our stance as researchers is to be neither naive about the forces that may push back on our hoped-for changes nor unnecessarily adversarial, creating an unwanted "us versus them" situation. Our hope with action research is that *communities of inquiry* could be developed in school sites, where an institutional stance embraces data gathering and analysis as tools of professional development, because this seems to be the most probable way that authentic changes can come about.

CRAFTING A QUESTION FOR STUDY

Research questions are often formalized versions of puzzles that the practitioner or persons involved have been struggling with for some time and perhaps even acting on in terms of problem solving. The decision to do more systematic inquiry on a puzzling issue is one of asking, "What issue or problem am I really trying to solve? How might data shed light on this?" It is, in essence, a stepping back a bit from what is often a daily struggle or puzzle to gain perspective through systematic inquiry. Formalizing the puzzles of practice into research is a way of working better rather than doing more of the same only harder.

A question for practitioner action research may come out of a frustration, a practice puzzle, or a contradiction in a setting (this is what we say we do, but do we?). Often these are things a practitioner has been giving thought to for some time. The research question most often addresses something the practitioner wants to do better or understand more clearly.

Our own experience indicates that there is probably nothing more important to action research than getting clear on the question being asked. Our experience also indicates that this can take a bit of time, that questions shift and evolve. We in fact expect this as we gather data and begin a cycle of the research. Part of the process of action research is this ongoing focusing on the issue in relation to the data gathered. So we are suggesting a conundrum of sorts here—that there is nothing more important than continuing to get clear on the research question and that this could continue to evolve and morph in relation to the data and problem solving. We start with our current understanding of the research question and see where the data and analysis push us. We have learned that we can trust the action research process to bring into sharper relief the issues for study and change, that the process will deepen our understanding of the question as well as the complexity of moving toward potential changes. This kind of deepened understanding is in fact one of the validity checks we propose for insider action research (see Chapter 2).

Individual or Collective Questions

The distinction between an individual's question and a collective one may not be as stark as it appears. Our own experience is that an individual's research question often has a spillover effect. Just doing inquiry in a site seems to send ripples through the environment, where others become interested, threatened, or intrigued (Herr, 1999c). It is also common that, as data are gathered, the researcher wants to talk about it, furthering the conversation in the larger school community. The questioning stance seems to lend itself to asking why we carry out business as usual and provoke new conversations about the status quo.

Because insiders doing action research in their own sites is such a complex undertaking and because it can become quite political, we have suggested that, if possible, it is best undertaken collaboratively. Action research can move at a rapid pace—schools move ahead on various issues based on demands placed on them rather than a researcher's schedule or even a researcher's findings. It can be helpful to have another researcher who is in ongoing conversation regarding both how to proceed and how to share the findings with the school community. Pragmatically, it can speed up the research process, since action researchers are typically not hired in their sites primarily as researchers; instead, it is something we do in our spare time. Having another colleague or two to help gather data can move the research process ahead in a timely way.

Sometimes as the research evolves and gains greater visibility, others want to become a part of it. While collaboration may start at the onset of a research project—for example, teachers come together in an inquiry group and decide on a focus of what they will pursue together—it can also become a part of the research as it progresses and others become interested. Because action research takes place in a local context with a goal of change, we see this development of increased interest and desire to collaborate as potentially part of the change process, of perhaps helping to establish a community of inquiry in a school site.

This community of inquiry can cross hierarchical lines such as when a teacher and her students become coresearchers. As with the other forms of collaboration, this can be conceptualized at the beginning of the research, or it can evolve. For example, in Herr's research with the students of color recounted in Chapter 4, the students named themselves coresearchers, in essence claiming it prior to Herr understanding it. The shift was one of moving away from studying the situation *for* students of color to one of conducting research *with* them. As one of the boys aptly put it, "It's our school." In this case, the move was from the students being participants in the research to the role of coinvestigators.

A collective question across sites is also possible. In this case, the researcher has collaborators, but they are not necessarily in the same site. Rather, what they hold in common is a larger question that each researcher is interested in investigating in his or her own site. Researchers can share readings, share strategies, and act as critical friends (Bambino, 2002; Costa & Kallick, 1993) to push each other's thinking. In cases such as these, each researcher has his or her own research project, yet sees a benefit in accruing a larger data set or being able to discuss the same issue across sites. This approach can be particularly useful when there are no collaborators with whom to work in one's own site but the researcher would still like the support of thinking through issues with other researchers.

Questions Derived From Outside Assessments

Data gathering and analysis seem to be an omnipresent reality in an age of accountability in schools. This commonly results, for example, in aggregate test scores, comparing one school with another, noting overall strengths and weaknesses as reflected via the numbers. Schools—and the educators who work in them— face repercussions based on this data and, if the results are not positive, may face some imposed sanctions. Many of us insist that these scores give only a partial picture of the work done in schools and the achievement of our students. Others (see, e.g., Skrla & Scheurich, 2001) suggest that testing can expose inequities in school opportunities and can be an impetus for positive changes.

In any case, accountability through testing is the current lived reality in schools, and based on how the results are interpreted, practices are changed with an eye toward improving these measures. Ironically, this is often a truncating of the action research process, where new practices are put in place (this could be a change in curriculum, a change in the arrangement and emphasis of teaching during the school day, etc.) without a step back that asks, "What other data might we need to understand these results or to design effective interventions?" But schools are often under pressure to quickly make changes and have the results of these changes reflected in the next cycle of test scores. It seems that there is no time to pose these other questions that might lead to fruitful problem solving.

In situations such as these, it does not mean that those in the school community itself cannot embrace some of these questions and deepen the process. As mentioned earlier, educators problem solve all the time. Action research provides the vehicle to systematize this process as well as ground it in data. So, given the example outlined above, where interventions are being put into place, educators may decide on a concurrent set of data they would like to gather, addressing the questions, "So where is this taking us? Are these interventions improving practices for our students? Are there unintended consequences? What are the trade-offs?" This kind of questioning would easily lend itself to fostering collaborative inquiry in a wider school context via an inquiry or study group.

Is It Feasible?

Earlier we suggested that researchers assess the potential risks in pursuing various questions in their sites. Considering the politics and risks involved is one part of a more general assessment around the question, "Is it feasible?" By this we suggest asking questions such as, "What resources would I need to do this research? What access would I need to gather the data I might need? Could I design a methodology that would really address the research question? Is it doable, given everything else I have to do?"

Some of this will be hard to answer initially, given an action research spiral that continues to evolve in the face of initial data gathered and conclusions drawn. For example, when Herr first started her research on what she later called "institutional racism" in her site, the initial question being pursued was a "personal" one, one aimed at doing her job as a school counselor more effectively. But as she gathered data, she was drawn into wider spirals of data gathering that moved her beyond the day-to-day functions of her job to gathering data that were more schoolwide. As it became clear that this was the direction in which the action research was taking her, the whole question of risks and resources had to be reassessed and reevaluated as the research proceeded.

But some areas of feasibility are fairly predictable in insider action research. For example, time—not having enough of it—is virtually always an issue. Some data-gathering techniques are kinder in terms of the resources they absorb, and in this sense, researchers can ask whether there is a methodological design that is doable, given the other demands on their time and other resources. Beyond the primary data gathering we ourselves do, it is good to ask what data are already available that can be brought to bear on the research question. Schools currently gather an incredible amount of data, some of which may be useful for the action research project. For example, early on in Herr's study exploring the experience of students of color in her school, as she thought about their struggles to succeed, part of the data she was interested in was attendance records—Were the students she was concerned about attending school on a regular basis? This was easily accessible data that had already been gathered via the routines of the school. School records of "puzzling students" (Ballenger, 2004) are often another rich source of data, depending on the research question.

The last thing educators need is one more thing to do. The experience of action research should be energizing, not draining. For this to be a realistic aim, issues of feasibility need to be carefully considered. We suggest asking questions such as, "How can current functions in an educator's day be integrated into the role of researcher? What does the day-to-day operation of a classroom or school site offer in the way of data? What would I have to add to the data-gathering processes, and what would I need to be able to do this?"

Assessing Tacit Knowledge

It is assumed that the researcher is not starting on the research question as a tabula rasa. We bring to the potential question our past experiences and the conclusions we have drawn. Unearthing the tacit knowledge we bring to a question can be an important source of data, but it also needs to be critically examined. Our research questions need to be framed in ways that could lead to genuinely new knowledge and potential changes in educational routines, our own included. The process of action research is designed to bring about changes, and one site for these changes is ourselves as researchers.

We suggest asking, "What is it I already know, and how do I know it? How might this knowing limit or bias the way I am considering or asking my research question?" These are important questions to process early on with a critical friend. As Costa and Kallick (1993) suggest, a critical friend is a "trusted person who will ask provocative questions and offer helpful critiques" (p. 49). Often action researchers have been in their sites for quite a while prior to beginning a research project and need some help to step back and assess everyday practices with fresh eyes or to question assumptions. A critical friend poses questions such as, "How do you know it's that and not this?" and asks the researcher to interrogate her or his own ways of knowing.

Maria Mercado (2000) drew on Lytle and Cochran-Smith's (1990, as cited in Mercado, 2000) notion of the oral inquiry process when putting her critical friends in place for her study of her kindergarten classroom:

> During oral inquiry, teachers build on one another's insights to analyze and interpret classroom data and their experiences in the school as a workplace. For teachers, oral inquiries provide access to a variety of perspectives for problem-posing and solving. They also reveal the ways in which teachers relate particular cases to theories of practice. (p. 112)

Studying the impact of having native Spanish speakers in her bilingual kindergarten classroom, Mercado sought critical friends who could add their experience and insights to her study. One colleague, Fatima, was a well-respected bilingual educator who taught first grade. Mercado offers her rationale in tapping Fatima as a critical friend:

> Her classroom context was very similar to mine. It was an early childhood bilingual education setting with a large number of Latino children. . . . She was also interested in supporting bilingualism and biculturalism in the classroom. . . . I believed that our discussions would prove not only supportive in improving my instruction but also in helping me to further consider the research questions in relation to my practice. (p. 112)

Mercardo and Fatima met together monthly, centering their discussions on the themes from Mercado's teacher journal. Mercado notes that the "goal of the discussion was to bring a critical and reflective element to the study" (p. 113). She used the time to clarify the themes for the study as well as probe her instructional decision making. In addition, "these served to triangulate the data sources by allowing me to check my impressions and understandings related to other data collected for the study" (p. 112). While Mercado tape-recorded their interaction, she did not transcribe these tapes. Instead she "listened to them again after the session and listed salient themes in a notebook titled *Critical Friend*" (p. 113). She also kept a running record during the conversations themselves, listing the topics that came up for discussion. She says the running record "served to key my memory about the conversations" (p. 113). In keeping with Lytle and Cochran-Smith's (1990, as cited in Mercado, 2000) notion of the oral inquiry process, Mercado sees her collaboration with her critical friend as supporting her reflective process through a jointly constructed examination of educational issues in her classroom.

Several other examples of relying on critical friends are in Chapter 3. (See the examples of Christman et al., 1995; Evans et al., 2000; Russell, 1992. In addition, see Andreu et al., 2003; Costa & Kallick, 1993; Fayden, 2006.)

Positionality

We discussed the issue of researcher positionality in Chapter 1. Here we revisit the issue in relation to framing a research question. When considering positionality, we are essentially posing questions such as, "Who am I to this proposed research and to this site? Am I in a position of power over others in the institution who might potentially be involved in this research?" Positionality can literally mean one's position in a school, that is, teacher, counselor, administrator, and so on, or where one is located in the institutional hierarchy, or who one has contact with on an ongoing basis. But it can also refer to one's positionality in reference to a proposed research question. In this latter case, the researcher could be an insider to the site but not necessarily an insider to the proposed study, meaning it is not the researcher's lived experience. For example, while Herr had worked extensively with students of color and had become concerned with their experiences in her school, when she formalized the research process initially, she asked two other colleagues, one African American and one Hispanic, to join in the research. In this case, she was an insider to the school but an outsider to what it meant to be a person of color in it. On the other hand, as the research began to rename the issue as one of institutional racism, with much work to be done with white faculty, she was a member of that group and could bring those insights to the table.

While it may be tempting to study our own school or classrooms for issues of convenience, it is important to build a case—to ourselves too—as to *why* it has to take place in our own sites or with our own students. If one of the purposes of our research is to improve our own practices, then it makes sense, obviously, to propose action research where we are located. Otherwise, if we are interested in a study *about* a certain topic in education, there is no compelling reason to conduct the study in one's own site, and in fact it may be much simpler to conduct the study elsewhere. We are making the distinction here, for example, between the following research questions: "How effective is mentoring for new teachers?" versus "How effective am I as a mentor to new teachers?" or "How well are we mentoring new teachers in my building?" The former is a policy question and asks about the effectiveness of an educational intervention or practice; the latter asks about one's own practices as an educator or mentor or about practices in one's site and how they might improve. So potential researchers need to ask themselves the question, "Why does the study have to take place in my own site/my own classroom?"

The answer should be one beyond our own convenience or simply that we are located in a particular site and have easy access.

We also assume that if we are conducting action research in our own sites, we are in the study ourselves, meaning we also are a focus of the study and will appear on the page. We are warning here against the "outsider-within" position (Herr & Anderson, 2005), where, although in the position of an insider, researchers write about the process as though they are outsiders. Action researchers as we are discussing them here are in the site as well as a site themselves for change.

Action research is a systematically evolving process, a living process changing both the researcher and the situations in which he or she acts. Neither the natural sciences nor the historical sciences have this double aim: living the dialectic of researcher and researched (Kemmis & McTaggart, 1982, p. 21). The researcher's role is characterized by the immediacy of the researcher's involvement in the action process. The researcher becomes as much a subject and learner as the participants. Action research is therefore not simply research done on other people (Heydenrych, 2001, p. 1).

Summing Up

We are not necessarily suggesting that any particular answers to the questions posed earlier in this section are "fatal" to the research process. Rather, our suggestion is that they be taken into consideration early on, since, as the researcher considers where she or he is "located," it may impact how the research question is framed or whether we invite others to collaborate with us in the process. It can also impact the methodological design of the research. Our own positionality also comes into play when considering issues of ethics and the granting of permission for the research. We take these up in the section that follows.

ETHICAL CONSIDERATIONS

Each research approach brings its own ethical challenges, and action research is no exception. Action research is a dynamic, evolving practice, and we should assume that there is no foolproof plan to avoid ethical dilemmas as the research develops. Cassell (1982) suggests that perhaps most important to the process is the ability to recognize an ethical issue when it arises so that it can be taken into consideration. The work, then, is not to anticipate every possible ethical conundrum as much as to commit to addressing them both before the research is begun and as they arise. Every researcher should assume that he or she will face ethical decisions as the research proceeds. At the same time, it is worth thinking through initially how to minimize any ethical dilemmas the researcher may face.

The conversation about ethical research sometimes becomes conflated with gaining approval for the research (from the district, from the university, from parents, etc.). While getting approvals can certainly be a significant part of beginning the research process, it should not be confused with the ongoing questioning that researchers must pursue as the research develops, where we commit to continued interrogation of *ourselves* regarding what makes for ethical research in the sites in which we carry it out. Since action research unfolds and develops in unanticipated directions, this kind of interrogation is an ongoing process for researchers.

Balancing Risks and Benefits

Ethical considerations initially ask, "Who might be harmed or put at risk by the research? If the research potentially puts some-one in harm's way, how do I minimize that possibility?" It may be startling to think of our research harming anyone or putting people at risk. But possible harms are broadly defined and may be physical, psychological, legal, social, or economic. For example, harms could include damage to the professional reputation of someone who works at the site or inadvertent exposure of a par-ticipant's identity if the site under study is very small.

The idea is to anticipate any possible harms and work to minimize them; some of this can be done methodologically. For example, Fayden (1998, 2006), in a study of four students in her kindergarten classroom, capitalized on classroom routines and methods of gathering data that did not single out the four children on whom she focused. She commonly, as part of her teaching practices, videotaped her classroom. Fayden (1998) set up the video camera when the children were out of the classroom and only had to record when the children reentered the class. She writes in her dissertation, "The videocam was set back in a corner on a tripod . . . so that the children had little interference from it. . . . Because I taped as part of normal classroom assessment and the children were used to this practice, there was very little comment on the procedure. I simply told the class I was 'taping,' which is how I usually approach a regular taping session" (p. 50). To enhance the recording of conversations during the videotaping, Fayden bought microphones and small tape recorders for *all* the tables of kindergarteners even though she was only transcribing the conversations at the one table where her four participants were sitting. She did this, she explains, so that "the other children should not feel preferential treatment was given to the participants" (p. 49). An ethical goal in this example of teacher research was that no child would be given preferential treatment and that, in singling out any children in a classroom, the researcher would minimize the risk that others might feel excluded. Just as physicians are guided by the Hippocratic oath, requiring them to "do no harm," "according to their best judgment," this same sense of exercising professional judgment is required of action researchers (National Commission, 1979).

Researchers, and the bodies designed to review and approve research, are asked to perform a balancing act. They are asked to take into consideration the possible risks and benefits of a course of research and make difficult decisions when the ratio is ambiguous. Benefits of the research are balanced against possible risks. As we will see in the next section, this equation is one that comes into play in gaining necessary approvals for the research to move ahead. Most school districts have particular priorities in terms of areas they are focusing on for improvement. It can help action researchers gain permission for their research if they demonstrate how their projects might further insight or knowledge toward meeting the school district's goals or priorities.

Gaining Needed Approvals

Codes for conduct in research came out of atrocities that came to light during the Nuremberg war crime trials at the end of World War II. This history of research abuses led to the creation of ethics policies focusing on the protection of human subjects from exploitation or exposure to unacceptable levels of risk through their participation in research. In addition, some populations, such as children, were declared in need of special protections. Federal regulations to address these ethical concerns have their origins in the Belmont Report, issued by the National Commission for the Protection of Human Subjects of Biomedical and Behavioral Research in 1979. This report set out the basic ethical premises that are embodied in current regulations (Hammack, 1997). While the Belmont Report has been codified into "rules" of sorts, it is acknowledged in the report itself that it was intended as a guide rather than a clear-cut blueprint. The creators indicate that the rules "often are inadequate to cover complex situations; at times they come into conflict, and they are frequently difficult to interpret or apply" (National Commission, 1979, p. 3).

Educators do research for all kinds of reasons: to further their own professional growth and development, to improve their practices, to fulfill the requirements of a course or a degree, or to generate knowledge for the larger field of education through presentations and publications. The question of whether or what approvals are needed to proceed is related in part to why the research is being done. Researchers should assume that if the research involves human participants and is going to be publicly disseminated (presented at a conference or to a public audience, written up for publication, etc.), there is a high probability that some kind of permission will be needed to move ahead with the research. It is also not uncommon that initially researchers do not anticipate presenting their work publicly but may change their minds or later have opportunities to present. It can be worthwhile to get any necessary permissions initially to have the freedom to go public with the results later if the opportunity should arise.

School districts typically have a research office whose role is, in part, to review proposed research. Communities sometimes require a part in consent giving, as in the case of, for example, Indian pueblos. Private schools often have their own internal process to approve research. If the research is being proposed to fulfill, in part, course work for a degree, it may also fall under the purview of the university's Institutional Review Board (IRB). One of the first tasks for the researcher is investigating what permissions might be needed to move ahead with the research. The paramount purpose of the IRB and other research review offices is to protect the rights and welfare of "human subjects," anyone who might be a participant in the research (McCarthy, 1998). Many university IRBs have a special approval process for professors who have students do action research projects as part of course requirements.

There are typically different levels of possible review: exempt, expedited, and full reviews. While it is beyond the purview of this chapter to discuss these fully, it is generally helpful to know that the first two categories typically move through the review process more quickly, since they are not dependent on assembling the whole review board. "Normal educational practices" that are "of minimal risk" to the participants potentially fall within the guidelines of exemption. The idea here is that educators study practices or routines that they typically employ in their daily work in their sites. Studies considered appropriate for expedited reviews are those that are considered "minimal risk," even though they are in addition to the educator's typical daily practices. Any research that is considered beyond minimal risk in light of the perceived benefits is typically reviewed by the full committee.

While charged with applying federal guidelines, permission-granting bodies operate in specific, local contexts. It behooves any researcher to explore the local climate and get a sense of how action research is considered by those granting permissions and what the time frames are to go through the process. If more than one permission is required (e.g., local school district and the university), time frames can stretch out longer than the researcher anticipates. Typically, these permissions need to be in place prior to beginning the research.

While individual proposals are considered and decisions are rendered, any researcher's work can collect the history and dilemmas of other researchers who have previously approached the review boards. Permission-granting bodies typically have considerable folklore surrounding them that may include horror stories of those who have gone before in the process of requesting permission to proceed with proposed research. It can be helpful to get ideas and suggestions from those whose research has gone through the process. It can also be a good idea to go directly to the sources, to ask any questions or ask for examples from the decision-making body. In the best case scenario, the researcher can forge an alliance with members of ethics boards, and both the researcher and the board can benefit from this kind of exchange. If, as hoped, action research has become increasingly common in universities and in school districts, those interested in seeing it facilitated are encouraged to work with the review boards to have some agreements as to how ethical research might be carried out and permissions typically granted. IRB offices and district research offices usually also have their own manuals to offer guidance to the researcher as well as templates of forms to be submitted.

We would be remiss here not to mention that many action researchers are apprehensive that their research proposals are being reviewed under guidelines that were designed with traditional scientific experiments in mind (Zeni, 2001) rather than action research. We have taken up the work of IRBs and district research offices and the dynamics of the permission-granting process and action research at length in previous works (see Herr & Anderson, 2005), and in the following section we will discuss some common concerns. Action research is a fundamental shift away from some standard research conventions, and because of this, it calls into question some conventional safeguards devised out of these alternate paradigms of research. The thing that action researchers and institutional reviewers hold in common is a desire for ethical practices in the research process. We have become increasingly convinced that the pushing into clarity of just what this means in terms of action research must be done *jointly* between practitioners and the local bodies that are in place to review proposals and research.

The federal regulations require that the boards involved in the review processes possess sufficient expertise to judge the research proposals they review (Hoonaard, 2001; Pritchard, 2002). Although it is important that these bodies develop an understanding of the risks and pressures peculiar to action research and specific populations, others with specific expertise may be brought in as consultants at the request of either the committee or the researcher (Pritchard, 2002). Researchers may submit the names of individuals specifically qualified to review their proposals to their local boards for consideration.

Many suggest that the ethical guidelines need to be rethought for action research (Zeni, 2001). The question is one of whether it is appropriate to judge the ethical merits of an approach such as action research using criteria derived from other paradigms of research (Hoonaard, 2001). Many action researchers see their IRBs as gatekeepers or as a hindrance to their research or, worse, as irrelevant. Action researchers can play a part in educating their local research boards to the complexities of action research. For example, when reporting our findings, we can also report our thinking through of the ethical situations we encounter in the field. This kind of information could be used to assist in a reading of the federal guidelines in light of the evolution and development of action research.

Common Ethical Concerns

As educators, we commonly want to study our own practices with an eye toward improving them. This means that we are adding the hat of researcher to our regular roles as educators, which involves a more systematic study of our practices. It also means that we are potentially rearranging our relationships with those we are in contact with daily in our sites. We can ask ourselves how our on-site relationships may change once they are transformed from working together or being together in fairly well-defined ways to ones redefined by the research process. This is particularly important to think through when there are hierarchical relationships (e.g., principal and teachers, teachers and students) where one typically has institutional power over another.

In a traditional research framework, the research relationship is one of researcher and "human subjects" or "participants," the latter meaning the informants or sources of data for our studies. We have written elsewhere (Herr & Anderson, 2005) about the potentially powerful—and positive—rearrangement of relationships through action research. Those who initially start out as participants may become coresearchers, or the research may be more participatory than is described in the binary terms noted above. But the traditional researcher/"researched" relationships are those that commonly come to mind when initially planning for proposed research. While we consider established relationships a strength of the action research methodology in terms of access and trusting relationships, there are cautions that come with this, particularly from the point of view of permission-granting boards.

A common concern of those approving research is that potential participants voluntarily consent to being part of a study, that there be no sense of coercion involved. An issue often raised with insider action research is that with the investigator in multiple roles (e.g., a teacher as well as a researcher of one's own classroom), voluntary consent will be compromised and potential participants will feel coerced to be part of the research, whether they want to be or not. Because the researcher is often in a position of power over the potential participants, the critique is that, for example, students will feel pressure to be part of their teacher's research or fear some kind of reprisal or falling out of favor.

But proposed research, and whether it moves forward, is a balance of weighing risks and benefits. Earlier we discussed the fact that researchers' questions are often derived from struggles in daily practices. Thinking back to one of the examples we offered in Chapter 3, that of Monica Richards and the "bums of 8H," the opening question that Richards wanted to address was, "How am I going to motivate students who do not want to learn?" The focus is on her own teaching practices and how she might improve them, to the benefit of her students. At this stage, her study is in essence a self-study, one that might lead Richards to make some changes in the classroom.

Her initial data gathering involved a daily, reflective journal, where she interrogated her own teaching practices. She also shadowed the "bums," essentially walking in their shoes through the school day, to experience it as they might. This took her to the point of sharing her observations with the class and forging a partnership to explore how school life might be different for them. She did two particular things that moved her out of the expected, hierarchical teacher roles: first, she enlisted their help in the problem-solving process, and second, she opened teacher behaviors for exploration, shifting the problem solving to the dynamic between the students and their teachers rather than only holding students accountable for their miserable grades.

In the case of their class with Ms. Richards, she was giving herself a failing grade of sorts and modeling to them that she wanted the learning to increase all around. She made explicit a stance of being colearners and then coinvestigators together. This flattens and muddies what we have come to expect in traditional, hierarchically arranged school and research relationships. We would suggest that the teacher is also vulnerable in the process—at "risk" via ceding being the all-knowing authority in control of the learning process. Instead she invites the students to also investigate how they best learn—a wonderful gift to any student—and casts herself in the role of learner also. The current arrangement of the classroom was clearly not benefiting the students, as illustrated by their frustration level and poor grades. The first level of risk was in the teacher admitting that she had a part in the poorly performing classroom. It is not that she let the students off the hook in terms of their own responsibilities, but rather that she shifted the classroom dynamic to one of shared responsibility, learning, and teaching.

Just as hierarchical relationships were muddied, we are suggesting that the notion of coercion is muddied as well. We have by now many examples, in print, where educators have explored their school practices, to the benefit of all concerned. This rich accounting of insider action research can be used to our advantage now as we make a case for calling into question typical practices in schools that consistently fail students. Just as action researchers may want to link their proposed research to district goals and priorities, a linkage to improved teaching practices and student outcomes can be a compelling argument for the research. Demonstrating that others have embarked on this kind of process in their sites, with positive outcomes, helps bring the possibilities of action research into focus.

We are suggesting, then, that the status quo can put students at risk, and that this is part of the rationale for proposing research that might be of benefit to them. This in essence begins to move from possible coercion to possible opportunity through the research process as weighed in the risk/benefit ratio. We are also suggesting that self-study is a good starting point in action research, where inside action researchers interrogate their own practices in relationship to the puzzles they are experiencing in their practices. They then are not putting anyone in the position of being possibly coerced into participation in the research but rather are putting themselves under systematic scrutiny.

If, on the other hand, the initial proposed question is one that concerns the larger school community (e.g., "How do we improve our standardized test scores and preserve authentic learning?"), it makes sense from the beginning to set up a more participatory research approach where, together, members of the school community design the inquiry. This moves the research to one of multiple researchers who may also be participants in gathering and generating the data. They are not consenting to be participants in the research so much as coresearchers, fully involved in the research decision-making processes. This rearranges relationships from researcher/researched to coinvestigators.

So where IRBs may see coercion and risk, the action researcher sees participation and benefit. In fairness to IRBs, they are [often] unaccustomed to dealing with the complex issues that action research surfaces. This is why proposals for approval of research must carefully lay out the benefits to the participants and the ways in which possible feelings of coercion among participants have been handled. Informed consent is one of the ways researchers deal with this issue.

Informed Consent

A cornerstone of traditional research approvals is informed consent, in which participants voluntarily agree to be part of the research. Toward this end, potential participants must be given enough information regarding the proposed research to form this judgment. Typically, researchers are asked to initially describe the purposes of the research and the procedures to the potential participants. If they express interest in participating, potential participants are then given a consent form. The consent form is a clear spelling out of what participants can expect should they be involved in the research.

What can appear to be a fairly straightforward process is not necessarily as clear in action research. Researchers themselves are not sure where the research is going. When employing the action research spiral (see Chapter 2), the research is organic to what has been discovered initially and what interventions have been tried. Depending on where this initial inquiry takes them, the next steps will be created as a result of this initial data gathering and decision making. So rather than being able to spell out exactly what the research will entail, the action researcher can discuss the aims of the study and the initial approach. The researcher can also explain that, given the results of the first rounds of data gathering, the participants may be approached again to consider consenting to their continuing participation in the study.

The consent process as currently laid out through the approval-granting procedures is a fairly static, one-time consent that poorly captures the possibility of the evolving research relationships and processes. Instead, action researchers are increasingly seeing the initial consent to participate in the research as the first of ongoing interactions around continued participation (Zeni, 2001). Standard consent forms clearly state that participants may voluntarily withdraw and cease participation in the research at any time, and this, of course, applies to action research as well. But beyond this, action researchers are suggesting that it behooves us to keep participants continually apprised as to how the research is evolving and, if they are not involved in the research decision making, to explain what might be asked of them next. This feeding back to the site of inquiry and to the participants what has initially been learned through the research helps foster the idea of a learning community based on inquiry. It also gives the participants a sense of the benefits of the research as they ask themselves whether or how they want to continue to participate.

The idea of "processual consent" (Rosenblatt, 1995, as cited in Tisdale, 2003, p. 26) is seen as a supplement to traditional informed consent. The goal in the case of action research is to repeatedly make clear the ongoing direction of the research itself as well as the next steps that would be involved for participants. In addition, Smith (1990, as cited in Zeni, 2001, p. 163) stresses the need for ongoing dialogue between the researcher and the participants, to move beyond what he terms "contract" relationships toward "covenants" of trust. Howe and Moses (1999) note that some have "proposed construing informed consent on the model of an ongoing 'dialogue' and have suggested periodic reaffirmations of consent . . . as the procedural embodiment of this notion" (p. 42). The notion of processual consent, where all are continually informed and thinking through where the data gathering has taken the research process so far, is within keeping with the tenets of action research and principles of respect in research relationships.

While the next chapter contains an in-depth discussion of various methodological possibilities, suffice it to say here that methodological decisions can be part of the ethical safeguards built into a study. For example, when insiders do research in their own site, they are already known to many potential participants and they are not seen as neutral entities. Some methodologies (e.g., interviewing) typically require face-to-face interaction and, depending on the position of the researcher in the school setting, may constrain what a participant feels free to share as data. Teachers may be very aware that they are talking with their "boss" when their principal asks to interview them regarding the effectiveness of various inservice activities. If, on the other hand, teachers are asked to fill out an anonymous questionnaire or answer open-ended questions in a survey format—which go into a pile of responses along with those of others—the information gathered may be of a different nature. It can be helpful in insider action research to offer anonymity where we can. It gives a bit of a buffer with the researcher and may put participants more at ease. It is worth thinking through, as the researcher designs the research, the possible approaches to the same end. There are typically multiple methodological approaches that could work, and some offer more possibilities for anonymous data than others. Where face-to-face data gathering is necessary or preferable, researchers need to consider their own positionality related to the participants and how they will minimize any possible discomfort.

Supports for Ethical Practices

We would suggest that part of the work of action research is keeping track of ourselves and the decisions we make in the field as we are faced with various quandaries. We would also suggest that this is probably done most easily when we commit to being transparent with other researchers or parties interested in our research, laying out with them the things we are facing and how we are considering proceeding. It is not uncommon, for example, for educators to join inquiry or study groups that also act as critical friend groups, that is, groups whose members agree to pose challenging questions to each other or to help think through the various dilemmas we face as action researchers. Many researchers, recognizing the complexity of action research processes, arrange for this kind of group involvement as a safety net of support for themselves before they actually start the research process.

If a researcher is joined by other colleagues in actually doing the research, these colleagues may serve as folks who agree to pose hard questions to each other. Sometimes, since all are very immersed in the research process, it is difficult to step back and take a challenging stance for each other. Some researchers decide to put themselves in another situation (a class, an outside inquiry group, etc.) where they can count on their needing to offer explanations for ethical issues and the decisions being considered.

It is also common that action researchers keep a research log or journal documenting how they have considered various issues that arise and the decisions they make in the face of them. This is a reflective tool that invites self-interrogation as well as a documentation of research dilemmas and decisions. Many researchers put this in place as they begin to think about their research and make methodological decisions. Other researchers also use this journal to record their own thinking and reflections as a form of data.

THE INITIAL DESIGN OF THE STUDY

While our understanding is that insider action research is an iterative, emergent, ongoing process of planning and implementing, at the same time, researchers need a plan as they formally begin their studies. Action research is a systematic study of an area of interest or concern, and as such, a beginning design is necessary to get started.

In its methodology, action research is not about hypothesis testing or about using data to come to conclusions. It differs from the traditional research approach in that it is based on intersubjectivity and therefore collective meaning-making and action—in other words, it is about praxis. As far as analysis and collecting data and evidence are concerned, action research is open-ended. We need not only to keep records that describe what is happening as openly as possible but also to collect and analyze our own judgments, reactions, and impressions about what is going on (Heydenrych, 2001, p. 1).

Action research is often described as a spiral encompassing a few, ongoing steps. These steps, while varying to some degree, are often described as planning, acting, observing, and reflecting. This is not necessarily a linear process, with one step discretely following after another. Rather, in the research process, the researcher will carry out all of these, but there can be a push/pull among the component parts, moving ahead, stepping back, as the researcher tries to move along. It is assumed that the steps are ongoing and iterative. Once the researcher has been through the whole cycle, it begins again. Cycles are pursued until the researchers are satisfied that they have gotten as far as they possibly can with the research and/or the issues are "solved" or resolved. What is most typical is that because questions and inquiry open up understanding, researchers may be in an ongoing inquiry stance, satisfied that they are finished with a part of the research but on to other areas of inquiry.

The following are the component parts typically delineated in the action research literature. We lay them out briefly while also suggesting there is nothing sacred about this layout. What is important to keep in mind is that focusing on an issue in a systematic way, building in critical self-reflection, and including multiple perspectives can deepen the researcher's understanding of the issue being studied.

Planning: The idea is to develop a plan of action to improve the area of interest or concern. Typically, this involves an analysis of the issue, querying what is already known and what else needs to be explored. A plan of action is developed based on what is learned. To do this well, the researcher needs to ask what data are already available, what else is needed, and how the needed data might be collected. It is also linked to the idea of tapping multiple perspectives to get a firm sense of the issues being tackled and to craft a plan that reflects these multiple realities.

Acting: Based on the emergent understanding of the issue, the researcher(s) and any collaborators and/or stakeholders devise a plan and take action to address the area of study. Typically, we do not get a plan absolutely "right," and in fact, as we implement a plan, the very implementation raises new issues or things we hadn't expected or anticipated. A plan is being implemented in the real world of a local context, and it is not uncommon that negotiation and compromise may be a part of the implementation process.

Observing: Kemmis and McTaggart (1988, as cited in Heydenrych, 2001) make the case that inside researchers need to be persistent about monitoring the proposed change process and plan well the process of documentation. The evidence collected will lay the groundwork to allow people to learn from the implemented plan through critical self-reflection. This process involves ongoing data collection to study the implemented plan and get a sense of what worked and what needs further refinement.

Reflecting: The researcher is reflecting on the data gathered from the implemented plan and reflecting on the action and research processes or, in other words, making sense of the evidence. This process may lead to the identification of a new problem or a new part of the prior issue being investigated, at which point a new cycle of the process is begun.

Considering Validity/Trustworthiness Criteria in Research Design

The ongoing planning of the research has to include validity or trustworthiness considerations. As we stated in Chapter 2, how practitioner action research demonstrates that it is credible or believable research that can be trusted and should be taken into consideration is an ongoing, emerging conversation. As stated earlier, there is not even agreed-upon language in outlining the criteria. Awkward though it may be, we continue using both validity and trustworthiness to hold the space until we have newer terminology that better describes the criteria by which practitioner action research can be judged. But in the midst of this emergent dialogue, we continue to work to plan for "good" research. It is not that all the conditions to meet the validity or trustworthiness criteria have to be planned for initially; rather, the demonstrating of validity or trustworthiness is a parameter that the research must meet eventually if it is to be taken seriously. By meeting the criteria of establishing validity or trustworthiness, the researcher signals that the research is credible. So the eventual meeting of these criteria must be planned for overall. We take these issues up below, first reiterating the various validity/trustworthiness criteria and then suggesting some ways of meeting them in the plan of the research. It quickly becomes obvious that these criteria are intertwined and that a single strategy may help meet more than one of the criteria outlined below. We do not ask here that the researcher hold these discretely or even separately. We do ask that the researcher holistically ask whether the spirit of the criteria has been taken into consideration and then indicate to the reader how they were addressed.

Democratic validity/trustworthiness: This asks to what extent the various stakeholders' points of view are taken into consideration in the research. This can be done through collaboration—involving others in the research process—or through a commitment to collect multiple perspectives and take them into account. Researchers want to ask themselves who they need to hear from and who will help them access various points of view. The idea is to planfully access multiple perspectives and voices. Several things need to be taken into consideration overall. First, of the various possible stakeholders, who will be selected as a participant in the research? This involves issues of sampling, that is, who and how participants will be chosen. Second, how will the researcher capture the stakeholders' points of view? Third, what data-gathering methods will allow their points of view to be heard?

The answers to these depend on the initial research question. For example, if researchers are concerned with issues involving their whole class, then any and all of their students could be considered participants. If, on the other hand, researchers are concerned with low achievers, then the focus may be on gathering their perspectives as participants. Beyond choosing the participants, the researcher will want to plan for how to best capture their perspectives. There are multiple possibilities in this regard, which will be described at length in Chapter 6. The idea is that the researcher has many data-gathering methods from which to choose.

Researchers' positionality comes into play in some of these initial decisions as well. In launching a study, researchers may ask who it is they have easy access to or who they initially feel comfortable approaching to participate in the study. This can be a good starting point, to stay within their comfort zone, as long as researchers realize they will not be able to stay there throughout. It is assumed that data gathering will stretch researchers and possibly take them into new territories or collaborations.

It is also not uncommon that people participate in varying ways in the research. Perhaps initially the researcher decides to interview some participants but then later wants a broader swath of points of view and decides a community survey serves that purpose. As the design is developed, various data-gathering methodologies come into play and are added as appropriate. Some perspectives of participants may be represented in more depth than others, depending on the data gathering employed (e.g., an interview provides depth, a survey typically provides breadth). It is also not assumed that researchers have to create all their own data-gathering tools. In the current example, others before us have created community surveys, and what they have developed may serve our purposes well (see, e.g., Johnson, 2002).

As the research evolves and develops, the answers to the initial questions of who should participate and how data are gathered may change too. These are ongoing questions for the researcher to pose. As the question is focused and refocused, it may become apparent that others need to be tapped as participants or that other data-gathering methodologies are more appropriate. In practitioner action research, the researcher may eventually determine that the first data-gathering plan was not realistic or that it needs to be further adapted to be effective and manageable. Researchers will want to document how they approached these issues and the rationale behind the decisions they made. This will help others understand how they came to the approach they are taking in the research as well as lay out the process for others who may be considering pursuing their own research.

Outcome validity/trustworthiness: To demonstrate outcome validity/trustworthiness, the researcher must address whether actions occur, based on the data gathering, that lead toward the "resolution" of the issue under study. The researcher is asked to address whether the actions lead to another round of data gathering and problem solving beyond the initial diagnosis of the problem and the implementation of a single solution strategy. Action research should not typically be aborted at the end of a round of data gathering and problem solving. Rather, the process typically deepens the researcher's understandings, leading to further data gathering and the ongoing pursuit of the action research spiral. Employing the action research spiral may happen a number of times until the researcher is satisfied. This is not to infer that the resolution of the problem has to be "successful." Instead, it implies that the researcher has pursued the issue and the problem solving as far as possible, given local conditions for the researcher and the context.

This also obviously relates to the issue of democratic validity/trustworthiness described previously. Researchers want to ask themselves, "Solved for whom?" It is not uncommon that as researchers put things in place to create change, we solve some problems and create other, perhaps unexpected ones. This is, in part, why we continue the action research process, asking, "Where did that intervention take us? Are we satisfied that this is a workable solution for multiple constituencies?" The typical answer to these questions is that the interventions need further refinement to "work" as well as possible in the realities of the site and for a variety of stakeholders.

Process validity/trustworthiness: Here we are asking to what extent the research process is adequate. What methodological adaptations were utilized to fit the realities of the setting and foster and capture the flow of action? The researcher is laying out how the methodology was carried out and how it was developed and adapted over time. It relates to outcome validity/trustworthiness, described above, in that it is understood that if the process is superficial or flawed, the outcome will reflect this superficiality.

A lot is required of the practitioner action researcher in that the process asks that the researcher also serve as a site for change and evolution. The researcher is asked to grow and change while also asking the same of the local site. It is possible to carry out action research procedures superficially, without really engaging in the process in a way that develops a depth of understanding or change, but this would be considered a flawed research process.

Dialogic validity/trustworthiness: This addresses the "goodness of fit" in terms of the researchers' findings, the research process, and the setting. How did you find what you found? Does it make sense in terms of how you gathered the data in this particular setting? In other words, how did you come to conclude what it is you concluded as a researcher, and does it make sense to others in the setting? Typically, this is "tested" and documented through the ongoing presentation of the process and findings to others in the site as well as any others tapped to help with the research process (e.g., critical friends).

Because practitioner action research depends on folding back into the site the ongoing findings of the research, the researcher wants to build in opportunities for presenting initial thoughts and findings and gathering responses to the data. This kind of presentation of the data and findings can be to a critical friend, a devil's advocate who pushes back on the conclusions, or to a larger group of stakeholders who are also concerned with the research question. Groups of collaborators or a group of researchers could also do this with each other.

As you explain your research approach to others—those in the setting, a critical friend, an inquiry group—and the findings that are a result of your data gathering, does it make sense to others? Are they able to see the goodness of fit in what you did and the findings and actions that evolved from the data-gathering process? This involves presenting back to others your thinking, process, and findings. The researcher is building in ways to make the research transparent. For the purposes of practitioner action research, where the goal is the folding of the data and analysis back into the site, this is often an ongoing process. Dialogic validity/trustworthiness can be a corrective of sorts, where researchers can check whether they are on course. This does not imply that research will not expose new understandings or things that participants and stakeholders did not anticipate. Rather, dialogic validity requires that researchers be able to demonstrate how they came to the conclusions they are drawing and how they have been and are open to alternative explanations that might fit better. It implies a presenting of data understandings and allowing these to rub up against others' perceptions or questions. This refinement process is a safety net of sorts for researchers, requiring them to consider multiple possibilities and refinements.

Catalytic validity/trustworthiness: Catalytic validity relates to the depth of the process. If the researcher has pursued spirals of research activity and has allowed the data to unfold new realities in the site, a new depth of understanding should also emerge. Catalytic validity/trustworthiness asks whether the research process has reoriented and refocused the researchers' and participants' understandings of their local context. This implies a deepening understanding—sometimes called *transformative learning*—of the social reality under study and a better grasp of the change process in the site. As multiple realities come into focus, this is often an energizing process for the researchers and various stakeholders involved. Catalytic validity/trustworthiness asks researchers to address how understanding has deepened and changed over time.

This includes their own reorienting toward themselves and their roles and practices in the site and the research.

Methods of Establishing
Validity or Trustworthiness

As we stated earlier, the validity/trustworthiness criteria are not discrete; hence, neither are the methods of establishing them. Methods of research can serve in various capacities in terms of the research design process and the establishment of various criteria for validity/trustworthiness. Most researchers choose some combination of the options outlined below. However, this should not be considered an exhaustive list. Initially, as the design of the research is being considered, the researcher may put in place a few of these approaches, adding more as the research design unfolds.

Since this book is oriented toward qualitative approaches to practitioner action research, some of the suggested approaches will appear familiar to those acquainted with the qualitative approach. At the same time, it is important to not lift wholesale qualitative approaches, since the criteria above depart from the criteria for establishing trustworthiness in qualitative studies. We both share and depart from methods of qualitative research.

Triangulation: Triangulation can mean using different sources of data (multiple participants and multiple perspectives), different methods of data gathering, or different researchers or collaborators to provide varying angles on the research question. For example, perhaps researchers interview teachers and then administrators. Following this, they decide to survey students about their thoughts on the research question. The researcher has built in different sources of data (teachers, administrators, and students) and also used varying data-gathering methods (interviews and surveys). In the study described in Chapter 4, Herr and her coresearcher experimented with doing multiple interviews with students. Would, for example, an African American student share different things with an African American interviewer versus what she might tell Herr? In this case, they used the idea that different researchers may, with participants, co-construct different responses to the interview questions. The combination of these approaches offers differing vantage points from which to view the research question and the data generated. Triangulation is very commonly used as one step in establishing the validity of a study.

Reflexive journal: On a regular basis, investigators record a variety of information about themselves, their thoughts on the study, the methodology, and the data. This often includes a record of the ongoing data-gathering schedule, the logistics of the study, and the methodological decisions, as well as a more personal section recording the researchers' reflections, insights, and challenges. Because action research evolves and because researchers are so intimately involved in the change process, keeping track of themselves and their decision-making process is essential. A reflexive journal helps the researcher keep track of the process of the research and make ongoing decisions in light of it. It is also valuable in terms of catalytic validity, where researchers can trace their own reorienting and refocusing in light of the evolution of the research.

Critical friend: As demonstrated earlier in this chapter, a critical friend is someone willing to push on the researcher's assumptions, biases, and understandings. He or she poses alternative explanations or offers ideas of alternative analyses of data, with an eye toward furthering the analysis. A critical friend allows researchers to hear themselves out loud as they make a case for their decisions and analyses. Because action researchers in the kind of studies we are discussing here are insiders and therefore involved in their sites—and often have a wealth of tacit knowledge to be interrogated and problematized—a critical friend can help provide some perspective and distance from taken-for-granted assumptions.

Member checking: Data, analyses, interpretations, and conclusions are brought back to stakeholders for verification and input. This can be done formally as well as informally. This approach is very compatible with action research, where we want to fold into the site insights from the research process as well as account for multiple perspectives.

Persistent observation: The researcher identifies the areas most relevant to the research question and focuses on them in depth to fully understand all the elements of the area and get a full picture. The tension in this is to fully explore one area in depth and bring it to a level where the researcher confidently understands it without screening out other relevant areas. The researcher is looking to balance depth and breadth.

SUMMING UP

Again, we remind the reader that this is not an exhaustive list. In addition, the researcher is not expected to use all the strategies outlined above. What we are suggesting, though, is that each researcher give thought to how to demonstrate that he or she has conducted a credible study, one that in good faith has tried to keep to the conventions of a valid action research study. We reiterate this because important decisions are being made based on the results of the research. If the study is flawed, the decision-making process will be compromised as well. In addition, much can be learned from an insider's research, but to move it to print or publication, researchers will be expected to have conducted a study that meets the criteria for validity/trustworthiness.

Final Thoughts on Getting Started

When we teach courses in practitioner action research, we often find that teachers or administrators set out to "prove" what they feel they already know. Typically, these are biases or prejudices, particularly in low-income schools, about why kids fail, why they misbehave, why parents don't seem to care about their kids, why kids miss school, and so on. It is possible to conduct a study that does not challenge the alleged certainties with which we enter the study. However, we find that typically an educator who enters a study with a deficit view of students or their families discovers through data gathering a greater complexity than their superficial observations previously indicated.

It is worth noting how, particularly in middle and high schools, administrators, teachers, students, and their parents can remain relative strangers to one another. Noguera (1995) observed that when teachers and administrators remain unfamiliar with students' and their families' lives, they fill the knowledge void with media stereotypes and are more likely to misunderstand and fear their students. Perhaps the key disposition that one must have upon beginning a practitioner action research study is the openness to being surprised by what one discovers. In such cases, data do not merely confirm what we already know but rather force us to deepen our understanding, challenge us to rethink our previous assumptions, and allow us to make decisions based on a more complex understanding of the needs of our students and their families. This, in reality, is the real test of whether we are conducting "good" research.

C H A P T E R   S I X

Qualitative Research Approaches for Practitioner Action Research

Teacher researchers can revolutionize professional practice by viewing themselves as potentially the most sophisticated research instruments available. The cult of the expert will undoubtedly be uncomfortable with such research populism.

—Kincheloe (1991, p. 30)

In this chapter we discuss a wide variety of data-gathering methods that qualitative and practitioner action researchers use. Other authors have described, in detail, each type of qualitative method, but we present a more general approach and give ample references to enable the reader to pursue a particular procedure in more depth. We also incorporate examples of how these various approaches have been adapted and used by practitioner action researchers.

Research methods and approaches must always be tempered by practice and seen through a filter of one's own environment and needs. How you can improve your practice, what you can contribute to the field of knowledge about learning, curriculum, teaching, and running a school necessitates an adaptable research methodology. It is important for action researchers investigating their own sites to remember that, despite traditional qualitative techniques, "[t]he 'sedentary wisdom' of long-established traditions offers legitimation rather than liberation; the biggest breakthroughs in scientific thinking have often required a break with investigative traditions rather than blind allegiance to them" (Wolcott, 1992, p. 17). Blind allegiance to traditional qualitative methods by insiders doing action research would quickly lead to frustration. Issues like time demands and multiple roles (e.g., simultaneously functioning in the roles of educator and researcher) quickly make apparent that the wearing of these multiple hats demands some adaptations of methodologies.

At the same time, qualitative and action researchers often *share* similar data-gathering methods—interviewing and observations, to name just two. As action researchers, we may adapt and borrow qualitative methods but not take on the mantle of, for example, an ethnographer just because we share some data-gathering techniques in common. A rich ethnography gives a window into a culture under study from the vantage point of an outsider. It documents a community—perhaps a school—from an outsider's point of view. A practitioner action researcher is trying to accomplish something different from the typical qualitative researcher. We fold the results of our data gathering and analysis back into our sites to move them toward change. At its best, action research is *disturbing* research, potentially interrupting day-to-day practices. The researcher is also an actor in the site, so rather than strictly documenting the culture of the workplace, researchers are using data in such a way as to inform their own actions as well as contribute to knowledge production in education.

As we describe the various data-gathering methods in qualitative research, remember that, as a practitioner action researcher, you will adapt, refine, and build upon these "traditional" approaches in order to conduct your inquiry. Cochran-Smith and Lytle (1993) articulate this view:

We argue that we need to develop a different theory of knowledge for teaching, a different epistemology that regards inquiry by teachers themselves as a distinctive and important way of knowing about teaching. From this perspective, fundamental questions about knowing, knowers, and what can be known would have different answers. Teachers would be among those who have the authority to know—that is, to construct Knowledge (with a capital K) about teaching, learning, and schooling. And what is worth knowing about teaching includes teachers' "ways of knowing" or what teachers, who are researchers in their own classrooms, can know through systematic subjectivity. (p. 43)

Traditionally, the three core techniques in qualitative research have been broadly labeled interviews, observations, and archives and documents. Practitioner action researchers are already adapting these methods, as well as developing new ones. For example, a newer approach is the use of personal narratives or stories as data. Another is the use of journals and diaries, begun in high school English and writing classes and now an important part of many practitioner studies. These examples come from the humanities rather than the social sciences, where much of the rest of qualitative research originates. Many practitioner action researchers are pushing the edges of what has heretofore been accepted as "appropriate" data and creating new areas that enhance the research process and the data gathered. We have given examples in different parts of the book and hope to give more examples throughout this chapter.

ADAPTING THE CHARACTERISTICS OF QUALITATIVE RESEARCH

In their classic work *Naturalistic Inquiry*, published in 1985, Lincoln and Guba laid out characteristics of good qualitative research. They were making a case for the legitimacy of naturalistic inquiry as well as outlining the basic tenets of this approach to research. We take the 14 characteristics they laid out for qualitative research and discuss them here in terms of adapting and applying them to practitioner action research that draws on a qualitative approach.

Characteristic 1: *The work is conducted in a natural setting.* Practitioner action researchers are obviously already situated in their school environments. At the same time, as we suggested in Chapter 5, the issue to be addressed in insider action research is why the study *has* to take place in the site in which we work versus another setting. What is it about the question being posed that demands that it be insider action research? Our desire is typically to improve our own sites and/or practices in them, in which case the research is idiosyncratic to our own sites of practice.

Characteristic 2: *You as a person are the primary research instrument and primary data-gathering tool.* At the time they wrote these characteristics, Lincoln and Guba were trying to justify qualitative research to a more positivist audience. While their characterization of living, breathing researchers as "instruments" and "tools" would seem to mirror the idea in more statistical studies regarding the "objectivity" of the research process, they make clear their appreciation of the researcher's sensitivity and subjectivity as an asset in the research process. We suggest that all that we register and record is important data. This could include subjective impressions, thoughts and emotions, and responses to things that occur. At the same time, these impressions must be captured systematically and must be interrogated and problematized in the data-gathering process. What qualitative and practitioner action researchers share is that as researchers, we are not distanced from that which is being studied; data are registered in our beings and systematically recorded. You may, of course, use any other additional instruments or tools to help gather and record the data. This could be anything from open-ended surveys and observational charts to equipment such as digital or video recorders, tape recorders, and so on.

Characteristic 3: *You utilize tacit knowledge in addition to knowledge expressed in language.* We suggested in Chapter 5 that the task of an insider doing action research is to ask, "What is it I already know, and how do I know it? How might this knowing limit or bias the way I am considering or asking my research question?" Because as insiders we have often been in our sites of study for some time, we have accrued a lot of information, which needs to be both welcomed and questioned. The work is to make the familiar strange, that is, to step back and explore what it is you know.

Characteristic 4: *You utilize qualitative methods.* We will spell out more fully in this chapter some of the choices in this regard, since there are multiple possibilities. Part of what you will want to consider is the kind of time you have, everyday activities that can be turned into data-gathering opportunities, and so on. Qualitative methods are typically open-ended in that they expand our understanding. They are characterized more often than not by open-ended questions and approaches that allow participants to express themselves. You will also want to consider how you are establishing that your research is meeting the criteria for "good" research.

Characteristic 5: *Your sampling logic is purposive sampling over random sampling, for the most part.* In purposive sampling you select participants for their relevance to the research question. As the data gathering evolves in response to what you have already learned, who is relevant to the question may shift and change. The issue of sampling also relates to the criteria for validity/ trustworthiness already discussed in Chapter 2, in that you are trying to tap multiple perspectives on the issue you are studying. The idea is to be careful not to select participants just because they might agree with your point of view.

Characteristic 6: *You utilize inductive data analyses, which will help you identify all the multiple realities to be found in those data.* This gets to the heart of practitioner action research in that data collected on-site should help us come to new understandings of both the issue being studied and possible ways to improve on-site practices. We would expect that our assumptions and the things we already know will be unsettled and that a more complex understanding will take place as we make meaning out of the data. This is in contrast to looking at the data with an eye toward "confirming" or "disconfirming" evidence of what was already deduced previously.

Characteristic 7: *You utilize grounded theory in which you allow your data to lead in finding a theory, rather than going into the research with a set theory.* Our work takes place in relation to a larger body of knowledge and research that can help us think about and understand our sites and practices but that also is limited in terms of our particular contexts. As we push on these limitations and come to new understandings, our knowledge moves beyond the local to connect to the larger research conversation taking place in research publications. Practitioner action research, as we continue to publish it, can contribute to theory building and generation.

Characteristic 8: *You utilize emergent design, which allows the design of the research to emerge as you move through the research process rather than be rigidly stated at the beginning of the proposal.* Practitioner action research as we define it implies an ongoing spiral of research where the research design continues to develop in relationship to the data gathered and the meaning made of them. As discussed in Chapter 5, this emergent, evolving design is part of what makes permission-granting research review boards uneasy about action research; neither they nor the researcher know quite where things are going ahead of time.

Characteristic 9: *You utilize negotiated outcomes with the members of your study.* We have suggested throughout that action research is best undertaken collaboratively. We have also suggested in our criteria for a valid study that to satisfy or demonstrate democratic validity/trustworthiness, the researcher needs to ask to what extent the research has been done with all the parties who have a stake in the problem being studied. And in process validity/trustworthiness, triangulation or the inclusion of multiple perspectives guards against viewing events in a simplistic or biased way. Practitioner action researchers then have an ethical stance that welcomes and solicits the perspectives of stakeholders throughout the process.

The cycles of inquiry suggest a feeding back of tentative conclusions and meaning-making to the site and the stakeholders, to assess where the data have taken the research so far in terms of deepening understandings. The ongoing feedback loop helps generate mutual understanding among various stakeholders, which should help protect against surprises at the conclusion of the research, that is, inferences drawn that stakeholders were not aware of throughout the process. The hope is that the data and analysis are helpful to all concerned, that they result in more complex community learning. Still, stakeholders have the right and invitation to give input throughout the research and into the "final" conclusions drawn.

Characteristic 10: *You write up your study as a case study or narrative rather than a scientific or technical report.* Practitioner action research easily lends itself to a narrative accounting of the process and the ongoing meaning-making. The write-up is akin to the bread crumbs left along the path to guide you on the way back: you can retrace your steps, remember where you have come from, even though you have traveled a long way on the journey. In this sense, then, action research is most typically a narrative accounting of what has taken place and the growing understanding coming to the researcher.

Characteristic 11: *You interpret the data in terms of the particulars of the case rather than in terms of lawlike generalizations.* The practitioner action research process involves the unique collection of data and meaning-making in a particular site. Actions to be taken are derived from this understanding of the local context with its possibilities and realities taken into account. What makes "sense" in one setting may not be possible or even a good plan in another.

Characteristic 12: *You make tentative application instead of broad application of the findings, because realities are multiple and different and your findings are always dependent on the interaction between yourself and your participants.* Again, the very process of the practitioner action research spiral asks you to consider an issue, gather data around it, thoughtfully consider possible action, and then reflect on where that has taken you in relation to the issue you are researching. Often this process takes place in collaboration with other stakeholders involved. All weigh the possible pathways of action, sift through the possibilities, and come to a choice of what to try. There is also a commitment then to study what the chosen action does in terms of the realities of the site.

Characteristic 13: *You utilize focus-determined boundaries based on the emergent focus; this permits the multiple realities to define the focus.* We spent considerable time in Chapter 5 discussing the creation of a research question. We also made the case that the focus of the study continues to expand and shift through the various cycles of action research; the data gathered and actions taken impact understanding and next directions. As with any qualitative study, the focus of the study determines the approach to the data gathering and research, but in practitioner action research, the research approach continues to evolve and be scrutinized through the various cycles of the research.

Characteristic 14: *Establishing the trustworthiness of the study.* This is a very important characteristic, because it defines how we determine if a study has merit and is believable and truthful. We have made the case in Chapter 2 that action research pushes us to reconceptualize what are considered validity criteria or trustworthiness. Much as Lincoln and Guba designed criteria for qualitative research that are in contrast to those established earlier for more positivistic research, we have suggested in Chapter 2 criteria for practitioner action research.

DEALING WITH SUBJECTIVITY

Subjectivity is a necessary component of all research and is, obviously, a part of practitioner action research. The systematic nature of inquiry allows researchers to speak from their lived experiences as long as this is identified. This is often evident in discussions of reflexivity and emotion in research (Ellis & Flaherty, 1992). When speaking from the subjective self, positionality must be emphasized to be useful to the educational community. Possibilities regarding positionality were discussed earlier in Chapter 1.

Practitioner action researchers can work with subjectivity by presenting both initial assumptions and subjective reactions to events, in effect, presenting audiences with both preconceptions and postconceptions. Qualitative researchers address subjectivity by incorporating and openly discussing it. Quantitative researchers address subjectivity by attempting to exhume it from themselves and their study by design and methodology (LeCompte & Preissle, 1993; Patton, 2002). In action research, the researcher is an inextricable part of the research and is, in reality, part of the site to be interrogated and included.

One point should be made about some use of language when discussing subjectivity in research: it involves the use of the terms *emic* and *etic.* An emic study is one in which a researcher describes cultural and behavioral patterns as they are *viewed by the participants in the study* rather than by the researcher and the research literature. The people studied (the members of that community) create the categories of their experiences, not the researcher. This is called, variously, emic, phenomenological, or subjective research and is considered a critical juncture in the difference between the paradigms of qualitative and quantitative research (LeCompte & Preissle, 1993). The etic perspective is the view offered by the outside observer who makes meaning *about* the community under study. The concepts and categories derived are those that have meaning to the scientific community. Cochran-Smith and Lytle (1993) make a strong argument for the uniquely emic positioning of a practitioner researcher: "Teacher researchers are uniquely positioned to provide a truly emic, or insider's, perspective that makes visible the ways that students and teachers together construct knowledge and curriculum" (p. 43).

Cochran-Smith and Lytle (1993) present anthropologist Geertz's (1973) discussion of the difficulties nonpractitioner researchers have in truly representing the emic categories of their participants. Geertz feels that anthropologists cannot really represent "local knowledge"—what inhabitants see—but can only represent what they see through, that is, their interpretive perspectives on their own experiences. Cochran-Smith and Lytle turn this around for practitioner action researchers and elaborate on the fact that local knowledge is what teachers come to know through their own research and what communities of teacher researchers come to know when they build knowledge collaboratively. Practitioner action research can contribute a fundamental reconceptualization of the notion of knowledge for teaching. Teacher researchers can reinvent the conventions of interpretive social science much as feminist and minority researchers have done by making problematic the relationships of researchers and researched, knowledge and authority, and subject and object (Buendia, 2003; Cochran-Smith & Lytle, 1993; Smith, 1999).

PURSUING THE RESEARCH QUESTION

In Chapter 5 we discussed at length some of the considerations to be taken into account as a research question is formulated. We suggested that this process of coming to a research question is in itself a complex undertaking and that typically the question continues to evolve as data are gathered and analysis and actions are undertaken. We also touched on research design and how that relates to the issues of validity/trustworthiness we originally discussed in Chapter 2. Our focus now is on the tools of data gathering, that is, how one gathers and uses data to "answer" the research question. In the case of practitioner action research, as we discussed in Chapter 2, the answer often comes in the form of understanding the issues involved in a more complex way. Often it involves gaining new insights into the issues so the problem can be reformulated or be more effectively addressed.

In the following sections, we describe what is commonly meant when interviews, observations, and archival and document retrieval techniques are utilized by a researcher. Each method can be done separately as a study. However, combining the techniques in different ways, called triangulation of data, allows the researcher to maximize time and to see the same scene from different angles. For practitioner action researchers, this can provide a very important perspective. It helps researchers separate from a classroom or school that they know intimately, and it allows the researcher to "make the familiar strange" (Erickson, 1973)—strange enough to see with new eyes instead of the usual perspective.

To begin, we offer an example of a teacher researcher's study to unpack how she adapted data-gathering methods in the face of her data and the realities of her teaching situation. In this she needed a way to observe her familiar classroom routines through fresh eyes. We use it to illustrate that, in utilizing qualitative methods, practitioner action researchers begin a practice of adapting them to the realities of their work sites, and as action researchers, the data and analysis inform the ongoing steps in the inquiry process.

Ann Strommen is a literacy and early childhood specialist. She worked with four groups of kindergarten and first-grade children in a Chapter I Reading pullout program. The children who came to her room for one hour each day were referred by their teachers because of problems in reading. Strommen, with a colleague, developed a series of contracts that the children worked on each week perfecting skills introduced at the beginning of the week. All contracts involved reading and writing.

After fulfilling the tasks of the contract, the children were free to engage in one of the many free-time activities in the room. Strommen (1991) did not have a clear sense of which activities the children were most often engaged in. Her research question, therefore, was developed to enhance her exploration of what the children did during self-selection time. She says:

I wanted a question that would be helpful to me as a teacher and would be within my capabilities. I had little time to observe the room and the sixteen children in it at any given time. Ann (Nihlen) visited the classroom and together we devised a spot observation technique. I then worked on a recording sheet that allowed me to scan the room at various predetermined times and record where the students were and what they were doing. I began this observation and immediately found it necessary to revise and refine the recording sheet. I had originally thought it would be most advantageous to know in what areas of the room the children were. I felt location would tell me what they were doing. I quickly remembered that children could, for instance, write in the reading area, and solve puzzles in the art area. My revised recording sheet now listed the activities the children could be engaged in. The qualitative approach allowed me not only to modify and change my observations, based on the reality of my classroom, but to feel comfortable changing my focus as the data led me. The research class supported my efforts to be led by, rather than lead, the data. Later I added the category of sex to the recording sheet to see if any gender differences would show up. (p. 34)

In her reflection above, it is easy to see how Strommen's initial methodology evolved. She front-loaded her lived reality in the classroom: that she had little time for observations. She needed a tool that she could work with quickly. She revised her observation tool once she used it, based on her assessment of its helpfulness in addressing her research question.

One of the many things Strommen discovered was that half of the children were not finishing their contracts in time to have self-selection. This came as a surprise to her until she realized that it also meant that the other half were finishing and making self-selection choices; this group became her database. From a pilot study Strommen had conducted earlier in the semester, she knew that all the teachers in the school thought that self-selection was important and that most of them provided for it daily. Working inductively, Strommen went to the library and began a review of the literature:

If research supports self-selection activities as a vehicle to help develop literacy in kindergarten and first grade students, my teammate and I would probably need to make some adjustments. One would be to change the schedule to allow time for more students to participate in self-selection activities. Another change might be to separate or rearrange their block, puzzle and game activity areas since it is so popular. (p. 35)

In terms of the action research spiral, Strommen first started out exploring what it was her students did in their self-selection time. What she discovered was that not all of the students had the opportunity of self-selection. This led her to consider the importance placed on self-selection and the question of whether the larger research conversation supported this emphasis. She allowed herself to question her own practices, what she had put into place to benefit her students. Strommen's research began to question the concept of self-selection itself. She needed to satisfy herself of its worth if she was going to put effort into rearranging her classroom structure to make it accessible on a more widespread basis.

Strommen learned through this process that she could do research that was directly relevant to her classroom and her teaching. She came to realize that her data could be analyzed in many different ways and provide a variety of answers, sometimes to questions she did not initially know she had. Strommen decided to let the data lead her. She also discovered that she could use what she learned immediately for the benefit of her students. In addition, she could share the general results with a wider audience of teachers and researchers by talking about and publishing the data.

DATA-GATHERING METHODS

We move now into the methods section of the chapter, where we give examples of various kinds of interviews, observations, and document/archival research. Following this section, we focus on analysis of the data and offer examples of how to analyze the data collected. Because both data gathering and analysis are immediate and ongoing, it is important to have approaches to both in mind going into the research process. The following sections can be read chronologically and/or later consulted as a reference for using particular methods as they become relevant to a particular study.

Interviews and Surveys

The interview has been variously described as a conversation with another person, a verbal questionnaire, or a life story. This wide-ranging definition implies the variety of techniques one could use in conducting an interview with another person or persons. Interviews are a good tool to use when one wishes to know how another person feels about events that have happened or are happening. They are also important in gaining a perspective on how others understand and interpret their reality. Interviewing assumes a skill in listening and a nonthreatening manner in asking questions.

We discuss several types of interviews here: ethnographic or open-ended; oral histories, narratives, and stories; structured; surveys and questionnaires; and checklists, rating scales, and inventories (see Figure 6.1). In addition, we discuss products of interview studies. Regardless of the type of interview you choose, certain tasks must be accomplished before beginning to ensure a successful product.

First Steps

1. To begin, you should contact the potential participant and discuss the possibility of interviewing him or her. Tell the participant why and what you hope to accomplish and the purpose of the research. It is best to have had face-to-face contact before the interview; that makes both of you more comfortable. Both you and the participant must see you as a researcher as well as a practitioner. This is an additional role for you as a practitioner.

2. In recent years, researchers and the researched have developed certain courtesies to protect each party. The consent form is one of these; it may be required by your district or school.

Figure 6.1   Types of Interviews

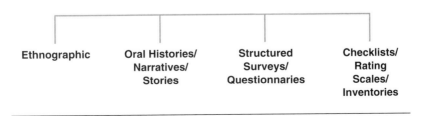

As a researcher, you must provide some kind of consent form for the interviewee to read and sign. As discussed in Chapter 5, many action researchers have moved to the idea of processual consent, that is, an ongoing process of asking participants to consent to the next iteration of the research. The consent describes the research you will be conducting and what you currently know about the data-gathering procedures. It can include items such as the ways you are asking the person to participate in the research (e.g., being interviewed), the use of recording equipment, some guarantee of the person's anonymity if he or she desires this, reassurance that he or she can quit the research at any time, and phone numbers where he or she can reach you outside of school. Both you and the interviewee should sign two copies; then you keep one and the interviewee keeps one. The form should be signed prior to the first interview. You should be there to answer any questions the interviewee may have. This assures you that he or she has read the form and understands the serious intent of your research and the gift of permission to interview him or her. Since some school districts require such forms, check to ascertain what needs to be done and how to do it to meet whatever guidelines apply. See Chapter 5 for more on this subject.

3. Prepare your questions for the interview based on your research question and what this person might know about your issue. No matter how general or how specific you intend to be, be sure that you have more than enough questions or topic areas to fill the time. Try to make them expository questions rather than yes-or-no questions. Start out with a question that is easy to answer, usually about the interviewee himself or herself. Interviews done on the run in the hallways, the teachers' lounge, or even the playground or other informal settings usually are not taped. You must try to jot down the main points as soon as possible after the interaction. It is amazing how quickly one forgets.

4. Check your equipment before you start the interview. Cassette tape recorders are inexpensive and common, and most are battery powered. A cassette recorder with a tape counter is most useful for later analysis. If you are planning on a half-hour interview or an hour interview, use a 90-minute tape so you do not have to turn the tape over often or replace it. Carry extra tapes and batteries.

5. Make sure that the room you have chosen is as quiet as possible. If it is in the school, try to find an out-of-the-way place where few people walk through and try to position the participant so that people cannot catch his or her eye.

6. Chat with the participant while you set up and arrange the tape recorder. This will make both of you feel more relaxed. If you are using an external microphone, be sure to explain this to the interviewee.

7. Begin the interview by starting the tape, checking to see if it is running, and speaking into the microphone, giving your name, the participant's name or pseudonym, and the date and location of the interview. Ask the interviewee to say something into the microphone, stop the tape, rewind it, and check to see that both voices are being heard. Then proceed with your first question. If you take notes during the interview, keep them brief; you want to be a good listener. Keep your eyes in an interviewing mode—depending on the culture, on or off the participant or to one side.

8. As you end the interview, ask the participant if he or she would like to add something to what was said. After that, turn off the tape and thank the person for his or her time and thoughts. If you plan another interview, talk briefly about when you will call to set up another interview.

9. Label the tapes before or as soon as possible after the interview. Label clearly and precisely the name, date, and project.

10. Now that you have a taped interview, begin to transcribe and analyze it. Allow approximately four hours of transcribing for each hour of recorded interview. Many researchers pay professional transcribers to do this task, for it is labor-intensive. Good typists and transcribers can make short work of it, and they certainly earn their money.

Another technique to handle reviewing and analyzing tapes, particularly if you have a lot of tapes or little money or time for transcribing them yourself, is to index the tapes. First listen to all the tapes. Then pick out themes of interest and relevance to the research question. Record on an index card the interviewee name, the date, and the number on the tape counter where the section you are interested in occurs. As you develop categories based on the data, you may have to listen again to the tapes, but this is a less expensive way to analyze the interviews.

In the latter sections of this chapter we discuss various methods for analyzing the interview. It is important to read these sections before conducting an actual interview. They will help you formulate questions to ask and to structure the analysis of your data.

Every data-gathering method has advantages and disadvantages. In terms of interviewing, some disadvantages or challenges are the following:

1. It is a time-consuming process to interview people and even more time consuming to transcribe the taped interviews to be able to work with the data.

2. In school settings, interviews often have to be worked around the time slots available in the day-to-day schedule: a teacher's prep period, lunchtime, recess, and so on. As such, the length of the interview is often determined by these constraints rather than a sense of having finished the interview. In the same vein, it can be difficult to find a space to interview where you will not be interrupted and where it is quiet enough to talk.

3. Interview questions are challenging to construct so that they are clear and effective in terms of tapping the area you want to explore.

4. Not everyone approached will want to be interviewed. Some fear discovery or lack of anonymity, particularly within a school or district where many people know each other well and are likely to identify each other. Their responses may be guarded because of these concerns. Others will not want their thoughts or responses recorded or put into written form.

5. Recording an interview depends on good equipment and using it well. All of us have had tape recorders malfunction or microphones positioned poorly, producing inaudible speech, and so on. These just come with the territory, even when you carefully check your equipment.

But interviews have advantages as well:

1. It is important to get the actual voices and thoughts of teachers, students, parents, and others in order to truly understand the issues that you are studying and to gain multiple perspectives. This can be particularly true for those not typically heard or those who have trouble relating to the research process or are disenfranchised from it (people of color, the poor or working class). Soliciting a wide range of participants can be part of the establishment of validity of your study.

2. Responses to open-ended interview questions often go in directions you hadn't thought about as a researcher or hadn't considered. They often contain surprises that enrich the study.

3. Interview data is often very rich because you as a researcher have the opportunity to hear participants' narrative experiences around the topic you are pursuing.

4. The interview process is often very cathartic or therapeutic for participants, particularly when being asked about topics they care about or painful or meaningful experiences.

Ethnographic Interviews

The open-ended interview is also called an ethnographic interview because of its original home within ethnographic research in anthropology. To grasp the design and intentions of this interview strategy, it is helpful to understand a few things about ethnography. Ethnography is considered both a process and a product. As a product, it gives a reader a comprehensive, holistic description of a cultural scene such as a tribal village, a homeless shelter, or a classroom. The core of ethnography is its concern with the meaning of actions and events to the people we seek to understand. The purpose is to provide a cultural interpretation of a scene within a culture. Culture in this sense refers to the acquired knowledge that people use to interpret experience and generate social behavior (Spradley, 1979).

The ethnographic interview is a technique for gathering data for an ethnography, but it also can be, and frequently is, used in other types of qualitative research and practitioner action research. In the process of interviewing, practitioner researchers develop descriptive open-ended questions, or what Spradley (1980) calls "descriptive" and "grand tour" questions. These types of questions enable the participants to talk about what they do and to build their own emic categories for their stories.

An example of this can be found in the Emerson Elementary School Oral History Project. This project came out of the work of teachers developing a Professional Development School (PDS) who wanted, after the first five years, to reflect on their practice over the years (see Nihlen, Williams, & Sweet, 1999). The teachers and Nihlen collaboratively conducted a series of interviews, the former as practitioner researchers, the latter as a university professor. An interviewer asked a staff member, "Tell me about your experiences at Emerson School." The answering of such a question can lead to what Spradley calls *"mini-tour"* questions (e.g., "You indicated that Emerson was a PDS. Can you describe its history for me?") as well as *"example"* questions (e.g., "Can you give me an example of site-based management?"), *"experience"* questions (e.g., "Could you tell me about some of your experiences on the School Leadership Team?"), and *"native-language"* questions (e.g., "What would teachers call this self-governing group?"). In this case, because the interviewer and interviewee were often both teachers and both knew things about the school, the interviewee was allowed and encouraged to tell her or his own story about the school (Nihlen et al., 1999).

There are a few caveats to keep in mind regarding the process. Because both the interviewer and the participants share experience in the same site, there can be an assumption that the interviewer *knows* what the participant is saying and need not ask him or her to elaborate on it. This is one of those situations where it is a good idea to check whether shared assumptions and meanings are truly shared by asking participants in the interview to elaborate on what it is they mean or are saying. And second, after each interview, the researcher must analyze the data already collected before conducting further interviews. This ongoing process of collecting data, analyzing and reflecting on data, and then going forward with additional collection of data is called "grounded theory" by Glaser and Strauss (1967). We also call it good common sense. When collecting qualitative data, one should pause frequently to reflect and analyze and allow the analysis to inform the next questions asked. This is tied directly to the action research model or spiral of plan, act, observe, reflect, and revise, where we ask where the first data might inform our perspective and actions and then how the analysis opens the possibilities of actions and the question itself (see also Stringer, 2003).

Spradley (1980) describes two other kinds of questions: *structural* and *contrast* questions. Structural questions, asked in the second interview with a participant, enable the interviewer to discover information about how participants organize the knowledge they described in the first interview. For example, interviewees might be talking about their classrooms and mention that they have six reading groups. The interviewer could ask, "What characterizes the different groups you mentioned?" or "What other kinds of groups do you have?"

Contrast questions are asked in later interviews to understand what participants mean by the terms they use. If the above teachers are talking about their reading groups and mention that they also have groups for other activities, the interviewer could ask a contrast question to help understand all the things the interviewees mean when they talk about groups (e.g., "What is the difference in the groups for art and the groups for reading?"). Or principals might discuss their PDS and their staff's participation in governance, and the interviewer would ask, "What's the difference between governance at your school and other schools?"

Spradley (1980) carefully leads a new interviewer through the steps of asking questions and then analyzing the data produced. His book is an excellent resource for the beginner. Later in this chapter, in the Approaches to Analysis section, we discuss Spradley's ideas, and we suggest that you read this section before undertaking any interviewing. Knowing how you might construct categories out of your data to analyze it is important information to keep in mind when interviewing. It can save many unnecessary hours of extra analysis.

The ethnographic interview is a core technique and can be used alone or in combination with other techniques such as observation. An offshoot of this type of research and interviewing is autoethnography, a technique of studying your pedagogy, curriculum, or classroom at the same time that you study yourself. Ellis and Bochner (2000) suggest that the aim in composing an autoethnographic accounting is to simultaneously keep the subject (the knower) and the object (that which is being examined) in view. The stories thus written aim to have the reader relive the experience rather than interpret the event (Ellis & Bochner, 2000; Schwandt, 2001).

A teacher researcher, Barbara DuPré (2005), writes about how she made decisions on how to design and implement her study combining elements of autoethnographic, ethnographic, and teacher research:

> The next step in designing this study was to determine how teacher research and ethnography interrelated. This inquiry led to Hayano's (2001) examination of autoethnography or the study of one's "own people" (p. 75). Hayano emphasizes that autoethnography is not a specific research technique, method, or theory, but that all of these elements are affected by the "researcher's involvement and intimacy" with his/her informants. He cites the incorporation of non-Western societies into urban social systems, minority and foreign anthropologists' desire to study their home communities, shrinking research funds, and increased competition for those funds as the impetuses behind this trend. If auto-ethnography is viewed as a continuum (Lewis, 1973, as cited in Hayano, 2001), then the teacher-researchers who are conducting ethnographies in their own classrooms must be positioned somewhere on that line. Teachers fit Hayano's criteria that the researcher must have "some prior knowledge of the people, their culture and language, as well as the ability to be accepted to some degree, or to 'pass as a native member' (p. 77). In addition, teacher researchers have acquired an intimate familiarity with the occupational group being studied, the school community. In all cases, teacher/ethnographers, as I will refer to my role from now on, among other autoethnographers, "possess the qualities of often permanent self-identification with a group and full internal membership, as recognized both by themselves and the people of whom they are a part" (p. 78).

Hayano poses three possible future paradigm shifts in direction for autoethnographers: 1) a search for entirely new theories, 2) emic or subjectively oriented data analysis, and

3) applied, action, or radical anthropology in support of one's own culture. I knew that I wanted to assert the value of teacher-research/ethnography to meet rigorous data analysis criteria and support the culture of a curriculum that the students and I had designed. Whether new theories would emerge was unknown, but anticipated.

Autoethnography also facilitated my critical (in the sense of discerning judgment) view of the hegemonic nature of the social and cultural hierarchies present in a middle school community. On the other hand, I hesitated to classify myself as a critical ethnographer because I was constantly mindful of the directive nature and the danger of speaking "*to* an audience on *behalf* of [my] subjects as a means of empowering them" (Thomas, 1993, p. 4, emphasis in original). However, I did encourage my students to learn to recognize and deconstruct the cultural beliefs and social practices that affected their own status as members of a middle school community as well as members of society at large. (pp. 75–78)

Oral Histories, Narratives, and Stories

Oral histories document the history of events and processes in the words of the people who participated. Carlos Vasquez (University of New Mexico, 1991) discusses their use:

Historians utilize them to get at the "truth behind the facts" of archival research, anthropologists to solicit ethnographic data attainable in no other way, linguists to document the uniqueness and fluidity of changing languages and dialects, sociologists to capture the most intimate and subjective nuances of social processes. For the scholar of human communications, oral history interviews provide the means by which to study how people understand one another and why that understanding so often breaks down. (p. 2)

Oral history is experiencing renewed interest from many researchers; practitioner researchers are no exception. Participants in the Emerson Elementary School Oral History Project sought a research technique that would tell the story of the staff in their own words and move them toward socially just solutions. Oral histories, conducted by teachers interviewing each other, allow voices to be heard clearly.

Many feminists and people of color are interested in this research tool because it helps keep the voice of the interviewee intact and reveals a story from the teller's own perspective. It is often a virtually uninterrupted accounting from the interviewee's point of view. In more traditional interviewing, questions are constructed by the researcher and essentially direct or focus the interview process. Some good references on oral history are Lanman and Mehafy (1988), Dunaway and Baum (1984), and Gluck and Patai (1991). See also the literary oral histories of Hurston (1935, 1985). Terkel (1974, 1980) provides wonderful examples of this technique as well.

The *narrative story*, on the other hand, has become a method for studying teaching that is concerned with "the personal histories of participants embedded within the social history of schools and schooling" and is solicited and collected not merely to describe a person's history but as a "meaning-giving account," an interpretation of that history as a way of explaining and understanding the participant's action in a classroom or other school setting (Connelly & Clandinin, 1987, pp. 130–131). It is written up in story form, often with a plot and temporal organization (Ellis & Bochner, 1996). Ziegler (1992), a teacher researcher, explains it this way:

> This may include a particular ordering of prior experiences brought to bear on new situations and these orderings bring about new ways of telling stories of who we are and how it is that we are doing what we are doing. This is something I have done as a teacher which has led me to do a dissertation and use narrative as method and mode. One story that I have told was about a student I had in my second year of teaching. As the class was talking about family responsibilities, Felix, a seven year old, had shared about how he helped his family by sweeping the dirt floor each morning. Later that day he was in a group with me reading *The Little White House*, a basal reader about an Anglo family of four who lived in their white house with their dog. Felix looked up at me and asked, "Why is Mother always smiling?" This story has since become an intentional story for me to illustrate how I need to match the

material to the child in order to make reading meaningful and relevant. (pp. 14–15)

Ziegler here uses a personal narrative to illustrate how she uses narrative to make points about the curriculum to teachers so that they can truly hear her.

Narrative, then, is a technique of interviewing and listening that relies on stories. Coles (1989) writes that as a psychiatrist, he comes to know patients through their stories. Teachers' stories are part of teachers' lives, and the study of their stories helps us understand the relationship between their lived experiences and their craft knowledge. As a research method, narrative was developed and used initially by teachers of English. They used it with students as well as with one another to understand better the effects of curriculum, the school, and their own teaching. Narratives raise the question of how best to learn from these stories, how to analyze them, and how to keep the speaker's voice intact.

The interest in narrative interview studies is fast growing. See Clandinin and Connelly's (2000) *Narrative Inquiry* and Witherell and Noddings's (1991) *Stories Lives Tell: Narrative and Dialogue in Education.* An author who speaks particularly about the politics and necessity for narratives of people of color is Buendia (2003).

Structured Interviews

The structured interview is also called a questionnaire-type or directed interview. In this type of qualitative approach, the interviewer asks prepared questions of the participant and controls the direction that an interview takes. Philosophically, structured interviews are very different from ethnographic interviews and imply certain epistemological differences as well. For example, ethnographic interviews discussed above imply that you as the researcher want the voices of the people you interview. In addition, their development of answers to the research questions can tell you a lot about them as well.

In a structured interview, the researcher more formally controls the questions, which, in turn, help shape the answers. This technique is best used when simpler, factual answers will suffice. It is often used, for example, as an initial probe of your participants to gather general information and locate any hot spots or areas of sensitivity. These interviews are commonly followed with more extensive ethnographic or narrative-type interviews.

To construct such an interview, the interviewer writes down a list of questions and sequences them so that there is a natural flow from one question to another. The wording of these questions should not deviate much from interviewee to interviewee. The interviewer tape-records or takes careful notes of the responses and later listens to or transcribes the tapes, goes over notes, and expands on them. In a less-structured interview format, the interviewer asks the same questions but does not worry about what order they appear in.

The fixed response is another type of structured interview. Here the interviewer lists the questions on a sheet, asks them of the participant, and then marks off predetermined answers or categories that the answer must fit into. For example:

How important is self-governance to you at the school? (put a check by one):

_____Very important   _____Important
_____Of little importance   _____Not important

Sociology is probably the original home of this type of interviewing. Sources for more information on how to do this include Brady (1979) and Whyte (1984).

Surveys and Questionnaires

A survey or questionnaire shares similarities with the structured interview because the questions are largely predetermined. With surveys and questionnaires, the intent is for the respondents to write answers; the interviewer does not have to be present when they do this. Surveys and questionnaires are a common instrument of practitioner research because they are interviews by proxy and are therefore easy to administer, they provide direct responses to factual and attitudinal questions, and they make tabulation and analysis of response almost effortless. But beyond this, they are also an easy way to promise participants anonymity. Identifying information is often not a part of a questionnaire or survey other than in the most general way. For example, participants may be asked to check whether they are male or female, a teacher or administrator, and so on. For busy teachers, this is a valuable tool that is often combined later in the research with the more extensive interviewing techniques discussed above.

With this kind of research, following a logical sequence of questions is most important but is often difficult to predict in advance. Questions that appear logical to interviewees are easier for them to answer. Most researchers develop an instrument, then field-test or pilot it on teachers or administrators not involved in the study. The results of the pilot can be used to revise the survey or questionnaire before administering it to the specific population of the study.

Initially, the researcher should decide the specific aim of the survey. Is it for an informal assessment or for more formal and external sources? The aim of the survey will help form the specific questions to be investigated and the corresponding sample of participants. It is important to remember that surveys and questionnaires cannot show causal relationships, but they can indicate associations or correlations. A survey can collect data that will help the researcher see the next step in the research.

Surveys come in two primary types: the descriptive or enumerative kind and the analytic, relational kind. The descriptive kind is similar to a census or public opinion poll, where the questions "how many" or "how often" are asked. The purpose is to count from a representative or class of people. A descriptive survey tells us how many members have a characteristic or how often an event occurs. It is not designed to "explain" anything or to show relationships between A and B.

The analytic survey explores the relationship between variables and is oriented to finding associations and explanations. It asks "why" and "what goes with what" kinds of questions. Analytic surveys are usually set up to explore specific working hypotheses.

The following is an example from the research notes of an adult education and literacy teacher. Liza Martinez (1993) is the coordinator and teacher of a program called Opciones para Mujeres, established to help immigrant women with limited English proficiency. The program uses a bilingual approach. Concepts are introduced in Spanish and reinforced with learner-centered and holistic activities in English. Martinez begins the semester with a descriptive survey-registration intake form:

> As part of the orientation, I had students complete a detailed registration form. This form has a multifold purpose: it has

provided me with personal information about the students; it has also helped me to determine whether a student is in need of other social services or should be referred to another educational program, for example. Finally, the registration form also asks students at the end in Spanish what they expect to get from the course. In this way, I have been able to determine whether they are functionally literate in Spanish. If they are not, they can be referred to a Spanish literacy class that is offered. After reviewing each registration form of the present students, I developed a checklist (for analysis) which I divided into several categories. Through the use of simple counting, I compiled the data and came up with a profile of the new group of students. (p. 7)

Martinez collected a great deal of data from her students during the initial meetings. She was then able to use this data to adapt her syllabus for the class and to suggest additional resources for her students. This is also a good example of information that a teacher might routinely collect for her teaching that can also be a data source for her research.

An example of a practitioner researcher using an analytic type survey technique involves a middle school teacher, Kathleen Cobb (1993), who used a qualitative research design as a tool to bring forth student perceptions. She asked her students what they thought about their own learning experience and about how teachers contributed to it. The purpose of her study was to hear students' voices about their own learning and what made it positive in their own eyes:

Initially, a general survey was administrated to 88 eighth graders in a science class. Questions were asked that probed topics such as: what should 8th graders know at the end of the middle school; what teachers and parents think middle school students should know; affective behavior of teachers that students value; strengths and weaknesses of the student; and perceptions of family members about the student. Next, from this larger group of students, a smaller group of 10 students were invited to participate in a group session to discuss questions about meaningful learning experiences and teachers. These students were chosen to reflect the multicultural characteristics of the school.

The survey was an instrument to give me a general "scan" as to what the students thought about their school experiences relating to subjects they thought important, teachers that had made an impression on them, how their families might influence their perceptions of what was important, and their image of themselves in a school setting. I found that the length of the survey was intimidating to some students as they felt they couldn't or wouldn't complete it fully. Also, more information was gathered than I could analyze in the time period allotted for the completion of this study. I chose to look at the questions that the students had most completely answered and that interested me the most. These questions can be loosely categorized into (a) academic subjects/topics considered to be of importance to the students, (b) elements of the teacher/student relationships that had influenced the students positively or negatively, and (c) situations that they remember as having been the worst or the best in their middle school experience. After studying this particular data from the survey, I decided to concentrate more specifically on the students' learning experiences. I wanted to know what they thought about their experiences. How did they define a good experience? I wanted to know how the students thought the teachers aided in the experience. From the survey, I had learned that good teachers listened, explained, understood, made learning fun, challenged and respected them, and most of all, were characterized as nice. I wanted to know in more detail what made a learning experience meaningful, significant. What was it that a teacher did, in the students' eyes, that made this happen. (pp. 2–3)

This example demonstrates the use of a survey to get a general picture of what students are thinking about their learning experiences. Cobb (1993) then interviewed a representative sample of the students to deepen her understanding of what they were saying. After the group interview, she had the students rate different factors that emerged on the surveys as important to a good learning experience. Last, she interviewed six of the participating students and focused on the factors rated highest. She concludes:

I went into this study with a curiosity. What goes on in a middle school student's head as he/she goes about the day? What makes an impression? What will remain in their memories when they are my age looking back on their experiences? As I asked the questions, I became profoundly aware of how students yearn to have someone listen to them, take their reflections seriously, and believe in them. I believe that on some level, most teachers who choose to teach middle school, and who enjoy it, know the importance of the student/teacher relationship and its significance to the learning process. It is the power of the students' own words, though, that brings this important relationship into focus. There are questions that this study has brought to my attention, and that perhaps later I can pursue. (p. 10)

The action research spiral worked successfully for Cobb. At this point, she is again in the reflective portion of the spiral, perhaps revising her research question in anticipation of future observations and study.

Checklists, Rating Scales, and Inventories

Checklists, rating scales, and inventories all utilize a "closed" type of question; the respondent does not have to write anything down. The response consists of a check mark or some other indication of choice, and the researcher then calculates some kind of score. These techniques are good for administering to groups of students or adults, and forms can easily be returned by dropping them in a box at the school.

Martinez (1993) taught an English as a Second Language class at a community center and developed a needs-assessment intake form. Students were asked to check off as many items as they thought applicable to the following phrase: "I need to improve my English because . . ."

The responses were then tabulated, and the number of people checking each item was placed in parentheses at the end:

- I want to enroll in a vocational or academic class (15)
- I want to speak with people who do not know Spanish (14)
- I want to read books and magazines (14)
- I want to get a job (13)
- I want to speak to a doctor (11)

- I want to read a newspaper (11)
- I want to go shopping (11)
- I want to ask for information (11)
- I want to speak on the telephone (11)
- I want to use public services (10)
- I want to speak with my child's teacher (10)
- I want to speak with coworkers at my job (8)

Martinez used this information to continue planning the class for her students as well as to ponder the assumptions of previous work that indicated that these types of students were more interested in general educational degree work than in preparing for jobs in the English-speaking community.

Observation

The second core technique in more qualitative action research is observation. As with interviews, observational research offers many different ways to gather data, and the research question acts as the guide in selecting the best method. The varied ways observations can be done greatly enhance how busy teachers in the classroom can find time to do them. In this section, we give an overview of observational techniques, then focus on participant observation, mapping, material cultural inventories, and visual techniques such as the use of video and photography.

Observations focus on what is happening, for example, in a classroom, a playground, or a hallway, or on what a student or faculty member does in a specific situation over a delimited amount of time. They can help demystify what is actually going on as opposed to what one might hope or assume or what a participant says is happening. It is a way of double-checking or gaining a different vantage point on what someone says versus what she or he does.

Ideally, observations are recorded and written down in some form, with many using some sort of a field notebook. Try to be as systematic as possible, with clear, unbiased language that avoids high-inference descriptors such as "nice," "pretty," "angry," and "stylish" and focuses on letting words paint a clear picture of the event for the reader. This helps re-create the scene at a later date when the researcher is reviewing notes and needs to understand what happened, not what he or she thought or perhaps wished happened. Time constraints for practitioner researchers often mean that a researcher jots a quick observation down in a journal, then later elaborates on it.

Anecdotal records, for example, help when you are juggling multiple roles in the classroom. They are often written after the fact and in a reflective manner. You can systematize them by avoiding high-inference descriptors and trying to keep the focus related to your research questions.

The basic rules for good observation are as follows:

1. Set clear goals, limitations, and guidelines for the observation.

2. Observe the entire event or incident, called a "stream of behavior."

3. Record observations completely and carefully in a field notebook in as systematic a manner as is possible; elaborate later when you have a moment.

4. Try to be as objective as possible. In other words, strive to be clear and unbiased, and try to recognize when this is not possible.

When an outside researcher begins any observation, as a newcomer he or she will initially try to see as much as possible in order to gain a general understanding of the situation and the observational research possibilities. However, practitioner researchers already have this general understanding, and it is this enormous amount of tacit knowledge that must be made explicit in order for researchers to see it freshly and openly. They are also stepping outside accustomed roles and stepping back to observe and see with fresh eyes. Recording this information as field notes or in a research journal separate from the field notes helps this process.

Armed with a general view of the school, and with a particular question, the researcher then begins the process of focusing on a particular situation or stream of behavior. A common mistake at this point is to look only at interesting events or situations. For example, if you are observing in your elementary school classroom and you are watching a reading group led by a student teacher, you might be inclined to record only the student teacher's encouragement and positive comments to students. If you are more systematic in your observations and listen and record everything the student teacher says and does with each child, you will gain a more inclusive and whole picture of the reading group's dynamics and the student teacher's abilities. An important point to remember about observations, regardless of where you are observing, is that if an event is truly significant, it will reoccur. If not, then focusing on it to the exclusion of other events can often lead you down a blind alley.

As with other data-gathering methods, conducting observations has its disadvantages or limitations:

1. Rarely are observations a "stand-alone" source of data. They are most commonly used in conjunction with other forms of data gathering. While we can carefully document what we see, as we ascribe meaning to what we have seen, typically we'll want to check our understanding against other data. In other words, observations do not typically speak for themselves.

2. Sometimes our roles as educators do not allow us the leisure to step back and assume the role solely of observer. To systematically observe over time so that we have more than snapshot impressions takes time that practitioner researchers may not feel they can spare. Or we may, as in the Mercado (2000) example later in this chapter, be able to observe our students in situations such as recess but not during class time. Sometimes action researchers utilize tools such as video cameras to document what they want to observe over time (see, e.g., the Fayden example in Chapter 5). To then utilize this data requires us to systematically view the tapes, perhaps even transcribe the dialogue in the tapes, all of which is very time consuming.

At the same time, observations are particularly beneficial in terms of the following:

1. We are able to see practice theories in action, that is, people tell us what it is they do and an observation amplifies that explanation. It can either substantiate the explanation or raise more questions for our participants.

2. Observations allow us to literally "see" things that had not occurred to us in terms of our research questions, things we would not have thought to ask about without seeing them.

3. Systematic observations force us as inside researchers to step back and view the familiar through new eyes.

Participant Observation

The first observation technique is participant observation. Its opposite is usually done in a laboratory or experimental environment and implies that the researcher has no contact with the people he or she is observing and is not interested in observing people in their natural surroundings. For practitioner researchers, this is not possible or desirable.

Why is it called participant observation, even if the researcher did not intend to interact with the participants? This term comes from anthropology and refers to the time when anthropologists were called armchair anthropologists. In the late 1800s and beyond the turn of the century, anthropologists in this new field initially wrote about cultures they had never visited. Information was culled from documents written by captains of passing ships or from missionaries and colonial administrators who were colonizing a particular culture. Malinowski (1922) was the first anthropologist to conduct fieldwork. His observations of the Trobriand Islanders were later called participant observation because he was there, in the field, rather than home in England in his library reading other people's descriptions of that culture. The term remains, though today we differentiate many varieties of participant observation.

An example of participant observation will provide an idea of the general category. Nihlen (1976) did her research for her dissertation in a first-grade classroom. She tried to be unobtrusive and not a participant, but this was unrealistic; the teacher and the children helped her become a participant observer. She was slowly incorporated into the children's classroom, first by tying shoes and zipping jackets, later with more responsible tasks such as reading to them and participating in the Friday art project. This broke the rules of anthropology for the 1970s but allowed her to be more realistic in her position in the class and to learn a great deal more about the culture of the classroom. Sometimes, however, it was overwhelming, and the teacher, trying to help her, pinned a sign on her blouse that said "INVISIBLE." This was a big word for the kids, but they caught on and loved the game. Nihlen realized the children never stopped seeing her but allowed her to sometimes watch them as if she were invisible.

Participant observers have varying degrees of involvement from passive or uninvolved to total and complete participation (see Figure 6.2). Moderate participation means that the researcher tries to maintain a balance between participation and observation. Active participant observers seek to do what the participants in the research scene are doing to understand the process better. Depending on their research question, practitioner action researchers are considered total participant observers, because they are already regular participants in the school (Spradley, 1980). However, when researchers step outside their role as teacher to study something else in the school, the role changes, and they are not inherently the total participant observer. Mercado (2000) describes this process for herself in observing her kindergarteners during their recess play:

> Lupita and I took turns at recess duty during mid-morning recess sessions. While Lupita was on duty I did observations of the children at play. I had already explained to the children that I would also be out for recess when Mrs. Martinez was on duty in order to observe them at play. I explained that I was doing this in order to help me think more about how I could teach better. I asked for their help in doing this by ignoring me when both Lupita and I were out on the playground. Most of the time this worked well, although at times the children had difficulty not considering me the duty teacher. Also, at other times it was necessary that I intervene when children engaged in play activities that I perceived to be unsafe. Although I was

Figure 6.2   Types of Participant Observations

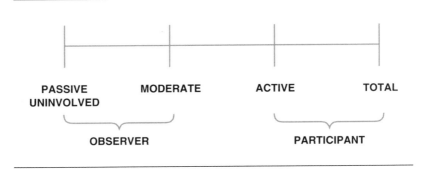

able to observe during this time, I found it difficult to be totally disengaged. I accommodated this difficulty by trying to keep some disengagement during at least part of the recess time. This forced me to be more conscious about remembering my impressions during the observations and record them at the end of the day in my teacher journal. (p. 106)

Spradley (1980) does an excellent job of describing the difference between a participant and a participant observer. He discusses such things as crossing the street at the light or getting a cola from a vending machine as examples of tasks we are participants in and have cultural knowledge about. However, this is tacit knowledge after the first few times, and we hardly think about it. Following are Spradley's six major categories of differences between the ordinary participant and the participant observer, differences that are very important for action researchers to consider as they try to do research where they are everyday participants.

First is the issue of *dual purpose.* A participant observer comes to a situation with two purposes: to engage in activities appropriate in the situation and to observe the activities, people, and physical aspects of the situation. The ordinary participant comes to that same situation with only one purpose: to engage in the appropriate activities.

Second is the issue of *explicit awareness.* Ordinarily, participants in a situation practice selective inattention as a way to escape experiencing overload. For example, if you are in the school cafeteria, you will not pay specific attention to all the children, only those for whom you are responsible. You may not closely watch how far or how close each child stands from another in a given line, and you may not closely observe how they make their selection of food. You have unconsciously selected certain stimuli to be more aware of and some to be less aware of. However, if you are a researcher interested in the line-standing behavior of children, you will watch the spaces between children as well as a host of other things. (And, of course, there is the issue of how to explain your presence in the lunch line when it is not your turn to work in the cafeteria. This gets into the issue some practitioner researchers have discussed concerning what it means when you turn up in your school where you are not "normally" expected to be. This creates problems of role definition.)

Third is the issue of a *wide-angle lens.* At the same time participant observers are selecting things in the environment that do not
warrant attention, they are using a wide-angle lens to conduct
observations. As a staff member in a school, you may not have
lunchroom duty, but if you are studying the line-standing behavior of children, that is one place you will want to go. You will try to
observe everything about the lines: distance and closeness of
children, straight versus crooked lines, shoving and pushing, hug-
ging, voices of children and of adults, and any other behaviors
that may occur.

Fourth is the *insider-outsider experience.* Practitioner researchers
interact in various activities at their schools. They are insiders; this
gives the activities a meaning and coherence understood to insiders. Participant observers need to be both insiders and outsiders
simultaneously. As a teacher, you are an insider in your classroom.
As a researcher, you try to be an outsider and view yourself and the
classroom as a stranger would. This will help you understand the
unspoken and hidden curriculum in the classroom. You are also an
outsider to many settings within the school and must adapt and
understand your multiple roles as a researcher and help others to
adapt to this changing situation.

Fifth is the issue of *introspection.* In observational research,
researchers become the research tool and must constantly analyze their own feelings and subjective reactions to this role.
Participant observers can take nothing for granted, and an intro-
spective and reflective stance helps gain perspective on events.
This also helps researchers understand new and old situations
and gain skill in learning the rules of the cultural scene.

The sixth issue is one of *record keeping.* Participant observers
need to keep a detailed record of events they observe. Sometimes
teachers cannot do this at the time. Then it is important to jot
down a key word or words that will help jar the memory later
when the researcher can write down a more comprehensive
record. The longer one waits to record an event, the harder it is to
re-create an accurate picture. Many teacher researchers use an
open notebook on their desks in which they make passing comments as they work with children. Others jot down things while
children are involved in group activities or when another adult is
working with the class. Some of us used index cards, which were
always handy and could be thrown into a shoe box on the corner

of a cabinet and examined and elaborated on later. See Hubbard and Power (1993) and Mills (2000) for further examples of ways to gather and store data.

We offer initially a somewhat traditional format of using one side of the notebook page for observations and the other side for personal feelings, comments, and hunches. We have already discussed the importance of keeping observations and feelings separate. But is this really a useful way to record data? Following is an example from a practitioner researcher and kindergarten teacher, Judith Pearson (1993), who tried to develop a way to observe three children who were identified as behavior problems. The traditional ways were not helping her.

> Why did I choose to observe three children? I needed to start somewhere, and if my basic question had to do with behavior management, observing behavior seemed a logical place to begin. It also gave me an entry point at which to try changing my focus of the classroom, having been fascinated with Spindler's [1982] and Erickson's [1973] ethnographic principle of "making the familiar strange." If I understood better how children thought, would I more easily be able to change my reality of how I saw them? If I understood the child's reality, would my idea of how to manage their behavior change? The child learns early on how to say what adults want to hear—a form of translation competence, I suppose, on the part of the child. Spradley defines it as "the ability to translate the meanings of one culture into a form that is appropriate to another culture" (Spradley, 1979, p. 19). I am attempting to see their culture sans the translation.
>
> Although I began with observations of three boys, the pursuit invariably led to observation of myself, teetering back and forth as I attempted to make sense out of what I saw and said and did. I am still, at this writing, struggling to comprehend what I've seen and heard this semester.
>
> As I began my observations, I realized that I had not yet learned the "tricks of the trade." Time and energy restraints constantly plagued me. I began taking notes on what I saw. I found that I was writing all the time instead of interacting with the children. Although I'd plan to have time in the afternoon where others could take over (the classroom), it rarely worked

out. Like the day I had planned to finish the sociograms. It seemed simple. I would do them after quickly helping the children put together our cookie recipe that had to chill. With my teacher's aide in the room I would have the rest of the hour. Ha! One interruption after the other delayed the cookie making and I ended up with no time at all. Next, I went to PE class. This was a perfect place to observe since the children didn't run to me. However, even knowing this, I wasn't willing or able to get away again for this kind of observation.

Whenever I could I took notes during class, but even as fast as I wrote, I wasn't using nearly enough detail; the words did not come swiftly to me and the event was over before I could record it accurately. Also, using a notebook was clumsy and it got lost easily, as I'd set it somewhere when things needed attending to.

The next problem was getting a recording system that worked for me. I tried a divided notebook but it was too awkward to carry around. So I went to a legal pad. I could usually find one of these and I could easily whisk the pages into a notebook. I'd write observations only on one side, saving the other side for my own thoughts. The system still lacks easy and quick use and access. Trying to solve this problem has given me a new insight into myself. I always thought of myself as organized, even though I have trouble remembering which organized file something is in. I think there are levels of being organized, something like the levels of thinking skills. I'm still at the factual level. I'm obsessed with doing it, but haven't the understanding of it yet.

So, I abandoned the notetaking and turned to the video camera. I planted it on a tripod and got what I got, which wasn't always my three boys. Nevertheless, it was surprisingly revealing. Every taped session had interesting interactions. I found the drawbacks to be: (a) finding a convenient place for the tripod where the children wouldn't trip over it, (b) placing it where I could see the whole scene, yet still be close enough to get the scene's voices, (c) taking the time to transcribe (each tape took 4 to 6 home viewing hours). I ended up with countless pages of observations but I wasn't sure how to abstract from them for data. My first idea was to use them to form a profile of one boy, which I did. (p. 6; reprinted with permission)

This is a good example of a practitioner researcher trying to work within a traditional framework of qualitative research to conduct research, then adapting various methods to the reality of her site. When she has trouble reproducing the traditional technique, she concludes that she is not organized or does not know the tricks of the trade, when in reality she needs more realistic and usable research techniques that take into account the frenzied pace of her day. With that in mind, she moved toward the more manageable videotaping, "where I got what I got."

Another example, with the actual text of her field notebook (personal communication, 2000), is from Barbara DuPré, the middle school language arts teacher mentioned earlier:

The entrance through which most staff and many of the students entered was directly south of the staff parking lot. My typical morning began with "duty" five times per month. I used this time as an opportunity to interact with students in a less formal way than I do in the classroom. Often, parents on their way to work brought students to school an hour and a half before the bell rang. Since students were not allowed in the building until after the bell rang, they had established traditional locations outside the school building where they gathered to socialize and await the bell. One of my participant observations described my duty location in this way:

This morning, the sun is peeking through the clouds, so there are more students outside. They are clustered in small groups of 6 to 14, lining the perimeter of the parking lot, waiting near the alcove-style entrances to the sixth grade science classes, resting on the rail along the side of the steps that lead to the school's basement, and milling on the patio between the shop/art building and the science building. Their voices echo through the patio, calling to each other from group to group. Single students break off as individual students walk up, the girls grabbing each other's hands or giving a rapid lean-to hug with arms grabbing each other's shoulders.

Yesterday's group is again stationed on the left cement bank of the entrance that leads into the sixth grade hall. An educational assistant shows up to help me with duty. She begins pointing and shouting in a gruff, commanding voice, "Move back! Off the ramp! Don't push!" In anticipation of the bell, a throng of students surges forward. The bell beeps five times in a high-pitched electronic tone.

I struggle to the left side of the entrance, but the assistant is trapped against the door, shouting repeatedly, "I said, 'Don't push!'" My voice joins hers in a continual cry for everyone to back off the steps. Eventually, they all do so, grumbling about tardies, lockers, first period teachers, lack of fairness, your fault. Only after the steps are clear do we reopen the doors. Students rush up the steps, but without pushing.

I greet students I know as they swarm into the crowded space, reminding some of them with "Hat!" to remove their baseball caps before they enter the building. When the last of the remaining students have trickled through the doors, I pat the flustered aide on the shoulder. As we pass through the doors, the woman continues to complain about the students' behavior. She turns and walks slowly into the Teachers' Lounge, located to the right near the sixth grade hall entrance. I call out to her, "Remember, it's Friday!" Then I begin the long swim upstream through the sixth grade hall then down another hallway to my classroom in the seventh grade hall.

Another kind of participant observation was developed by a practitioner action researcher at Emerson Elementary School. Geraldine Garcia, a Title V academic tutor for Native American students, did a series of critical environmental observations as part of anecdotal records. She had a tiny room to meet with students, more like an enlarged closet than a real room. When Native American children were identified by their regular teachers as needing help in subjects such as reading, math, and social studies, they were sent to Garcia for a half hour each day. At any given time, she had up to six students, each needing help in a different academic area. She worked with whatever assignments the children brought to her from their homeroom teachers.

When Garcia (1991) began teaching at Emerson, she was not aware of its professional development program. She enrolled in an on-site teacher researcher course:

I was surprised and pleased to discover that a university class was to be offered on-site as part of the professional development for the staff. I read with interest the initial articles about qualitative research and thought about how it would be relevant in my room. The research coursework and the discussions with the other teachers provided an opportunity to look critically at my room and I decided to change the environment. At the same time I began to realize that this transformation of space to enhance learning provided a unique source of research data. I recorded data by drawing pictures and writing descriptively about each stage of the changes and what process I went through in order to see the room as a place I could manipulate to enhance learning. I moved furniture, pushed back bulletin boards, and utilized a refrigerator, which was in the room, as a place for magnetized letters of the alphabet. (p. 10)

Garcia developed a method that combined mapping and observation along with anecdotal records and drawings. Each week she made a picture of the room and wrote descriptive field notes. When she changed something in the room, she noted the children's as well as her own responses to the change. This way each change helped promote a new change in the curriculum as well as in the physical structure of the room. At each juncture, she explained to the research class both her own transformation and the changes in the classroom. They were able to give her encouragement as well as additional suggestions. Garcia speaks about her classroom environment:

Within that week I looked at my environment carefully and tried to find ways to enhance learning. I started rearranging the furniture so it would not be cluttered and crammed like before. In the arrangement I noticed how the students were eager to use the chalkboard. The students would be trying to squeeze on both sides of the table to get to the board. After rearranging the furniture, the students noticed the blackboard space. There was more room to walk around the table. Their eyes just beamed when they saw the space. "Wow, you changed the room." "It looks nice in here." "Now we can have a place to use the blackboard." The environment made a difference in the way the children developed work and play. The students used the blackboard for doing math problems. It invited other students to join them. It was exciting to see the students being

excited about learning and sharing. The blackboard also created the freedom to draw and explore one's ability. (p. 46)

Garcia reports that she grew professionally as well as personally in the process of researching and implementing change in her
classroom. Of the research class and her work in it, Garcia says
that it "has brought about great sparks and challenges. The class
has created a spiraling effect in the way I view learning and environment within myself and the Title V program. We as educators
need to take time and become aware of the things around us and
learn from our students" (p. 46).

Mapping

Another tool in the category of observations is mapping.
Mapping has long been used in the study of proxemics, which is
the development of categories of distances that people place
between each other (Hall, 1974). Mapping is most useful for doing
quick observations in a classroom or playground that lead to plen-
tiful data. The technique involves creating some sort of map of
your research space. Some people make an approximation of the
space while others find it useful to use graph paper and make an
exact map to scale of the scene. Think about your research question and let that be a guide to your decision, what you need to
know about what is happening in the space, and what kinds of
data will help you answer your question. Below is a description of
how to create an exact map and some examples of how mapping
has been used by teachers.

A classroom is an easy example: the researcher can do the
measuring when the room is empty or let the kids help and make it
a lesson in measurement. If the room has old floor tiles, many are
one-inch square and need only to be counted. If not, the floor
should be measured with tape. The outside walls should be measured first, then doors and windows should be marked on the
map, other objects that are permanent along the walls should
be marked, and finally the furniture should be marked. Many
researchers designate immovable furniture, rarely moved furniture, and regularly moved furniture such as student desks, chairs,
and tables. Each should be carefully recorded and drawn on the
graph paper.

One middle school teacher researcher made a map of the floor plan, including the permanent and rarely moved objects. Each week she recorded where the student desks were. She then compared these maps after several months and learned a lot about student preferences for the shape of desk areas when they were combined, who wanted to be next to whom, and how separate the girls and boys wanted to be. She was startled to find that all students wanted to be closer to her in the front of the room and that the boys actually got closer.

A map can help chart adult movement in the classroom. You, as the researcher, can create the map, and you and a colleague can chart each other. For example, one elementary school teacher charted a colleague every two minutes for half an hour over several weeks. He put a number on the map where the teacher was standing at that moment. This helped the teacher see how she utilized her room and which children got more attention through simple proximity.

Hall's proxemic categories (1966, 1974) range from closer than six inches to twenty-five feet and beyond. The four categories are intimate, personal, social, and public. Hall bases these four categories on manifestations of territoriality in both animals and humans. Staples (1993) observes that the kinds of interactions that occur within each category are culturally influenced.

Following is an example from the journal of a kindergarten teacher who tried to use mapping to gather data on the playground:

> My plan was: check every three minutes to see where children were, what they were doing, and with whom they were playing. At first I tried to chart everyone. I found that it was very difficult to keep track of who was where and to maintain a systematic span. They moved and changed groups too fast. So I disregarded the time intervals and tried to note groupings, placements, and interactions. Still it was too much. I couldn't keep track of all the children along with doing my playground duties.
>
> Some problems interfere with this observation method: (a) The children's needs and my supervisory duties, (b) the windy weather, making note-taking awkward at best, (c) infrequent recess duty—only twice a week. The other days I would try to get outside, but so many other things got in the way, not

the least of them being a need for a breather. Nevertheless, I feel this type of record keeping would be valuable with as much time as I could manage. If I concentrated on only four children a week, I wouldn't be so overwhelmed. That way I would be tracking each child every six weeks or so, giving me a pretty good picture of that child's patterns.

I started observations of classroom play and interaction during Choice Time. I didn't get very far with this, finding it so hard to sacrifice the time it took away from my personal interactions with the children. Moreover, I didn't discover an easy system for recording the data. First I made a map of the classroom, intending to write children's names directly on the map. It took too much time to find the location on the map. So I numbered the locations, intending to write the location number after the child's name—it took too much time to find the number and transfer it to the name [see Figure 6.3]. Finally, I made an alphabetized list of all the possible Choice Time activities and wrote the abbreviated child's name after the location. This worked the best. I think that if I combine the playground and classroom observation, doing only four children a week, it might be workable. I made up a data sheet that would work for both indoors and outdoors to keep track of the four children observed, their choice of companions, and their choice of playing place. (Pearson, 1993, p. 22)

This example places the struggles of the practitioner trying to conduct research in her own classroom at the center of the question of which techniques are most useful.

Material Culture Inventories

Material inventories of a culture were a standard technique used by early anthropologists in their attempts to understand differing cultures. The technique involves recording everything that people use or make or adapt. Today educational anthropologists use these inventories in the classroom and school to record how people move around a space and create their environment in classrooms and schools. In conducting such an inventory, researchers should carefully mark the boundary of observations and inventory. For example, a classroom, a particular part of a hallway or entryway, or lavatory graffiti can be

Figure 6.3   Mapping Examples—Pearson

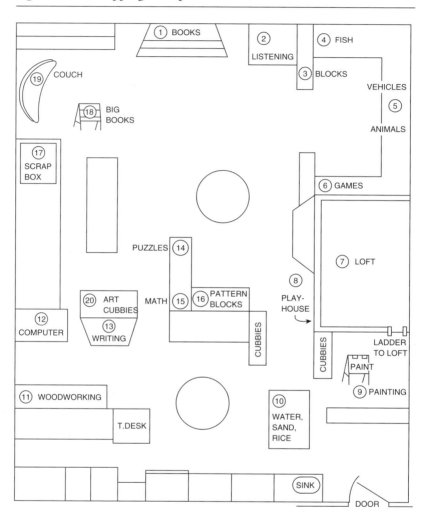

selected. Researchers must decide how frequently they will observe and record data and how they will describe its placement.

Visual Recordings and Photography

A final technique of observation is visual recordings. Photography and videotaping are excellent ways for practitioner researchers to record data from situations in which they are also participants. Practitioner researchers take off their participant hats, put on their researcher hats, and analyze the data at their leisure.

The camera acts as an extension of our senses; it records not only what we want it to see but all the surroundings as well. The camera has been used since its invention as a clarifier and a modifier of ecological and human understanding. As a precise recorder of reality, it can turn raw circumstances into data (Collier, 1967). Margaret Mead and Gregory Bateson were the first to use photography as part of research in anthropology (see Bateson & Mead, 1942), and Mead continued to use photography in her work in child development.

In the last 20 years, educational anthropologists have begun to use video to analyze discrete events in the classroom. Gearing and Sangree (1979) delineated aspects of cultural transmission in the classroom; they also worked with teacher researchers in this area. Erickson (1986) labels his video analysis in the classroom "microethnography."

With the movement of VCRs into schools and homes, the use of videotaping a classroom has increased enormously. Teachers or counselors can run the video camera themselves in their rooms or get a colleague to help. The video camera can be focused on a small group activity so that the teacher can participate in the activity, or another person can scan the room, moving the camera slowly from one end to the other and back again over a period of time. The teacher can do timed observations of certain segments of the room. The list is endless, and the camera will follow the researcher's imagination.

If you decide to videotape your room, test the camera and your tape before starting. If you use a microphone, make sure it can pick up the group or activity you want, or consider using an additional microphone. Slow, steady camera moves are most effective; fast moves make for difficult viewing.

Children are accustomed to the video camera and the VCR. What becomes irresistible to them is that one is now in their classroom looking at them. The researcher needs to habituate students to the camera. Letting it run for a few days before beginning to tape will normalize it for the students and enhance data gathering in a naturalistic setting. The researcher should find out the district's policies on videotaping children, even for personal use. Figure 6.4 is a checklist for video camera use and analysis in the classroom.

Elliott (1991) suggests that researchers review the entire tape initially, stopping at insightful events and carefully marking them using the numbering system on the VCR. Then they should transcribe, loosely or precisely, depending on the intended use, the

Figure 6.4   Checklist for Video Camera Use and Analysis

Qualitative Research Approaches for Everyday Realities

1. What do you wish to observe?
2. What are the features of the event?
3. Are the goals of the lesson clear?
4. What is the role of the teacher?
5. Are students involved/interested?
6. Who is doing the talking?
7. What type of utterances are made?
8. What type of questions are asked (convergent/divergent)?
9. What type of pupil involvement is there?
10. What is the pace?
11. What style of classroom/pupil organization is used?
12. What negative features of this performance present themselves?
13. What nonverbal behavior is present?
14. Are the voices clear?
15. Is the language formal/informal?
16. What mannerisms are evident?
17. Do any distractions occur?
18. What things have you learned from this analysis?

relevant events for the research question. Transcribing videotapes by hand is a time-consuming and exhausting job, though well worth the effort. But examples from practitioner action researchers' journals and research reports indicate that videotaping is seen as an extremely useful tool. It is fairly easy and often less stressful to collect data this way, and one can find the time later to index and analyze the footage. It provides a comprehensive record that is reliable and accurate and can be used as an exemplar for demonstration to students and other staff. However, its disadvantages include the difficulty of transcription, the need for expensive equipment that a school district may not have, and the possible distortion of aiming the camera only at certain things.

Following is an excerpt from a study of surface and hidden curriculum in a science class for sixth graders:

This is my first attempt at an in-depth look at my teaching. I am searching specifically for insights into how I am attending to the various aspects of the politics of the learning experiences

I provide for my students. This is a first experience with participatory research. It was an exercise in "making the road as I was walking" (Horton et al., 1990).

    The data for this investigation was taken from a video of a lesson on germinating seeds. The students are 6th graders in my class who are with me for a three period block each day. I am responsible for teaching science, math and Spanish to these students. My primary focus in all I undertake to teach is to provide opportunities to use language, the language of science (or math or Spanish) in the four domains of literacy.

    Before I began to analyze the video of this class I wanted to look at social interactions between the students and myself. I wanted to look at the complexity of the material I was asking them to spend time on. I wanted to see if I could get any insight into what the students thought about their learning. I began by looking at the video with the students, because they asked to see it on the day it was filmed. They were given the option to respond in writing about what they saw. (Ortega, 1993, p. 20)

Ortega used this videotape to reflect on her presentation of curriculum as a teacher as well as to show the students their behavior in class and to have them reflect on their work in the room. As an action researcher, she was able to revise the curriculum and then move ahead. This also became part of a larger study she conducted for a practitioner research class.

    Following is another example from a middle school language arts teacher who extensively used video in her data collection. DuPré (2005) offers the following:

Studying my own practice required technological equipment beyond a pen and paper. Although I recorded field notes in my researcher's journal, the demands of the curriculum intruded on my opportunities to script my observations as often as I had planned. Therefore, I relied on audio- and video-recordings to help produce participant observations. Having read Hubbard and Power (1993), I anticipated the student's initial nervous reaction to the presence of an audio- or video-recorder. However, during the course of my pilot study, I had discovered that students soon became accustomed to the presence of the recorder and participated in classroom activities with minimal self-consciousness. This was also true in this year's study.

Mapping activities suffered from the limited scope of the video camera's lens. When I zoomed the lens far enough away to reveal more of the room, I lost resolution in the students' and my faces. Nevertheless, I found mapping movement in the classroom to be indicative of the social structure of the classroom and my interactions with the students. To demonstrate how studying one's own teaching impacts that teaching, I noticed a marked increase in my movement within the aisles of student desks after analyzing my initial maps. I was trying to adjust my proxemics in order to encourage the less vocal students to participate in class.

I used a digital camcorder to film classroom activity one to three times per week for 39 weeks. I also frequently recorded audio in the classroom on a digital audio recorder. I transcribed the tapes myself in order to provide time for reflection that led to future curricular choices as well as interview questions. Before I transcribed each digital tape, I reviewed LeCompte and Preissle's (1993, pp. 199–200) guidelines for directing observation. First, I identified the membership of the group or scene. Next, I narrated my observations of group social behaviors in the scene using "low-inference descriptors" phrased with concrete and precise detail. I also made verbatim records of what people said, especially when they used native terms. I identified the physical settings, and the "sights, sounds, smells, tastes, and textures" found in the environment as well as the pace of elapsed time. Later, I annotated these participant observations with "high-inference interpretive comments" (p. 228) that I used to analyze and interpret the cultural scenes to help me discover the meanings the students attributed to their behaviors. As a member-checking activity, I asked the participants to view captured film and listen to recorded audio to edit my transcriptions. (p. 56)

Still photography is an interesting and exciting way to capture data in a classroom or school building. Its primary advantage is that it is a quick and inexpensive method of recording data. Digital cameras allow the photos to be archived on the computer and supplement any presentation or report. Photos document artifacts and behaviors and offer a window into the school and its events. Walker (1985) argues that nonpractitioner "educational researchers tend not to treat schools and classrooms as culturally exotic or indeed as problematic settings" (p. 100) in which the use of photography would greatly enhance the research project and data collection. Thus, they do not consider photographing this environment.

Walker and Weidel (1985) used photography to collect evidence of children's experiences in a London secondary school. They photographed a range of subjects during the academic year. The project, *Pictures: A Collaborative Project (1977–1979)*, was placed in an exhibition with teacher and pupil interpretive comments juxtaposed. It was also used as a basis of discussion between teachers and students in the math department and for an evening meeting with parents.

Permission must be obtained of parents to photograph children in the school, as well as other adults, particularly if used outside of personal research. The researcher should check with the district and school.

Archives and Documents

This section examines a few of the various kinds of archival approaches and document-collecting techniques available to the action researcher. Archival refers primarily to researching the historical records. It is the process of critical inquiry into past events to produce an accurate description and interpretation of those events, their meaning and implications for the present day. There are two major sources of information in history. One is the primary source, which is an original or firsthand account of events. Examples are personal diaries, grade books, letters, and official records such as census materials, school board minutes, policies, and legislative actions. Secondary materials are at least once removed from the event itself. Newspaper accounts are a good example of this category of material.

Primary sources should be used for research whenever possible. All sources must be authenticated to evaluate the validity of the document to ensure that a document was written by whom and when it states. If the source is part of a public collection or record, this has commonly already been done. In addition, internal criticism helps evaluate the meaning, accuracy, and trustworthiness of the content of the document. For example, a personal document like a letter is written from a certain point of view or vantage point. How does the researcher take this into account when analyzing what it has to offer to the inquiry? The researcher's job, if he or she is using personal documents, is to try to understand what was actually going on and the context in which the document was created.

A single document can rarely stand on its own. Part of examining history is to cross-reference several documents before accepting a statement as fact. The researcher should evaluate each document in its chronological position and in light of comments that preceded it, not comments that appeared later.

The goal is to synthesize the information available from as many different sources as possible. Try to use differing types of information such as statistics, school board records, newspapers, diaries, and personal letters—anything that will add context to the situation under study. This is also another way of establishing multiple perspectives toward building validity for the project. Pull the central ideas together and see the possible continuity between and among them.

History is usually reported and written in a narrative form. It can provide an educator with a broad perspective about educational issues and problems. It can assist in understanding why things are as they are. Educational reform and social reform are functions often served by historical research. We are better equipped to predict and move into the future by knowing our past, which can perhaps help us avoid mistakes already committed. Gangs leave graffiti, and organizations provide mountains of records into which the researcher can delve. As a researcher in a school, Nihlen carefully kept everything delivered to her mailbox in chronological order; it proved invaluable to her collaborative's later investigation. In the 1990s, Patton (2002) "evaluated a 'free high school'" that had been created during the struggles and turmoil of the 1960s. Little about the program's current programming could be understood outside the historical context from which it emerged. Each current issue has its own historical context and, depending on the question being investigated, may be a significant area to explore.

Another example of how archival techniques and document searches are combined with oral history is in the Emerson Elementary School Oral History Project (Nihlen et al., 1999). As the researchers interviewed the staff about the last 10 years at Emerson, older staff also discussed the earlier years at the school. This necessitated a search for school board records mentioning Emerson or PDSs, newspaper articles on the school and public reaction, and school attendance records. The researchers sought primary sources when available and accepted secondary sources such as the local newspaper's mention of a document when that was what was available. They also sought personal documents such as diaries and journals written by early staff and parent participants in the school. These were combined with oral history interviews to broaden the view of the school and community and to help triangulate all the data. The varied sources kept all of the researchers involved in this project from assuming their reality as the only reality of the experience of Emerson Elementary School.

For a good discussion of historical methods, see Patton (2002), Tuchman (1994), and Whyte (1984).

There are several advantages to this methodology:

1. Schools exist in a larger context, specific to various points in time. Primary sources of data recorded as public documents can often provide this contextual lens.

2. Researchers do not have to "create" the data themselves, for example, conduct an interview or observation. Rather, they draw on data created for other purposes, often done by others— minutes of a meeting, for example. These documents can be less labor-intensive for the researcher in terms of their creation and be available already in some kind of archived format. For example, minutes of meetings throughout a school year are often already collected in one place and kept in a specific file.

3. This kind of information is typically generated in schools anyway. It is fairly easy to look through the kinds of documents a school archives or draw on its record keeping as a solid source of information.

Some challenges that come with using this kind of data-gathering approach include the following:

1. The records may be incomplete or inaccessible to the researcher. Or they may be poorly organized/unorganized (e.g., stacks of files in boxes that are not in chronological order).

2. The written accounts may not be as richly documented as the researcher might hope. For example, the minutes kept at a meeting may vary greatly depending on the recorder. In other cases, groups may agree to just briefly record the "facts," and it is difficult to glean context from the documents.

3. It may give the researcher a public lens or transcript without some of the other behind-the-scenes or closed-door accounts.

Journals and Diaries

The development in education of the diary and journal as research tools and as data has occurred primarily through teachers of English and in the field of anthropology. A journal is a personal document that can also be used as a research tool to capture reflections and encounters (see Ballenger, 1993; Elliott, 1991; Richards, 1987; and examples from Chapter 3). Journals are a good example of something a teacher might use in the classroom to promote educational objectives, yet they can also be used as a source of data for research. They encourage description, interpretation, and reflection on the part of the teacher as well as the student. In addition, many teachers routinely journal about their school day as a reflective tool in examining their teaching or documenting their thinking on a certain student or issue.

The journal acts as a narrative technique and records events, thoughts, and feelings that have importance for the writer. As a record kept by a student, it can inform the teacher researcher about changing thoughts and new ideas and the progression of learning. McKernan (1991) lists three types of traditional diaries or journals:

1. The intimate journal, which is extremely personal and full of personal sentiments, confessions, and a log of events as seen through the eyes of the individual writer, is written in almost every day.

2. The memoir, which is a more impersonal document, is written in less often and aspires to be more objective and not concentrated on personal feelings.

3. The log is more of a running record of events, such as a list of meetings attended and calls made. We also use it to augment our field notes. (p. 23)

The journal/diary can be kept by researchers to document the classroom or school and can also be used as a personal case history. The keeping of a journal/diary encourages a reflective stance on the part of the writer and can provide a rich source of data on the daily life of a classroom.

Raisch (1992) writes about secondary student teachers and their cooperating teachers becoming teacher-researchers. She used journal writing between each group and between herself and the teachers extensively. She found the most difficult part was in the analysis of the data and ended up coding for themes within the journals in order to guarantee participant voice.

Studies by teachers using journals and diaries increase daily. See Fulwiler (1987), Goswami and Stillman (1987), and Miller (1990) for exciting work by teacher researchers using diaries and journals.

A Word on Mixed Methods

Many studies become what is now called "mixed method studies" because they involve using both quantitative and qualitative data such as statistics from the school district as well as interviews with teachers. Suffice it to say that as we move more and more into a testing and "show me the numbers" mode in education, these mixed studies will gain more and more credence.

As we mentioned in Chapter 5, data that a site is gathering anyway or has imposed upon it can be used in the action research process. For example, many schools are implementing changes or having them imposed because of poor showings on standardized test measures. These "solutions" may or may not be the best ways to address to the problems posed by failing test scores. One way to find out is to begin the inquiry process, asking whether what is being implemented seems to benefit the students and the school in general. Depending on the answers to these queries, some modifications in the interventions may be warranted.

Herr worked for several years with an alternative high school that had some of the lowest literacy scores in the school district. The school was under a mandate to improve its standardized test scores or face consequences imposed upon it by the school district. In discussions among the faculty regarding the low scores, many of the teachers pointed toward the highly transient population in the school and "hypothesized" that the test scores were brought down by those students with whom they had not had much time to work. As the first step, then, in problem solving, we disaggregated the test scores to ascertain whether students who had been in the school for at least two years had higher test scores than did the more recent attendees. We were in essence testing a hunch as to what was "causing" the poor overall scores. In reality, the disaggregation of the data indicated that students who had been enrolled in the school over time were doing no better on the standardized tests than those who were newer to the school. This information led to an inquiry into the effectiveness of the curriculum conducted from a more qualitative approach to data gathering. This vignette is an example of how quantitative data, gathered outside the school—in this case, the scores from standardized tests—was the beginning of some important problem solving within the school. Toward this end it was combined with other qualitative data that the faculty elected to gather, and the whole thing became part of the action research.

Action researchers will always want to ask what data are available that can be used in the inquiry process, even if it is not data they gathered themselves. See Patton (2002) for good examples of how to integrate both kinds of data into solid studies.

DATA ORGANIZATION AND ANALYSIS

Organizing Data

Keeping all the data organized as you collect it is a major task in and of itself. Researchers seem to go about this in fairly idiosyncratic ways, with each having a logic of his or her own. Some researchers toss items like memos or papers to be archived in labeled baskets. Other people devise various color-coded files, with each representing a different kind of data. The key is that whatever you devise, it should work for you in terms of helping you find your data when you need it. In addition, you will want a way to keep track of your methodology—what data you have collected in some sort of chronology (e.g., how many interviews you have done on what dates, numbers of observations). Some people keep an ongoing record in a researcher's log. It can be helpful to construct organizational structures for both of these tasks—what data you've collected, when, and the actual data artifacts (transcribed interviews, field notes, etc.)—early on, since it is easy to become overwhelmed by mounds of data or stymied as to what you need to do next (more interviews? additional observations? etc.).

The following is an example of how one teacher organized her multiple data collection sources with dates and subject of material to help her see what she had. "PO" means observations and "J" means journal. At a later date, she incorporated video and tape recording, and they join the chart.

Data Collection Chart

Video/Audio/Documentation Record

Data	Date(s)	Subject	Documentation
J #1	8/2	Typed Journal Consent Forms	Consent forms
PO #1	8/27	Participant Observation Poems filmed for Open House	What Is a Middle Schooler?
PO #2	8/28 & 29	Participant Observation Poems filmed for Open House	Mid Schooler & This Is the Year & Study Skills Posters
Survey #1	8/29	Wrinkle Writing	
Survey #1	8/29	Class Culture/ Community	
Survey #1 Results: Ques. 1–4	8/29	Semantic Analyses	
PO #3	8/30 & 9/3	Participant Observation	MTR handbook Surveys MTR Step 6 Group rules, DLP Wk 3, Baseline Surveys, Step 7 Mirror
J #2	9/2	Typed Journal Open	Open House & MTR directions
PO #4	9/4	Participant Observation MTR	MTR Step 7 & butcher paper group rules
PO #5	9/5 & 6	Participant Observation	MTR Step 9 & 10 Sociograms Knee-to-knee stories of injustice
J #3	9/7	Audio Journal	Creative Drama

SOURCE: DuPré (2005).

There are, of course, many ways to highlight your data collection and organize it. Any systematic method will greatly help you keep track of what you are trying to do, particularly as you become immersed in the school year and become busier and busier. See Hubbard and Power (1993) and Mills (2000) for some good suggestions in terms of getting and staying organized.

Initial Analysis and Ongoing Reflection

When you begin to develop your study, it is important to recognize that at various intervals, you must stop gathering data and reflect on what you have thus far. For example, if you are doing observations of teacher proxemics in the classroom using a mapping technique, after having done a few you will want to stop until you have had a chance to look at the maps and see if this method is helping to address your research question. The worst case scenario is one where data pile up unanalyzed. The data gathering and analysis go hand in hand, because one informs the other, that is, the analysis will guide you in what to do next in terms of data gathering and actions to take.

As you first look at your data, you will want to ascertain whether your inquiry question still seems answerable and worth asking. What do the data tell you in terms of the research question so far? Have you gotten the question "right," or as you go about your inquiry, do you discover a layer underneath that original question that more accurately reflects what it is you want to know? As you begin to think about these things, you will want to record your thinking and insights in some way; often this is done in a researcher's journal. Do not assume you will just remember these insights, since they fade in light of new decisions you make based on them. Also, keeping a trail of the research decisions you are making is one of the ways of establishing the validity of your study.

You then need to check to see if the data methods you began with are gathering what you want as far as data are concerned: That is, are they catching the particular kinds of data you want and filtering out data that are not relevant at this time? Do they still seem the most appropriate, given the evolution of your research question? Are they doable in terms of your work routines? It is not unusual to tweak your approach some as you ask yourself these questions. When Herr first began the study presented in Chapter 4, she started with individual interviews but then moved to primarily a group interview format in part because it was so difficult to find time to interview students one-on-one. This turned out to be a serendipitous move, since the group was catalytic in terms of taking action together. You will want to keep revisiting these questions about the effectiveness of your data-gathering methods throughout the study and adjusting them accordingly.

You begin to answer the questions posed above through a preliminary review and analysis of your data. For example, if you as the teacher in the classroom were following your students' movements around you and you wanted to know how many students hung around you, by gender and ethnicity, you should have recorded student position and included gender and ethnicity or name (so that you could fill in the demographics later). You could then begin to count up the number of students in each category who were close or distant from the teacher. You might then link this to research from other proxemic studies that have shown that language ability and participation rates improve based in part on proximity to the teacher (Nihlen, 1976). This linking to other research, so that your analysis and data can "dialogue" with that of others, is an ongoing process throughout the research.

Next you can ask the question, "Do I need more of the same data, or do I change what I am doing?" Depending on the question and what data you need to refine it and provide answers, you can begin to develop other data-gathering strategies. One problem that frequently develops for practitioner researchers is the dilemma of not enough time and the practicality of the data-gathering techniques themselves. For example, gathering proxemic data might be impossible to implement in your site. If so, it would be time to regroup and figure out another strategy for collecting data. There are typically multiple ways to gain the data that you need, so if one approach isn't working, another one might.

Given the cyclical nature of action research, most of us are gathering data over a long period of time. One strength of practitioners doing research in their sites is the prolonged period of time spent there and the opportunity for the research to continue to unfold over time. Given the lengthy nature that is typical of this undertaking, it makes sense to pause periodically, see what has been collected so far, ask how it relates to the research question, and ask if there is anything that needs to be changed in the inquiry process. Typically, we are juggling multiple roles in our sites, and the research should not be an unmanageable burden or it will be too difficult to continue. It is legitimate to make shifts if or when the approach being used is too onerous in terms of time or energy or is simply unreasonable, given multiple roles.

As you continue, you will want to do so with an eye toward establishing the validity of the study. For example, you may want to begin to triangulate some of the various forms of data, such as interviews and observations, and see if there are different perspectives that you will want to further explore. You should be periodically asking yourself if you are constructing a study that others would find credible, given the inquiry approach you are pursuing.

Stopping periodically in the data-collection process also allows you to see if you have any gaps in the data, holes that you need data to address. Our initial understandings are partial, and typically the data analysis opens up other things we are curious about and will need data to address. Continuing to ask throughout what other data you need for the ongoing evolution of your question and your understanding will guide your next steps in data gathering. Again, it is imperative that your analysis keep up with your data gathering, since you are basing your next steps on the analysis.

Are We There Yet?

All that has been described in the previous section could continue indefinitely. How do action researchers know when they are done? There are multiple answers to this. Perhaps after a number of iterations of the action research spiral, you are satisfied that you have gotten as far as you can in your particular context. Perhaps your sense is that you have studied your site sufficiently and have made changes based on your analysis and data gathering. From this perspective, you may decide that you are finished with this particular inquiry. Or perhaps you changed curriculum or structure and your research work is paying off in your role as teacher or principal and you choose to stop. Or it could be that despite your most informed actions, the issues seem intractable and you stop. Or perhaps you change jobs or a class ends and the research project ends with it.

On the other hand, many of us adopt an ongoing inquiry stance to our work in general and continue with action research in one form or another throughout our careers. This is, in part, because it can be such an effective form of professional development.

If the question is, "When do I have enough data?" typically what we ask ourselves is whether the flow of new information has diminished. Are new insights no longer coming with the analysis of the data? Are the data seemingly repetitious? Does it feel familiar in terms of the territory the data are covering? Are we relatively satisfied with where the research has taken us in terms of the original question or puzzle we were trying to solve? Have we come up with solutions that seem to be effective? Depending on the answers to these questions, we may decide that we are "there": at an end point, at least for the present.

Approaches to Analysis

Depending on the length of time that you have been carrying out your inquiry, you probably have a large amount of data with which to work. Hopefully, you have periodically stopped data collection and reviewed where you are going, perhaps going forward in a straight line or perhaps changing direction to better answer the question. By organizing the data collected, you have filled in gaps in data to create the most holistic picture you can. You have a good start on the analysis of the data.

The first step is to pull all your data together, reread your initial question, and then reread all your data. Wander through the data, making notes of items that strike you.

A comprehensive scanning of all the data in one or two long sittings will provide some emerging patterns with which to begin the process of analysis. Take these initial emergent patterns and see what fits together, what converges. It is here that you begin to match, contrast, and compare the patterns or constructs in the data in earnest. Hunches or intuitive leaps are very important and usually extremely significant in the process of analysis and should not be ignored.

Various conceptual techniques are useful in poring over the data. LeCompte and Preissle (1993) outline them, as do Lincoln and Guba (1985) and Patton (2002). Here we present a few useful analysis techniques along with some examples of how they can be applied.

Initially, everything you have collected is interesting. Your job is to code data into initial constructs or aggregates of data and compare them to each other to see if they really are separate circles of information or if they can be placed together. Keep doing this with your initial categories and keep comparing and contrasting them. Examine how frequently they occur and in what order.

Developing Coding Categories

Developing coding systems for your data is of paramount importance. Coding systems enable you to see categories in the data; consequently, the data become more manageable. Differing research questions generate varying categories; every question needs some organization to address the data for answers.

Practitioner action research drawing on qualitative data is messy and comes in large containers. It lacks the slim portfolio of numbers. This is all the more reason to come to grips early on with notebooks full of observational data and boxes full of tapes and transcriptions. Earlier we suggested reading over all the data collected and refreshing yourself with the initial question. Next you will need to begin separating and isolating potentially interesting and important data. Remember, as you go along and develop codes or categories, you will always be cross-checking yourself to make sure the data are speaking more loudly than the researcher. Allow yourself to see if the data can fit into some categories; develop or use existing codes and see if the data fit. If they do not, no harm has been done, and you can try another angle. The more perspectives you gain on the data, the more you learn about them. Then you decide what you want to do about what you discovered, what recommendations and actions make sense to you for yourself and your school, and so on.

Following is a brief description of a family of codes that might suggest ways coding can be accomplished. They are based on the codes suggested by Bogdan and Biklen (1998). Mason also suggested an abbreviated form of coding in her book *Qualitative Researching* (2002).

Setting/Context Codes

Setting/context codes are fairly easy codes that encompass the large context of a study. Descriptive literature on the site goes here, as do newspaper articles. General descriptions by the participants, as well as descriptive statistics, fit here.

Situation Codes

Place data here that tell how the participants define the setting or particular topics. This is where participants' thoughts on their worldview and how they see themselves are placed. If you have various participants, such as students, principals, and support staff, you might want to have a code for each one. "Some 'definitions of the situation' codes in a study of women's perceptions of their own elementary school experiences included 'feminist awareness/image of present self,' and 'influences on interpreting past'" (Biklen, 1973).

Perspectives Held by Participant

This includes codes for shared rules and norms as well as general points of view that are a little more specific than above. Sometimes these perspectives are captured in particular phrases people use.

Participants' Ways of Thinking About People and Objects

These codes represent what participants think of each other and their understanding of one another and the objects that make up their world. Teachers' views about the nature of the students they teach is an example.

Process Codes

Process codes refer to words and phrases that facilitate organizing sequences of events, changes over time, and passages from one type or kind of status to another. To use this code, you must view people over a period of time and see changes occurring. This is commonly used in ordering life or oral histories, and the codes would be the stages in an individual's life that appear to separate important segments, such as early life, first day of school, junior high, or becoming a teenager.

Activity Codes

Activity codes are directed at regularly occurring kinds of behaviors. These behaviors can be fairly obvious and relatively informal, such as student smoking or joking, or school activities such as morning exercise in school, attendance, and lunch.

Event Codes

Event codes refer to happenings that occur infrequently or only once. Events such as the firing of a teacher, a teachers' strike, and a school pageant are examples.

Strategy Codes

Strategies refer to the tactics, methods, and techniques people use to accomplish various things. Teachers' strategies to control students' behaviors, to teach reading, and to get out of recess duty are examples.

Relationship and Social Structure Codes

Regular patterns of behavior not officially defined by the organization, such as cliques, friendships, romances, coalitions, enemies, or mentors, fit under this category. Formal relations, such as social roles and positions, also belong here.

Methods Codes

The researcher's comments about the process, procedures, joys, and problems go here.

Working the data into codes is labor-intensive and time consuming. Decide on what kind of piles, folders, or index cards you will use in advance. In an interview study with the homeless, Nihlen (1992) took all the interviews out and read them through several times:

> After reading 40 one-hour-long interviews fully transcribed you become desperate to reduce the work. The third time around I began to mark categories or codes which seemed to repeat from interview to interview. On index cards I recorded where these occurred in the text. For example, the category of "work" kept repeating itself. I made a code for "work," and put

all the references each person made to work in this pile. I had many piles of cut-up interviews on my desk and table after awhile and I began to think I needed to see what was in them.

I took the pile coded "work" and sorted it into several more codes. Included in these piles were coding categories similar to the above such as setting/context, definition of the situation, perspectives held by participants, participants' ways of thinking about people and objects, process codes, etc. One coded pile which struck me I labeled "kinds of work." This could be an activity code. Under "kinds of work" I listed 8 jobs they talked about, including canning (collecting cans), giving blood, signing (holding up a sign asking for work or money), and begging.

These codes and sub-codes helped me see that the homeless people I talked to were working, only at jobs that I had not considered as "real" jobs and therefore did not see until I was coding my data. These kinds of discoveries occur as you unpack your data in as many different ways as possible. (p. 17)

Ethnographic Analysis

This type of analysis uses language to help us see what is happening and helps us build categories of meaning from data. The method is based on semantic rules for aggregating differing units of data. Spradley (1979) developed three categories as tools for the analyzing and ordering of data: domain, taxonomic, and componential analyses. Many practitioners and university professors alike use portions of domain analysis to scan the data, then proceed with Spradley's or other analysis techniques. Following is a brief description of the three categories.

Domain Analysis

A "domain" of cultural meaning is a category that includes smaller categories. For example, schools have students and teachers and other staff. "Kinds of teachers" could be a domain category. Each domain has terms, cover terms, and a semantic relationship that links together two categories. "Is a kind of" is a phrase that links two categories into a semantic relationship; its job is to place terms inside the cultural domain.

For example, using the cultural domain term "kinds of teachers," teachers can be identified as grade teachers (1st, 8th, 11th), special education teachers, or Chapter I reading teachers (see Figure 6.5). If you were doing a study in your school, and during the interviews other teachers referred to the kinds of teachers mentioned above, you could place each term into the category "kind of teacher." Based on your interview and observational data, you would build numerous domain categories to help display and understand your data.

Figure 6.5   Example of a Domain Analysis

Included terms	Semantic relationship	Cover term
X	is a kind of	Y
Third-grade teachers	are a kind of	teacher
Resource room teachers	are a kind of	teacher
English as a second language teachers	are a kind of	teacher

Taxonomy

The next stage is to begin to ask questions that will help build a taxonomy. The researcher selects several cultural domains and makes sure that they include as many members as possible. Then the researcher seeks to find out how these domains are organized.

A taxonomy is a set of categories organized on the basis of a semantic relationship. It seeks to show the relationships between all the included terms in a domain. A taxonomy reveals subsets and how they are related to the whole. Using the above example of kinds of teachers, you could open the category of special education teachers to include C-level teachers, gifted teachers, resource room teachers, and full-inclusion teachers.

Consider the school building. It is full of cultural meanings: which door the parents enter and which doors staff most often enter, the students' lunchroom, the library, the staff lounge, the principal's outer and inner offices. Using a taxonomy of the term *school*, one could build a diagram of the particular organization to understand it better (see Figure 6.6).

For strangers, this taxonomic analysis would help them orient themselves in the building. For a researcher who knows the school intimately, it might help to make the familiar strange so the researcher could remember all the areas in which students are not allowed or in which they are only allowed during certain scheduled periods. For example, if you found two seventh graders hanging around out in front of the building an hour before school

Figure 6.6   Example of a Taxonomy of the Term *School*

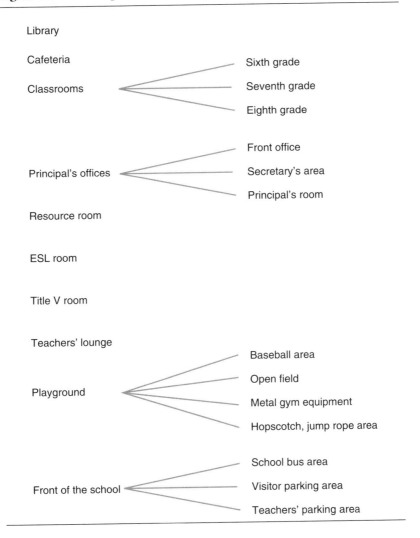

ended, you might come to certain conclusions about the appropriateness of their behavior and activity.

Another way to build a taxonomy is shown in Figure 6.7, using the domain "kinds of teachers."

Componential Analysis

The third category used by Spradley is the componential analysis, which is a systematic search for the units of meaning

Figure 6.7   Example of a Taxonomy of Kinds of Teachers

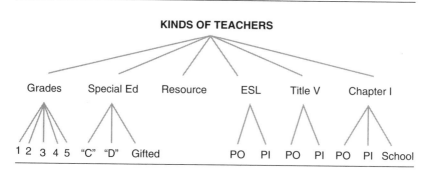

associated with the cultural patterns of people. When contrasts exist among members of a domain, those contrasts are attributes or components of meaning. *Component* is another term for *unit*. Thus, a researcher is looking for the units of meaning that people have assigned to their cultural categories.

Returning to the example of teachers as a domain category, what you seek to discover at this stage are the actual components of meaning the participants use when discussing kinds of teachers. Spradley suggests seeking out through interviews, observations, and your own notes the dimensions of contrast in, for example, distinguishing one kind of teacher from another. Location, training, tools of the trade, and status of subject taught, for example, would all be components of meaning, attributes associated with the cultural category of resource room teacher.

Constant Comparison and Grounded Theory

The constant comparison method of analysis comes from the work of Glaser and Strauss (1967; Strauss & Corbin, 1998). In this analysis, as soon as a researcher begins to collect data, he or she also begins coding it and examining it in the light of more data. Thus, the researcher is constantly collecting, coding, analyzing, and comparing data. Analysis generation also proceeds along this path. As newly collected data on events are compared with earlier notes, new typologies and relationships become apparent. (See Strauss and Corbin (1998) for a detailed description of this method.)

As in all methodologies, you are breaking down and closely examining your data. You systematically compare and contrast and categorize the data again and again. The whole process forms a spiral or dialectical pattern.

The procedure is to make comparisons and ask questions; thus the term *constant comparison*. It is useful to begin this analysis as soon as you have any data. Like Spradley's (1979) semantic analysis, this is an interpretive method of analysis. Unlike semantic analysis, you do not use the participant's own words; rather, you interpret the meaning and build a series of concepts based on your interpretation of a line of an interview or a bit of an observation. Thus, you immediately begin to assert your researcher self onto the data analysis, and thus, it is your interpretation of what the participant is saying or doing. Of course, in the end, it is always the researcher's interpretation of what is happening, but it is intensified by leaving the emic voice so early in the analysis process.

As you build concepts and categories, you are building theory for the work. The dimensions give variation to the theory. Following is a brief summary of the first three parts of the analysis. (For further information, read Strauss & Corbin's 1998 book, *Basics of Qualitative Research*. It is full of practitioner examples.)

1. Concepts: Don't summarize, but rather, conceptualize your participant's words. For example, if your participant talks about all the hard and difficult things about being a first-year teacher in the classroom, you might conceptualize this as "difficulties." This represents an abstract representation of an event, object, or action that the researcher identifies as being significant in the data (Strauss & Corbin, 1998).

2. Categories: Once you get a number of concepts, like "difficulties" above, you then group the similar categories together. For example, you might have added categories such as "mistakes," "problems," "problems with paperwork," and "issues with principal." You want to look for the salient issues with which to group them. You might link mistakes, problems, and difficulties together and administrative difficulties and issues with principal together. The first one you might categorize as "obstacles," and the second one you might categorize as "administrative problems." These "crunched" data now move into the third stage, properties.

3. Properties: The categories are analyzed further to form properties. You select attributes or characteristics of the categories to build properties that represent characteristics of a category, the delineation of which defines it and gives it meaning. For example, in the above example under Categories, you might combine "obstacles" and "administrative problems" and label them "issues of first-year teachers," or, depending on your research question, you might label these categories "problematic teacher."

Following is a long example that illustrates the complexity and the sometimes intuitive nature of analysis. For each of us, our research question guides us in determining which direction we see and how we work the data. This summary of data analysis comes from DuPré (2005):

> As the number of domain analyses I had generated increased, I created a taxonomy in an effort to unpack the terms further. Because of the pilot study I had completed three years ago, I had developed some strong "hunches" about what my research might say. It was very important for me to be aware of the influence of my own philosophical stance that fostered preconceptions so that the informants' constructs could frame the study in a phenomenological approach. LeCompte and Preissle's (1993) discussion of tacit theory was particularly relevant to my research. This influence included "life experiences, cultural ideologies, disciplinary training, philosophical commitment, and issues and problems identified by significant others that so clearly affect goals and questions" (p. 125). Acknowledging my own subjective bias in the selection of data, the transcription of observations, and the construction of interview questions, I consistently attempted to immerse myself in these multiple data sources with an open mind so that patterns could emerge. As I formed impressions, I constantly triangulated one source against another to search for validity in my interpretation (Guba, 1978, p. 13). Having prepared an ethnography that focused on my own teaching three years ago, I felt confident in Spradley's process to facilitate holistic analysis of the data, to examine similar and dissimilar phenomena so that theory could be induced.
>
> To support the trustworthiness of the analysis further, I followed Strauss and Corbin's (1990) guidelines for analytically

integrating the patterns that had emerged through my taxonomies. First, I wrote several pages that explicated the story
line as if I were giving a descriptive overview of the ethnography to my colleagues. Next, I searched through my taxonomies
to discover the "core category" that was abstract enough to
encompass everything that I had described in the story. This
category emerged as a conceptual shift from considering tolerance and intolerance as immutably embedded within "others"
who were not the responsibility of detached bystanders to an
awareness that knowledge, awareness, and the willingness
to work for change could positively increase acceptance and
respect in "others."

The taxonomies that I had created using Spradley's
guidelines helped me to write hypothetical statements
regarding paradigmatic relationships following Strauss and
Corbin's analytic ordering: "A (conditions) leads to B (phenomenon), which leads to C (context), which leads to D
(action/interaction, including strategies), which then leads
to E (consequences)" (pp. 124–5). Having written these
hypothetical statements, I then compared them against the
data to see if they fit. When they did not, I tried to identify
whether or not intervening conditions were causing the variation. These prototypical cases led to further informal conversations, structural questions in interviews, and reflective
writing. All of these strategies helped establish the trustworthiness of my findings.

Following Spradley's cyclical process of coding for terms,
creating domain analyses and taxonomies, member-
checking, reflecting on the data in my journal, and conducting new interviews and participant observations, I was able
to divide the classroom culture into small, descriptive chunks
of phenomenon that I then turned over and over before refit-
ting them into relevant constructs and categories. Using
Strauss and Corbin's guidelines helped to integrate the categories into theory. As I began to tell the story, to every extent
possible I used the participants' own terms with thick description so that comparisons could be "conducted confidently and
used meaningfully across groups and disciplines" (LeCompte
& Preissle, 1993, p. 47). I found reassurance in Clifford
Geertz's (1973) assertion that although one starts any effort
at thick description, beyond the obvious and superficial, from

a state of general bewilderment as to what the devil is going on—trying to find one's feet—one does not start (or ought not) intellectually empty-handed. Theoretical ideas are not created wholly anew in each study; as I have said, they are adopted from other, related studies, and, refined in the process, applied to new interpretive problems. (p. 27)

Writing Up the Research

The biggest question you might have is, "So what?" What will all this analysis get me? And that is, of course, a very legitimate question for busy and multitasking educators to ask. What we want to convey at this point is how these and other forms of analysis help us come to understand what our data have to offer in terms of addressing the questions that took us into doing inquiry in the first place. You may have decided to do practitioner action research for yourself and your own professional development; this is, of course, a legitimate approach to the process. At the same time, we revisit here the idea that practitioners can uniquely contribute to the knowledge base in education and that this is accomplished typically through disseminating your research to a broader audience.

Our own sense is that only through an ongoing, multilayered analysis of the data can an action researcher reap the benefits of all the effort and have something to offer to the larger educational community. This is not to imply that your action research has to be a "success" in terms of making positive changes in your school environment and/or practices. But it does imply that there is a contribution to be had out of the inquiry journey and where it has taken you. We could, in fact, benefit from accountings of the messy, muddy side of trying to undertake change in our own work sites.

Should you choose to write up an account of your research, you will want to do so with your intended audience in mind. Is it for other educators in your own site? Is it for a class or to fulfill a requirement in your graduate education (a dissertation? a thesis? a capstone experience?)? For a conference or publication? The way you approach the writing will depend on these intended audiences and what will be a compelling account of your research to them.

The following is an excerpt from Barb DuPré's (2005) dissertation. A middle school English teacher who utilizes an award-winning curriculum she developed, DuPré incorporates issues of social justice and tolerance into her curriculum through theater, movement, and lots of reading. In this excerpt, she talks about the many decisions she made in order to produce a document with which she was pleased and to address the various audiences for her work.

As a writing teacher, I also stress the acknowledgment of audience to my student writers. Writing to a target audience necessitates determining what they value so that they are more likely to value the work. For Spradley, this also entails determining the proportion of six different levels of ethnographic writing from the most abstract to the most specific: 1) universal statements, including all-encompassing statements about human beings' behavior, culture, or environmental situation; 2) cross-cultural descriptive statements that provide assertions that are true for some societies but may not apply to all; 3) general statements about a society or cultural group may refer to complex societies or to a particular culture or cultural scene; 4) general statements about a specific cultural scene or low-level abstract expressions often provided through interviews; 5) specific statements about a cultural domain, including folk terms and specific contrasts provided by informants, shown through a great deal of narrative description; and 6) specific incident statements that create a sense of immediacy of the informants' perceptions at the actual level of behavior and objects.

Who then is the selected audience for this ethnography? In my mind, as I wrote and revised these chapters, I found myself anticipating questions from other teachers and realized that I was answering their questions teacher-to-teacher. Focusing on their voices improved the translatability of phenomena across other teaching and learning communities while refining accessibility of cultural meaning to outsiders. Therefore, I attempted to focus on levels five and six, generalized through the abstractions of levels three and four.

Most notably, I also chose to write in an ethnographic style that honored the students as an important audience for this writing and invested participants in the project. They took an unexpected, long-range interest in the completion of this work. They demonstrated this through countless hours spent in interviews, in member-checking, in spending their lunch time participating in group coding sessions, and in revisiting my classroom, even after they have gone on to high school, to see "how the project is going." Several of them have read drafts of findings and have asked to attend my defense. I welcome their continued interest as evidence that they recognized the importance of the work that we did beyond my completion of a requirement for a degree. (p. 123)

In this excerpt, DuPré conveys the unique characteristics of writing up the data for a teacher researcher whose chosen audience will be other teachers, students, and also the university or community. This section is from her dissertation, perhaps the most academically formal of her various audiences, and in this she adheres to the conventions of academic writing, drawing on what other authors have established and situating her work in this stream. If she were writing for community members, this might be of less importance than other areas of the research process, such as if multiple stakeholders' views were included and how their voices and thoughts were represented.

We are fortunate that in the last decade many practitioner action researchers have agreed to the publication of their work. We reiterate that practitioner action research, then, is a significant way of knowing about schools and teaching. In addition, as Cochran-Smith and Lytle (1993) have observed, "[I]nquiry by individual teachers and communities of teacher researchers realign[s] their relationships to knowledge and to the brokers of knowledge and also necessitates a redefinition of the notion of a knowledge base for teaching" (p. 43). To address, then, the "So what?" question with which we began this section, we suggest that the writing of the research is for ourselves and our professional development, for our sites, but also for the larger research and educational communities. Our thinking is that the change process extends to the realignment alluded to above and to the ongoing redefinition of what it is we "know" in multiple spheres. We believe that all of these spheres can be influenced and informed by practitioners' action research.

References

Allington, R. (2002). *Big brother and the national reading curriculum: How ideology trumped evidence.* New York: Heinemann Press.

Altricher, H., & Posch, R. (1989). Does the grounded theory approach offer a guiding paradigm for teacher research? *Cambridge Journal of Education, 19*(1), 21–40.

Anderson, G. L. (1990). Toward a critical constructivist approach to school administration: Invisibility, legitimation, and the study of non-events. *Educational Administration Quarterly, 26*(1), 38–59.

Anderson, G. L. (2002). Reflecting on research for doctoral students in education. *Educational Researcher, 31*(7), 22–25.

Anderson, G. L., & Herr, K. (1999). The new paradigm wars: Is there room for rigorous practitioner knowledge in schools and universities? *Educational Researcher, 28*(5), 12–21.

Anderson, G. L., & Jones, F. (2000). Knowledge generation in educational administration from the inside-out: The promise and perils of site-based, administrator research. *Educational Administration Quarterly, 36*(3), 428–464.

Andreu, R., Canos, L., de Juana, S., Manresa, E., Rienda, L., & Tari, J. J. (2003). Critical friends: A tool for quality improvement in universities. *Quality Assurance in Education, 11*, 31–36.

Argyris, C., Putnam, R., & Smith, D. M. (1985). *Action science: Concepts, methods, and skills for research and intervention.* San Francisco: Jossey-Bass.

Argyris, C., & Schön, D. (1974). *Theory in practice: Increasing professional effectiveness.* San Francisco: Jossey-Bass.

Argyris, C., & Schön, D. (1991). Participatory action research and action science compared: A commentary. In W. R. Whyte (Ed.), *Participatory action research* (pp. 85–96). Newbury Park, CA: Sage.

Atwell, N. (1982). Classroom-based writing research: Teachers learn from students. *English Journal, 71*, 84–87.

Ballenger, C. (1993). Learning the ABC's: The shadow curriculum. In *Children's voices, teachers' stories: Papers from the Brookline Teacher Researcher Seminar* (Tech. Rep. No. 11). Newton, MA: Literacies Institute.

Ballenger, C. (1996). Learning the ABCs in a Haitian preschool: A teacher's story. *Language Arts, 73*, 317–323.

Ballenger, C. (1998). *Teaching other people's children: Literacy and learning in a bilingual classroom.* New York: Teachers College Press.

Ballenger, C. (2004). The puzzling child: Challenging assumptions about participation and meaning in talking science. *Language Arts, 81*(4), 303–311.

Ballenger, C., & Rosebery, A. S. (2003). What counts as teacher research? Investigating the scientific and mathematical ideas of children from culturally diverse backgrounds. *Teachers College Record, 105*(2), 297–314.

Bambino, D. (2002). Critical friends. *Educational Leadership, 59*(6), 25–27.

Barone, T. (2000). *Aesthetics, politics, and educational inquiry: Essays and examples.* New York: Peter Lang.

Bartunek, J., & Louis, M. R. (1996). *Insider/outsider team research.* Thousand Oaks, CA: Sage.

Bateson, G., & Mead, M. (Producers and Directors). (1942). *Balinese character: A photographic analysis* [Film]. New York: New York Academy of Science.

Berger, P., & Luckmann, T. (1967). *The social construction of reality.* Garden City, NJ: Anchor.

Biklen, S. (1973). *Lessons of consequence: Women's perceptions of their elementary school experience: A retrospective study.* Unpublished doctoral dissertation, University of Massachusetts.

Bochner, A., & Ellis, C. (2002). *Ethnographically speaking: Autoethnography, literature, and aesthetics.* Walnut Creek, CA: AltaMira Press.

Bogdan, R., & Biklen, S. K. (1998). *Qualitative research for education: An introduction to theory and methods.* Boston: Allyn & Bacon.

Bone, D. (1996). Quality management is collegiate management: Improving practice in a special school. In P. Lomax (Ed.), *Quality management in education: Sustaining the vision through action research* (pp. 152–165). London: Routledge.

Brady, J. (1979). *The craft of interviewing.* New York: Vintage.

Brause, R. S., & Mayher, J. S. (1991). *Search and research: What the inquiring teacher needs to know.* New York: Falmer Press.

Brookline Teacher Research Seminar. (2003). *Regarding children's words: Teacher research on language and literacy.* New York: Teachers College Press.

Brown, L. D., & Tandon, R. (1983). Ideology and political inquiry: Action research and participatory research. *Journal of Applied Behavioral Science, 19*(3), 277–294.

Brown, L. M., & Gilligan, C. (1992). *Meeting at the crossroads: Women's psychology and girls' development.* Cambridge, MA: Harvard University Press.

Buendia, E. (2003). Fashioning research stories: The metaphoric and narrative structure of writing research about race. In G. López & L. Parker (Eds.), *Interrogating racism in qualitative research methodology*. New York: Peter Lang.

Bullough, R. V., & Pinnegar, S. (2001). Guidelines for quality in autobiographical forms of self-study research. *Educational Researcher, 30*(3), 13–22.

Caro-Bruce, C., Klehr, M., & Zeichner, K. (2007). *Using action research to create equitable classrooms*. Thousand Oaks, CA: Corwin Press.

Carr, W. (1989). Action research: Ten years on. *Journal of Curriculum Studies, 21,* 85–90.

Carr, W., & Kemmis, S. (1986). *Becoming critical: Knowing through action research*. Victoria, BC, Canada: Deakin University Press.

Cassell, J. (1982). Harms, benefits, wrongs and rights in fieldwork. In J. E. Sieber (Ed.), *The ethics of social research: Fieldwork, regulation and publication* (pp. 49–70). New York: Springer-Verlag.

Chisholm, L. (1990). Action research: Some methodological and political considerations. *British Educational Research Journal, 16*(3), 249–257.

Chism, N., Sanders, D., & Zitlow, C. (1989). Observations on a faculty development program based on practice-centered inquiry. *Peabody Journal of Education, 64*(3), 1–23.

Christman, J., Hirshman, J., Holtz, A., Perry, H., Spelkoman, R., & Williams, M. (1995). Doing Eve's work: Women principals write about their practice. *Anthropology and Education Quarterly, 26*(2), 213–227.

Clandinin, D. J., & Connelly, F. M. (2000). *Narrative inquiry: Experience and story in qualitative research*. San Francisco: Jossey-Bass.

Clandinin, D. J., & Connelly, F. M. (1995). *Teachers' professional knowledge landscapes*. New York: Teachers College Press.

Clift, R., Veal, M. L., Holland, P., Johnson, M., & McCarthy, J. (1995). *Collaborative leadership and shared decision-making: Teachers, principals, and university professors*. New York: Teachers College Press.

Cobb, K. (1993). *Meaningful learning experiences: Perceptions of middle school students*. Unpublished manuscript.

Cochran-Smith, M., & Lytle, S. (1993). *Inside/outside: Teacher research and knowledge*. New York: Teachers College Press.

Cochran-Smith, M., & Lytle, S. (1998). Teacher research: The question that persists. *International Journal of Leadership in Education, 1*(1), 19–36.

Cochran-Smith, M., & Lytle, S. (1999). The teacher research movement: A decade later. *Educational Researcher, 28*(7), 15–25.

Coles, R. (1989). *The call of stories: Teaching and the moral imagination*. Boston: Houghton Mifflin.

Collier, J., Jr. (1967). *Visual anthropology: Photography as a research method*. New York: Holt, Rinehart & Winston.

Collins, P. H. (1990). *Black feminist thought: Knowledge, consciousness and the politics of empowerment.* New York: Routledge.

Connelly, F. M., & Clandinin, D. J. (1987). On narrative method, biography and narrative unities in the study of teaching. *Journal of Educational Thought, 21*(3), AQ: 130–131.

Connelly, F. M., & Clandinin, J. (1990). Stories of experience and narrative inquiry. *Educational Researcher, 19*(5), 2–14.

Corey, S. M. (1949). Action research, fundamental research, and educational practices. *Teachers College Record, 50,* 509–514.

Corey, S. M. (1953). *Action research to improve school practices.* New York: Teachers College Press.

Corey, S. M. (1954). Action research in education. *Journal of Educational Research, 47,* 375–380.

Costa, A. L., & Kallick, B. (1993). Through the lens of a critical friend. *Educational Leadership, 51*(2), 49–51.

Counts, G. (1932). *Dare the school build a new social order?* New York: John Day.

Cunningham, J. B. (1983). Gathering data in a changing organization. *Human Relations, 36*(5), 403–420.

Delpit, L. (1993). *Other people's children: Cultural conflict in the classroom.* New York: New Press.

De Schutter, A., & Yopo, B. (1981). *Investigación participativa: Una opción metodológica para la educatión de adultos.* Patzcuaro, Michoacan, Mexico: CREFAL.

Diegmueller, K. (1992, August). Dynamic duo. *Teacher Magazine, 8,* 23–27.

Dunaway, D., & Baum, W. (1984). *Oral history: An interdisciplinary anthology.* Nashville, TN: Oral History Association.

DuPré, B. J. (2005). *Creative drama, playwriting, tolerance, and social justice: An ethnographic study of students in a seventh grade language arts class.* Unpublished dissertation, University of New Mexico.

Eisner, E. (1997). The promise and perils of alternative forms of data representation. *Educational Review, 26,* 4–10.

Elliott, J. (1991). *Action research for educational change.* Philadelphia: Open University Press.

Ellis, C., & Bochner, A. P. (1996). *Composing ethnography: Alternative forms of qualitative writing.* Walnut Creek, CA: AltaMira Press.

Ellis, C., & Bochner, A. P. (2000). Autoethnography, personal narrative, reflexivity: Researcher as subject. In N. K. Denzin & Y. S. Lincoln (Eds.), *Handbook of qualitative research.* Thousand Oaks, CA: Sage.

Ellis, C., & Flaherty, M. G. (Eds.). (1992). *Investigating subjectivity: Research on lived experience.* Thousand Oaks, CA: Sage.

Erickson, F. (1973). What makes school ethnography "ethnographic"? *CAE Newsletter, 4*(2), 10–19.

Erickson, F. (1986). *Tasks in times: Objects of study in a natural history of teaching.* East Lansing: Institute for Research on Teaching, Michigan State University.

Evans, M. (1995). *An action research enquiry into reflection in action as part of my role as a deputy head teacher.* Unpublished doctoral dissertation, University of Kingston, UK.

Evans, M., Lomax, P., & Morgan, H. (2000). Closing the circle: Action research partnerships towards better learning and teaching in schools. *Cambridge Journal of Education, 30*(3), 405–419.

Fals Borda, O. (2001). Participatory (action) research in social theory: Origins and challenges. In P. Reason & H. Bradbury (Eds.), *Handbook of action research: Participative inquiry and practice* (pp. 27–37). Thousand Oaks, CA: Sage.

Fayden, T. (1998). *Writing time for a group of four Pueblo Indian kindergartners.* Unpublished dissertation, University of New Mexico.

Fayden, T. (2006). *How children learn: Getting beyond the deficit myth.* Boulder, CO: Paradigm.

Fenstermacher, G. (1994). The knower and the known: The nature of knowledge in research on teaching. In L. Darling-Hammond (Ed.), *Review of research in education* (Vol. 20, pp. 3–56).

Foshay, A. W. (1993, April). *Action research: An early history in the United States.* Paper presented at the annual meeting of the American Educational Research Association, Atlanta, GA.

Foshay, A. W., & Wann, K. (1953). *Children's social values: An action research study.* New York: Bureau of Publications, Teachers College, Columbia University.

Foucault, M. (1980), *Power/knowledge: Selected interviews and other writings, 1972–1977.* New York: Pantheon Books.

Freedman, S., Jackson, J., & Boles, K. (1983). Teaching: An imperiled profession. In L. Shulman & G. Sykes (Eds.), *Handbook of teaching and policy* (pp. 261–299). New York: Longman.

Freedman, S., Jackson, J., & Boles, K. (1986). *The effect of teaching on teachers.* Grand Forks: University of North Dakota Press.

Freire, P. (1970). *Pedagogy of the oppressed.* New York: Herder & Herder.

Fullan, M. (1982). *The meaning of educational change.* New York: Teachers College Press.

Fulwiler, T. (1987). *The journal book.* Portsmouth, NH: Boynton/Cook.

Gallas, K. (1993). *The languages of learning.* New York: Teachers College Press.

Gallas, K. (1997). *Sometimes I can be anything: Power, gender, and identity in a primary classroom.* New York: Teachers College Press.

Gallas, K. (2003). *Imagination and literacy: A teacher's search for the heart of learning.* New York: Teachers College Press.

Garcia, G. (1991). *Learning and culture: Teachers as agents of change in professional development schools.* Unpublished manuscript.

Gaventa, J. (1988). Participatory research in North America: A perspective on participatory research in Latin America. *Convergence: An International Journal of Adult Education, 21*(2–3), 19–48.

Gaventa, J., & Horton, B. D. (1981). A citizen's research project in Appalachia, USA. *Convergence: An International Journal of Adult Education, 14*(3), 30–42.

Gearing, R., & Sangree, L. (1979). *Toward a cultural theory of education and schooling.* New York: Mouton Press.

Geertz, C. (1973). *The interpretation of cultures.* New York: Basic Books.

Gitlin, A., Bringhurst, K., Burns, M., Cooley, V., Myers, B., Price, K., et al. (1992). *Teachers' voices for school change.* New York: Teachers College Press.

Glaser, B. G., & Strauss, A. L. (1967). *The discovery of grounded theory: Strategies for qualitative research.* Chicago: Aldine.

Glickman, C. (1993). *Renewing America's schools: A guide for school-based action.* San Francisco: Jossey-Bass.

Gluck, S., & Patai, D. (1991). *Women's words: The feminist practice of oral history.* New York: Routledge.

Goswami, D., & Schultz, J. (1993). *Reclaiming the classroom: Teachers and students together.* Portsmouth, NH: Boynton/Cook.

Goswami, D., & Stillman, P. R. (1987). *Reclaiming the classroom: Teacher research as an agency for change.* Upper Montclair, NJ: Boynton.

Graves, D. (1981). Research update: A new look at writing research. *Language Arts, 58*(2), 197–206.

Green, S., & Brown, M. (2006). Promoting action research and problem solving among teacher candidates: One elementary school's journey. *Action in Teacher Education, 27*(4), 45–54.

Greene, J. (1992). The practitioner's perspective. *Curriculum Inquiry, 22,* 39–45.

Greenwood, D., & Levin, M. (1998). *Introduction to action research: Social research for social change.* Thousand Oaks, CA: Sage.

Griffin, E., Lieberman, A., & Jacullo-Noto, J. (1982). *Interactive research and development of schooling* (Final Report). New York: Teachers College Press.

Gutièrrez, L. M. (1990). Working with women of color: An empowerment perspective. *Social Work, 35*(2), 149–153.

Habermas, J. (1979). *Communication and the evolution of society.* Boston: Beacon Press.

Hall, B. (2002). I wish this were a poem of practices of participatory research. In P. Reason & H. Bradbury (Eds.), *Handbook of action research: Participative inquiry and practice* (pp. 171–178). Thousand Oaks, CA: Sage.

Hall, E. T. (1966). *The hidden dimension.* Garden City, NY: Doubleday.

Hall, E. T. (1974). *Handbook for proxemic research.* Washington, DC: Society for the Anthropology of Visual Communication.

Hammack, F. M. (1997). Ethical issues in teacher research. *Teachers College Record, 99*(2), 247–265.

Harwood, D. (1991). Action research vs. interaction analysis: A time for reconciliation? A reply to Barry Hutchinson. *British Educational Research Journal, 17,* 67–72.

Hermann-Wilmarth, J. M. (2005). Listening to Anthony: The case of a disruptive preservice teacher. *Journal of Teacher Education, 56*(5), 471–481.

Herr, K. (1993). [Field notes]. Unpublished raw data.

Herr, K. (1999a). Private power and privileged education: De/constructing institutionalized racism. *Journal of Inclusive Education, 3*(2), 111–129.

Herr, K. (1999b). The symbolic uses of participation: Co-opting change. *Theory Into Practice, 38*(4), 235–240.

Herr, K. (1999c). Unearthing the unspeakable: When teacher research and political agendas collide. *Language Arts, 77*(1), 10–15.

Herr, K., & Anderson, G. L. (1993). Oral history for student empowerment: Capturing students' inner voices. *International Journal of Qualitative Studies in Education, 6*(3), 185–196.

Herr, K., & Anderson, G. L. (2005). *The action research dissertation: A guide for students and faculty.* Thousand Oaks, CA: Sage.

Heydenrych, J. (2001). Improving educational practice: Action research as an appropriate methodology. *Progressio, 23*(2). Retrieved July 8, 2006, from www.unisa.ac.za/default.asp?Cmd=ViewContent& ContentID=13277

Holly, R. (1989). Action research: Cul-de-sac or turnpike? *Peabody Journal of Education, 64*(3), 71–100.

Holmes Group. (1990). *Tomorrow's schools: Principles for the design of Professional Development Schools.* East Lansing, MI: Holmes Group.

Hoonard, W. C., van den (2001). Is research-ethics review a moral panic? *The Canadian Review of Sociology and Anthropology, 38*(1), 19–36.

Howe, K. R., & Moses, M. (1999). Ethics in educational research. In A. Iran-Nejad & P. D. Pearson (Eds.), *Review of research in education* (pp. 21–59). Washington, DC: American Educational Research Association.

Hubbard, R. S., & Power, B. M. (1993). *The art of classroom inquiry: A handbook for teacher-researchers.* Portsmouth, NH: Heinemann Press.

Huberman, M. (1996). Focus on research moving mainstream: Taking a closer look at teacher research. *Language Arts, 73*(2), 124–140.

Hurston, Z. N. (1935). *Mules and men.* Philadelphia: J. B. Lippincott.

Hurston, Z. N. (1985). *Spunk: The selected stories.* Berkeley, CA: Turtle Island Foundation.

Hutchinson, B., & Whitehouse, P. (1986). Action research, professional competence and school organization. *British Educational Research Journal, 12*(11), 85–94.

Hyland, N. E., & Noffke, S. E. (2005). Understanding diversity through social and community inquiry: An action-research study. *Journal of Teacher Education, 56*(4), 367–381.

Johnson, R. (2002). *Using data to close the achievement gap: How to measure equity in our schools.* Thousand Oaks, CA: Corwin Press.

Kelly, J. G., Mock, L., & Tandon, S. D. (2001). Collaborative inquiry with African-American community leaders: Comments on a participatory research process. In P. Reason & H. Bradbury (Eds.), *Handbook of action research: Participative inquiry & practice* (pp. 348–355). London: Sage.

Kemmis, S. (Ed.). (1982). *The action research reader.* Geelong, Victoria, BC, Canada: Deakin University Press.

Kemmis, S., & McTaggart, R. (1982). *The action research planner.* Geelong, Victoria, BC, Canada: Deakin University Press.

Kincheloe, J. L. (1991). *Teachers as researchers: Qualitative inquiry as a path to empowerment.* Philadelphia: Falmer Press.

Lanman, B., & Mehafy, G. (1988). *Oral history in the secondary school classroom.* Provo, UT: Oral History Association.

Lather, P. (1986). Research as praxis. *Harvard Educational Review, 56*(3), 257–277.

LeCompte, M. D., & Preissle, J. (1993). *Ethnography and qualitative design in educational research* (2nd ed.). New York: Academic Press.

Lee, C., Smagorinsky, P., Pea, R., Brown, J. S., & Heath, C. (1999). *Vygotskian perspectives on literacy research: Constructing meaning through collaborative inquiry.* Cambridge, UK: University of Cambridge Press.

Levin, B., & Rock, T. (2003). The effects of collaborative action research on preservice and experienced teacher partners in professional development schools. *Journal of Teacher Education, 54*(2), 135–149.

Lewin, K. (1946). Action research and minority problems. *Journal of Social Issues, 2*(4), 34–46.

Lewin, K. (1948). *Resolving social conflicts.* New York: Harper & Row.

Lieberman, A., & Miller, L. (1984). School improvement: Themes and variations. *Teachers College Record, 86,* 4–19.

Lincoln, Y., & Guba, E. (1985). *Naturalistic inquiry.* Thousand Oaks, CA: Sage.

Lindblom, C., & Cohen, D. (1979). *Usable knowledge: Social science and social problem solving.* New Haven, CT: Yale University Press.

Liston, D. P., & Zeichner, K. M. (1991). *Teacher education and the social conditions of schooling.* New York: Routledge.

Lomax, P., Woodward, C., & Parker, Z. (1996). How can we help educational managers establish and implement effective "critical" friendships? In

P. Lomax (Ed.), *Quality management in education: Sustaining the vision through action research* (pp. 152–165). London: Routledge.

Luna, C., Bothelo, M. J., Fontaine, D., French, K., Iverson, K., & Matos, N. (2004). Making the road by walking and talking: Critical literacy and/as professional development in a teacher inquiry group. *Teacher Education Quarterly, 31*(1), 67–80.

Malinowski, B. (1922). *Argonauts of the Western Pacific.* New York: E. P. Dutton.

Martin, N. (1987). On the move: Teacher-researchers. In D. Goswami & P. Stillman (Eds.), *Reclaiming the classroom: Teacher research as an agency for change* (pp. 20–28). Upper Montclair, NJ: Boynton/Cook.

Martin, R. (2001). *Listening up: Reinventing ourselves as teachers and students.* Portsmouth, NH: Heinemann Press.

Martinez, L. (1993). *Teacher research in the Opciones Para Mujeres Program.* Unpublished manuscript.

Mason, J. (2002). *Qualitative researching.* Thousand Oaks, CA: Sage.

McCarthy, C. R. (1998). The Institutional Review Board: Its origins, purposes, function and future. In D. N. Weisstub (Ed.), *Research on human subjects: Ethics, law and social policy* (pp. 286–300). Oxford, UK: Pergamon Press.

McCutcheon, G., & Jung, B. (1990). Alternative perspectives on action research. *Theory Into Practice, 29*(3), 144–151.

McIntyre, M., & Cole, A. L. (2001). Conversations in relation: The research relationship in/as artful self-study. *Reflective Practice, 2*(1), 5–25.

McKernan, J. (1988). The countenance of curriculum action research: Traditional, collaborative, and emancipatory-critical conceptions. *Journal of Curriculum and Supervision, 3*(3), 173–200.

McKernan, J. (1991). *Curriculum action research: A handbook of methods and resources for the reflective practitioner.* New York: St. Martin's Press.

McNeil, L. M. (2000). *Contradictions of school reform: The educational costs of standardized testing.* New York: Routledge.

McNiff, J., & Whitehead, J. (2000). *Action research in organisations.* New York: Routledge.

McNiff, J., & Whitehead, J. (2002). *Action research: Principles and practice* (2nd ed.). London: RoutledgeFalmer.

Mediratta, K., Lewis, A. C., & Fruchter, N. (2002). *Organizing for school reform: How communities are finding their voices and reclaiming their public schools.* New York: Institute for Education and Social Policy.

Mehan, H. (1979). *Learning lessons: Social organization in the classroom.* Cambridge, MA: Harvard University Press.

Mercado, M. (2000). *Three native Spanish speakers in the classroom: Interacting among themselves and with their English speaking peers.* Unpublished dissertation, University of New Mexico.

Miller, J. (1990). *Creating spaces and finding voices: Teachers collaborating for empowerment.* Albany: State University of New York Press.

Mills, G. E. (2000). *Action research: A guide for the teacher researcher.* Upper Saddle River, NJ: Merrill/Prentice Hall.

Mishler, E. G. (1986). *Research interviewing: Context and narrative.* Cambridge, MA: Harvard University Press.

Moller, J. (1998). Action research with principals: Gain, strain and dilemmas. *Educational Action Research, 6*(1), 69–91.

Myers, M. (1985). *The teacher-researcher: How to study writing in the classroom.* Urbana, IL: National Council of Teachers of English.

National Commission for the Protection of Human Subjects of Biomedical and Behavioral Research. (1979). *The Belmont Report: Ethical principles and guidelines for the protection of human subjects of research.* Retrieved June 13, 2005, from http://ohsr.od.nih.gov/guidelines/belmont.html

Nihlen, A. S. (1976). *The white working class in school: A study of first grade girls and their parents.* Unpublished doctoral dissertation, University of New Mexico.

Nihlen, A. S. (1992, April). *Views from the bottom: Homeless definitions of self.* Paper presented at the annual meeting of the American Anthropological Association, San Francisco.

Nihlen, A. S., Williams, M., & Sweet, A. (1999). Teachers' stories of Professional Development School restructuring: Decision making. In D. M. Byrd & D. J. McIntyre (Eds.), *Research on professional development schools: Teacher education yearbook VII.* Thousand Oaks, CA: Corwin Press.

Noffke, S. E. (1995). Action research and democratic schooling: A rationale. In S. E. Noffke & R. Stevenson (Eds.), *Educational action research: Becoming practically critical* (pp. 1–10). New York: Teachers College Press.

Noffke, S. (1997). Professional, personal, and political dimensions of action research. *Review of Research in Education, 22,* 305–343.

Noffke, S. E., & Brennan, M. (1991). Action research and reflective student teaching at the University of Wisconsin, Madison: Issues and examples. In B. R. Tabachnik & K. Zeichner (Eds.), *Issues and practices in inquiry-oriented teacher education* (pp. 186–201). London: Falmer Press.

Noguera, P. (1995). Preventing and producing violence: A critical analysis of responses to school violence. *Harvard Educational Review, 65*(2), 189–212.

Oakes, J., Hare, S. E., & Sirotnik, K. A. (1986). Collaborative inquiry: A congenial paradigm in a cantankerous world. *Teachers College Record, 87,* 545–561.

Oja, S., & Ham, M. (1984). A cognitive-developmental approach to collaborative action research with teachers. *Teachers College Record, 86*, 171–192.

Ortega, L. (1993). *Look at my teaching: Investigation of surface and hidden curriculum.* Unpublished manuscript.

Patton, M. Q. (2002). *Qualitative research and evaluation methods* (3rd ed.). Thousand Oaks, CA: Sage.

Pearson, J. (1993). *Whose classroom—Whose management?* Unpublished manuscript.

Polanyi, M. (1958). *Personal knowledge.* Chicago: University of Chicago Press.

Price, J., & Valli, L. (2005). Preservice teachers becoming agents of change: Pedagogical implications for action research. *Journal of Teacher Education, 56*, 57–72.

Pritchard, I. (2002). Travelers and trolls: Practitioner research and institutional review boards. *Educational Researcher, 31*(3), 3–13.

Raisch, M. L. (1992). *A description and analysis of secondary student teachers and their cooperating teachers as teacher-researchers.* Unpublished doctoral dissertation, University of New Mexico.

Reed-Danahay, D. (Ed.). (1997). *Auto/ethnography: Rewriting the self and the social.* New York: Berg.

Richards, M. (1987). A teacher's action research study: The "bums" of 8H (A humanistic view of motivational strategies with low achievers). *Peabody Journal of Education, 64*(2), 65–79.

Richardson, V. (1994). Conducting research on practice. *Educational Researcher, 23*(5), 5–10.

Robinson, V. M. (1993). *Problem-based methodology: Research for the improvement of practice.* Oxford, UK: Pergamon.

Rogoff, B., Turkanis, C. G., & Bartlett, L. (2001). *Learning together: Children and adults in a school community.* New York: Oxford University Press.

Roman, L. (1992). The political significance of other ways of narrating ethnography: A feminist materialist approach. In M. LeCompte, W. Millroy, & J. Preissle (Eds.), *The handbook of qualitative research in education* (pp. 555–592). San Diego: Academic Press.

Rose, S. (1990). Advocacy/empowerment: An approach to clinical practice for social work. *Journal of Sociology and Social Welfare, 17*, 41–51.

Rowntree, D. (1981). *Statistics without tears: A primer for non-mathematicians.* New York: Penguin.

Russell, R. (1992). Out of the silence: Developing teacher voice. In A. Gitlin, K. Bringhurst, M. Burns, V. Cooley, & B. Myers (Eds.), *Teachers' voices for school change* (pp. 89–117). New York: Teachers College Press.

Saavedra, E. (1994). *Teacher transformation: Creating texts and contexts in study groups.* Unpublished doctoral dissertation, University of Arizona.

Sanders, D., & McCutcheon, G. (1986). The development of practical theories of teaching. *Journal of Curriculum and Supervision, 2*(1), 50–67.

Sanford, N. (1970). Whatever happened to action research? *Journal of Social Issues, 26,* 3–23.

Schaefer, R. J. (1967). *The school as a center of inquiry.* New York: Harper & Row.

Schön, D. A. (1983). *The reflective practitioner: How professionals think in action.* New York: Basic Books.

Schubert, W., & Lopez-Schubert, A. (1997). Sources of a theory for action research in the United States of America. In R. McTaggart (Ed.), *Participatory action research: International contexts and consequences* (pp. 203–222). Albany: State University of New York Press.

Schwandt, T. A. (2001). *Dictionary of qualitative inquiry* (2nd ed.). Thousand Oaks, CA: Sage.

Shirley, D. (1997). *Community organizing for urban school reform.* Austin: University of Texas Press.

Short, K., Connor, C., Crawford, K., Kahn, L., Kaser, S., & Sherman, R. (1993, April). *Teacher study groups: Exploring literacy issues through collaborative dialogue.* Paper presented at the annual meeting of the American Educational Research Association, Atlanta, GA.

Sirotnik, K. (1988). The meaning and conduct of inquiry in school-university partnerships. In K. Sirotnik & J. Goodlad (Eds.), *School-university partnerships in action.* New York: Teachers College Press.

Skrla, L., & Scheurich, J. J. (2001). Displacing deficit thinking in school district leadership. *Education and Urban Society, 33*(3), 235–259.

Smith, G. (1975). Action research: Experimental social administration? In R. Lees & G. Smith (Eds.), *Action research in community development* (pp. 77–95). London: Heinemann.

Smith, L. T. (1999). *Decolonizing methodologies: Research and indigenous peoples.* London: Zed Books.

Smith-Maddox, R. (1999). An inquiry-based reform effort: Creating the conditions for reculturing and restructuring schools. *Urban Review, 31*(3), 283–304.

Spindler, G. (1982). *Doing the ethnography of schooling.* New York: Holt, Rinehart & Winston.

Spradley, J. (1979). *The ethnographic interview.* New York: Holt, Rinehart & Winston.

Spradley, J. (1980). *Participant observation.* New York: Holt, Rinehart & Winston.

Stake, R. (1986). An evolutionary view of educational improvement. In E. R. House (Ed.), *New directions in educational evaluation* (pp. 89–102). London: Falmer Press.

Staples, C. (1993). *Under the circumstances: A case study of a new teacher of "at-risk" students.* Unpublished doctoral dissertation, University of New Mexico.

Strauss, A., & Corbin, J. (1998). *Basics of qualitative research: Techniques and procedures for developing grounded theory* (2nd ed.). Thousand Oaks, CA: Sage.

Stringer, E. T. (2003). *Action research: A handbook for the practitioners.* Thousand Oaks, CA: Sage.

Strommen, A. (1991). *Teacher researcher.* Unpublished manuscript.

Terkel, S. (1974). *Working: People talk about what they do all day and how they feel about what they do.* New York: Pantheon.

Terkel, S. (1980). *American dreams, lost and found.* New York: Ballantine.

Tisdale, K. (2003). Being vulnerable: Being ethical with/in research. In K. deMarrais & S. Lapan (Eds.), *Foundations for research: Methods of inquiry in education and social sciences* (pp. 13–30). Mahwah, NJ: Lawrence Erlbaum.

Torbert, W. (1981). Why educational research has been so uneducational: The case for a new model of social science based on collaborative inquiry. In P. Reason & J. Rowan (Eds.), *Human inquiry: A sourcebook of new paradigm research* (pp. 141–151). New York: John Wiley.

Tripp, D. H. (1990). Socially critical action research. *Theory Into Practice, 29*(3), 158–166.

Tuchman, G. (1994). Historical social science: Methodologies, methods, and meanings. In N. K. Denzin & Y. S. Lincoln (Eds.), *Handbook of qualitative research* (pp. 306–323). Thousand Oaks, CA: Sage.

University of New Mexico. (1991). *The oral history program* [Brochure]. Albuquerque: University of New Mexico.

Van den Hoonaard, W. C. (2001). Is research-ethics review a moral panic? *Canadian Review of Sociology and Anthropology, 38*(1), 19–36.

Walker, R. (1985). *Doing research: A handbook for teachers.* London: Methuen.

Walker, R., & Weidel, J. (1985). Using photographs in a discipline of words. In R. G. Burgess (Ed.), *Field methods in the study of education* (pp. 121–147). Lewes, UK: Falmer Press.

Wallerstein, N., & Duran, B. (2003). The conceptual, historical, and practice roots of community-based participatory research and related participatory traditions. In M. Minkler & N. Wallerstein (Eds.), *Community-based participatory research for health* (pp. 27–54). San Francisco: Jossey-Bass.

Watkins, K. (1991, April). *Validity in action research.* Paper presented at the annual meeting of the American Educational Research Association, Chicago.

Webb, G. (1996). Becoming critical of action research for development. In O. Zuber-Skerritt (Ed.), *New directions in action research* (pp. 137–161). London: Falmer Press.

Weiner, G. (1989). Professional self-knowledge versus social justice: A critical analysis of the teacher-researcher movement. *British Educational Research Journal, 15,* 41–51.

Whitehead, J. (1989). Creating a living educational theory from questions of the kind "How do I improve my practice?" *Cambridge Journal of Education, 19*(1), 42–59.

Whyte, J. B. (1987). Issues and dilemmas in action research. In G. Wolford (Ed.), *Doing sociology of education* (pp. 28–49). Philadelphia: Falmer Press.

Whyte, W. F. (1984). *Learning from the field: A guide from experience.* Beverly Hills, CA: Sage.

Winter, R. (1987). *Action research and the nature of social inquiry: Professional innovation and educational work.* Aldershot, UK: Avevury.

Winter, R. (1991). Interviewers, interviewees, and the exercise of power (Fictional-critical writing as a method for educational research). *British Educational Research Journal, 17*(2), 252–262.

Witherell, C., & Noddings, N. (Eds.). (1991). *Stories lives tell: Narrative and dialogue in education.* New York: Teachers College Press.

Wolcott, H. (1992). Posturing in qualitative research. In M. LeCompte, W. Millroy, & J. Preissle (Eds.), *The handbook of qualitative research in education* (pp. 3–52). New York: Academic Press.

Wong, D. E. (1995a). Challenges confronting the researcher/teacher: Conflicts of purpose and conduct. *Educational Researcher, 24*(3), 22–28.

Wong, D. E. (1995b). Challenges confronting the researcher/teacher: A rejoinder to Wilson. *Educational Researcher, 24*(8), 22–23.

Zeichner, K., & Noffke, S. (2002). Practitioner research. In V. Richardson (Ed.), *Handbook of research on teaching* (4th ed.). Washington, DC: American Educational Research Association.

Zeni, J. (2001). A guide to ethical decision making for insider research. In J. Zeni (Ed.), *Ethical issues in practitioner research* (pp. 153–165). New York: Teachers College Press.

Ziegler, A. (1992). *Teacher research.* Unpublished manuscript, University of New Mexico.

Index

CORWIN PRESS

The Corwin Press logo—a raven striding across an open book—represents the union of courage and learning. Corwin Press is committed to improving education for all learners by publishing books and other professional development resources for those serving the field of PreK–12 education. By providing practical, hands-on materials, Corwin Press continues to carry out the promise of its motto: **"Helping Educators Do Their Work Better."**